CRISES OF THE

What is the relationship between internal states of psychological crisis and features of the external social world? This book explores that question, bringing psychoanalytic thinking and practice to bear on the more public spheres of culture and politics. The contributors argue that the problem with many of our present social arrangements is not that they cause emotional distress, but that they fail to contain it adequately. In many areas we find cultural forms and political practices which feed off and intensify – while perhaps offering spurious solutions to – the crises of the self. Are these fragmented identities an inevitable characteristic of our 'postmodernist' age or can a more hopeful set of political and cultural strategies be assembled?

This timely collection is an innovative contribution to that debate and touches on such basic questions as the origins and dynamics of racism, the experience and meaning of gender, the nature of morale and commitment in organizations and public life, the importance of romance in popular culture, and the social meaning of psychoanalysis.

Barry Richards is a Lecturer in the Sociology Department, at the East London Polytechnic, and Managing Editor of *Free Associations*. The contributors are Paul Hoggett, Barry Richards, Robert M. Young, R.D. Hinshelwood, Karl Figlio, Sheila Ernst, Marie Maguire, Amal Treacher, Jed Sekoff, Les Levidow, Valerie Sinason, Stephen Frosh, Philip Cohen, and Jane Temperley.

CRISES OF THE SELF

FURTHER ESSAYS ON PSYCHOANALYSIS AND POLITICS

edited by
Barry Richards

*'an association in which the free development of each
is the condition for the free development of all'*

Free Association Books / London / 1989

First published in Great Britain in 1989 by
Free Association Books
26 Freegrove Road
London N7 9RQ

British Library Cataloguing in Publication Data

Crises of the self: further essays on psychoanalysis and politics
  1. Psychoanalysis. Social aspects
  I. Richards, Barry
  150.19′5

ISBN 1-85343-095-1

Typeset by MC Typeset, Gillingham, Kent
Printed and bound in Great Britain by
Short Run Press Ltd, Exeter, Devon

CONTENTS

1 INTRODUCTION

Barry Richards

TO CALL SOMETHING a 'crisis' is nowadays a very ordinary description. There can be few areas of social life that have not been described as being in 'crisis' in recent years. The use of this word is now a warning sign that some clichéd and polemical analysis may be on the way. All the same, we do not have to abandon the word. We need to consider why its use has become so commonplace, and how it may still be possible, and desirable, to identify states of crisis.

The contributions to this volume are not attempting explicitly to rework or rehabilitate the notion of 'crisis'. Indeed, in most of them there is little use of the term. However, the notion of a 'crisis of the self' provides a useful rubric for these papers, one which can highlight the relevance of the psychoanalytic thinking represented here to a range of present-day concerns with social malaise, personal distress and problems of change: for example, the interest in 'postmodernism', the emergent 'politics of identity', the question of the moral condition of Thatcherite Britain, and the growing social role of psychotherapy and counselling.

In the sense proposed here, a 'crisis' is not simply a state of imminent mental collapse but is a psychic configuration in which something continually needs to be done, and is being done, in order to ward off a collapse, an immanence rather than imminence. As such it might be a long-term, even apparently fixed, state of affairs. This is not the same as the Freudian concept of repression, although that also refers to a continual process carried out in the interest of psychic order. The healthy Freudian ego is based on repressions firm yet permeable enough to contain unconscious strivings while utilizing their energies. The self in crisis is lacking this basic precondition of

1

psychic integrity, and needs instead to turn to other, more defensive ways of managing itself and its resources of primitive feeling. The projective expulsion of intolerable feelings is, as will be seen, foremost among the strategies of crisis-management to which it turns. ('Self' is being used in a largely non-technical sense to refer to the psychic totality of the individual, rather than in the narrower sense, given to it in some non-psychoanalytic psychologies, of the object of self-awareness.)

Intrinsic to all the accounts of 'crises' given here is the observation that the external social world is not an inert backcloth to individual enactments of crisis-management, but is an active constituent in them. Both in weighting the possibilities for management, and more obscurely in framing the origins of the crisis, the world of particular social institutions and specific cultural formations is constitutive of the self.

Here we encounter another cliché: the importance of 'society' in the making of individuals, or the assertion that inner and outer worlds are deeply interrelated. And here again we have to stick with the truth buried in the cliché and to find ways of elaborating and regenerating it. For over a decade now in Britain work has been in progress which has been trying to do this by drawing upon developments in psychoanalysis (particularly in the British traditions) and incorporating them into reflections on contemporary political experience. An earlier volume of essays (*Capitalism and Infancy: Essays on Psychoanalysis and Politics*, 1984) was a contribution to this task, which is also a central part of the project of the journal *Free Associations*.

In 1987, Free Association Books, the publishers of the journal, and the sociology department of North East London Polytechnic (since renamed the Polytechnic of East London) collaborated in the organization of a conference, designed to further the work of the journal and to build on the interdisciplinary teaching programmes pursued in the sociology department. Many offers of interesting papers were received; the conference was well attended and very successful. A second one was held in 1988, with similar results. A third is now scheduled for 1989, and the conference – under the standing title of 'Psychoanalysis and the Public Sphere' – seems set to become an annual event.

The papers in this volume are only a sample of the work that has been presented at the 1987 and 1988 conferences. There were many other papers which merited publication, and the journal editors hope in future to make better use of this resource. The present selection

2

was made on the basis of the thematic continuities and convergencies which, I argue, can be found here. Before proceeding to summaries of the papers, a few more general points about the collection are worth making.

Since the publication of *Capitalism and Infancy* things have moved on, both in the intellectual culture into which psychoanalytic ideas are diffusing and in the surrounding political culture. The general impact of and receptiveness to ideas from the Britain schools of psychoanalysis, especially the Kleinian, is much greater than it was. It could be claimed for the previous volume that it was breaking some ground in exploring the implications for social understanding of broadly object-relational ways of thinking in psychoanalysis, while in the present collection the influence of specifically Kleinian ideas, especially around the concept of projective identification (see p. 8), is more marked. At the same time there are major continuities, crossing narrower doctrinal boundaries, in the concerns with narcissism, splitting, and the prospects for containment and reparation.

Politically we are of course five years further into an administration which has been proceeding with its plans to transform British society into an 'enterprise culture' based on socio-economic restructuring, the reform of the state apparatus and of many other key institutions. The dismay of the Left, and of the opposition as a whole, had deepened. The project of reviving the socialist ideal, albeit in transmuted form, to which the earlier book in large part subscribed, seems even more remote. There is consequently rather less sense of political mission in this collection than was evinced in the previous one.

At the same time, the scope of the papers included here testifies to the vigour with which the public significance of psychoanalysis and psychoanalytic knowledge is being explored. The political open-endedness of this process has to be regarded as a strength at a time when very few closures seem to produce viable positions. None the less it will be seen that there are in individual papers powerful commitments to specific values: against racism and militarism, for the recognition of emotional needs, of their mediations by gender, and of psychological truth. A major contribution of psychoanalytic thinking to the public sphere seems to lie in following through these commitments, in the critical scrutiny of political passions and in the considered extrapolation of psychoanalytic values beyond the consulting room.

As a whole[1] these papers do not explicitly take a position in the debates presently surrounding the notion of the 'post-modern'.

3

However, the term 'post-modernist' has to some degree become a rallying point for arguments that the modern, humanist project of rational enquiry by a coherent, knowing and moral self is exhausted, or was always illusory. On this point these papers are of great relevance, in that they demonstrate this not to be the case, whatever difficulties that project finds itself to be in. The psychoanalytic traditions which they represent, or are influenced by, are entirely linked to the modern enterprise; even those developments possessing some affinities with the 'post-modernist' temperament (e.g., arguably, the phenomenologically and aesthetically oriented writings of the 'post-Kleinians') remain tied to a transcendent and normative vision of rationality and goodness (see Rustin, 1989). A general discussion of modernity, psychoanalysis and the self is not to be offered here; instead, the usefulness of these papers in casting light on the specific problems they address will have to be the test of the 'modern' assumptions underpinning the psychoanalytic work they illustrate.

The book is divided into three sections. In the first, some broad perspectives on the self in crisis are offered – political, historical and philosophical. The second and third consist of 'case studies', either in the clinical sense of being accounts of work with particular individuals or in particular settings, or in the sense of being analyses of specific segments of culture. The second section deals with examples from the fields of health and welfare, the third with phenomena in popular culture and political culture. These distinctions are somewhat blurred, especially since psychodynamic analyses tend to blur the boundaries between different areas of social life by focusing on processes common to all areas. However, this grouping has still been made, in the interests of both flagging the scope of the book to a number of potential readerships and reminding us of the need for other levels of analysis which address the *specificity* of different social domains.

The impact of modern uncertainties upon the capacity for political vision is the subject of Paul Hoggett's paper, which takes up some well-worn themes in a fresh way. There are two themes: the critique of political passion for its tendencies towards dogmatism and destructiveness, and the critique of political disengagement for its emptiness and irresponsibility. Blending psychoanalytic and political preoccupations in a distinctive fashion, Hoggett expounds the psychoanalytic critique of activism as based upon some degree of falsehood and splitting. Commitment to a path of action must involve

4

premature and at best partial apprehension of the truth of a situation, which in the complexity should give grounds for hesitation and hedging. Committed activism must also be powered by a splitting of good from bad, so that the costs of one's actions (for example the personal distress caused to one's opponents and their families, or on a more violent level the sufferings of war) do not disable the activist with guilt – the damage can be experienced as largely confined to bad objects. As in racism (see Chapters 12–14), the human world is divided into the Good and the Bad, though in the ideologies Hoggett is concerned with, those of the moribund ultra-Left, the split is usually articulated along lines of class allegiance rather than ethnicity.

Hoggett gives this critique its full weight, but is more immediately concerned with the apparently opposite form of malaise which, in the last twenty years, has come to predominate over the sickness of action. This is the condition of cynicism, of contempt for moral commitments of all kinds. This is as omniscient and narcissistic an attitude as the fundamentalisms to which it is superficially opposed; it is simply a different mode of resolution of the same crisis of the self which feels itself to be in a thoroughly disordered and uncontrollable world. Yet the institutional forms taken by these different modes of resolution will themselves be likely to be very different. Fundamentalism seeks to fill and control the public sphere with the Party or its equivalent, while cynicism evacuates itself from the public sphere, and the public from itself (a theme developed in Karl Figlio's paper). Also the choice between the two major modes will be determined at least in part by the immediate political context; Hoggett postulates that periods of recession will produce the resentful withdrawal of the cynic.

The problem with some such psychoanalytic interpretations of political culture is that they tend to overlook the specific, 'conjunctural' aspects of particular situations, and to imply that recurrent or cyclical feeling-states are the main thing, irrespective of the *unique* context. Hoggett acknowledges the recursive nature of political sentiments, but is concerned to address the specific features of present-day uncertainty, and the problem of overcoming it with some commitment to action which is not a pathological form of splitting. Fluently linking Gramsci and Bion, he brings a new theoretical energy to bear upon an old and deep problem.

In the second chapter I outline a way of thinking about the place of psychoanalysis in the context of the dislocations wrought upon social experience in and by the general processes of modernization. The cue for this is in the complementarity of certain key themes in sociological and literary writing about modern experience on the one hand and the nature of the therapeutic effort in psychoanalysis on the other. Specifically, the accounts of metropolitan experience to be found in early urban sociology (and since absorbed into popular lore about the horrors of city life) can be read as describing, on the social level, a meaninglessness equivalent to that of the individual's symptoms, dreams and associations, before these are analysed.

Through interpretive work upon the analysand's free associations, some sense is given to the motley nonsense of the phenomenal world. A mosaic is made of the pieces, and obscure strivings are brought to immediate life, often very painfully, and to reason. A restorative integration is performed upon a self confronted with the threat or actuality of its disintegration. In the private sphere of analytic therapy a cure or containment can then be found, at least for some people, for the fragmentational crisis of the self; in the public space of the modern city no such resolution is in sight. On the contrary, the development of consumer capitalism seems to be deepening the problem. The possiblities for individual enjoyment through consumer goods have so far been inversely related to those for individual enhancement and integration through communal purpose; as the former grow, the latter shrink. This at least is a common experience, and it yields two ways of looking at the practice of psychoanalytic therapy.

One is to see it as the purchase in the private sphere of what *cannot* be secured in the public, and therefore as fundamentally a kind of privileged retreat from the public world (whether this retreat is seen as being to a real and desirable goal or to an illusory condition of wholeness). The other is to see it as the preservation and development of a set of values concerning the possibility of meaning and coherence, not to be salvaged or sequestered from a hopeless public world, but to be carried into it.

The integrative goal of psychoanalysis can be distinguished from those offered by other theories and therapies. It is not the same, for example, as a Romantic holism, though it draws upon Romantic traditions. It also contrasts with other responses made in psychological theory to the anomie of the modern metropolis, responses in which the surface of experience – of dissociated and instrumental relations with others – is taken for the sum total of human possibility. Psychoanalysis is, at least potentially, a source of opposition to the disintegrative tendencies in modern culture; its explicit purpose of repairing the fabric of individual experience has implications for a number of political agendas.

The experience of knowing (or not knowing) is a central dimension of selfhood, and so epistemology, the theory of knowledge, is an important philosophical approach to the self. The implications of psychoanalysis for epistemology are examined by Robert Young. As the Frankfurt School writers stressed some time ago, the progress of scientific rationality has been contradictory. The application of reason to the world ultimately undermines itself, in that it nurtures doubt, scepticism and a belief in relativity, including ultimately the relativity of reason and its products. As a consequence of this, in the study of science and within some scientific disciplines there have crystallized in recent years a host of arguments to the effect that scientific knowledge has no special status, or that its special claims are largely illusory. Nor are these problems confined to science – once the possibility of absolute knowledge is forgone, the effects are felt at all levels, in everyone's attempts to understand the world.

Thus the epistemic self, the knowing subject, has been in the throes of a well-publicized and much-discussed crisis for some time. The dissolution of all absolute or transcendent frames of reference has been one of the main themes in the post-modernist vision of the de-centred subject. Lacanian readings of psychoanalysis, among others, have usually been insistent that psychoanalysis itself is a major contributor to this de-centring and dis-illusionment, in its revelations of self-deception and of unconscious wishes at the heart of what is taken to be knowledge of the world. Working as he does with a theory of the 'alimentary basis' of knowing, it might seem as if Young is striking out in a similar direction. Using the ideas of Bion and Winnicott, he sees our knowledge as inevitably grounded in emotional life, ultimately in the primitive psyche-soma of infancy. Furthermore, he suggests that the same analysis should be applied to our experience and use of consumer goods, especially the high-technology goods which are now so important a part of everyday life in many societies and of the global economy. As in the production of ideas about the world, so also in the consumption of comforting devices: the role of primitive processes is paramount. Young vividly describes the consoling and supportive functions that consumer durables can fulfil. If the consumer society has created a moral crisis of the self, as is often argued, it also provides a wide range of possibilities for checking and managing the crisis. In this way, perhaps, the crisis is routinized and perpetuated, and the post-modernist vision apparently confirmed.

This paper argues that Winnicott's concepts of transitional objects and transitional phenomena provide a necessary way of thinking about both scientific knowledge and personal consumption, and about the technology which is the link between these two. Young sees Winnicott's use of these concepts to say something about 'the whole cultural field' as one of the most important attempts made within post-Freudian psychoanalysis to address social phenomena. Winnicott would however be a difficult figure to recruit to epistemological or moral nihilism, representing as he does one of the most humanist traditions in psychoanalysis. And in fact the direction of Young's argument is not towards the vortex of relativism.

Tracing knowledge and consumption to their unconscious roots may seem as if it is going to be the final turn of the relativist screw, but it turns out to offer the possibility instead of an alternative to both objectivism and relativism. Young proposes that we need a 'psychoanalytic epistemology' to help us in the task of integrating the rational and the primitive. The aim of this task is not the final rejection of the possibility of a coherent knowing self, but a re-moralization of knowledge, an overcoming of the historic split between fact and value that has flawed modern rationality. It is a transformative enrichment of that rationality, rather than its overthrow. This is an ambitious project, as Young remarks, but it is probably no more than psychoanalysis is already asking of philosophy.

In the first 'case study' Bob Hinshelwood provides a succinct and vivid demonstration, using two examples, of how the troublesome concept of projective identification can be used to understand sequences of interactions and other events in social settings. Although in these examples the settings are both clinical ones, it is clear from the descriptions given that here is something which can be seen happening in any kind of social situation. Intolerable feeling-states are forcibly passed on from one person and interaction to another. Thus, in the tightly interrelated and sensitively poised complexes of feeling which constitute the emotional under-life of all ongoing social groups (whether in work, domestic or 'social' settings), the generation of affect at one point in the system may eventuate in surprising consequences for other people at later times.

This understanding of the geographical and temporal mobility of feeling is one of the major contributions made by psychoanalysis to the understanding of organizational and institutional life. It enables us to fix for inspection some moments in the bewildering processes of reflection and amplification between inner and outer worlds. We

8

can at least see some of the phases in the zig-zag of feelings from one person or grouping to another. And more than that, we can begin to think in terms of responses made along the way which help to reduce the momentum, possibly even to convert the process into a constructive one. In the concept of projective identification, the capacity for affective transmission which is identified as the basis of contagion and collective madness is also seen as the basis for communication and empathy, for the understanding and sharing of feeling-states as well as for their serial transmission. In this sense the group therapist represents one element of good citizenship, that concerned with delineating the common predicaments and the collective responsibilities underlying some social conflicts.

This restoration of an authentic collectivity paradoxically involves, in Hinshelwood's terms, freeing the individual from 'possession' by the malign series of projective identifications. He links the psychoanalytic account of disowning of parts of the self with the concepts of 'role' and 'alienation' from social theory, showing how the different perspectives converge upon an understanding of individuals as depleted, as having lost possession of vital parts of themselves when they resort to evacuation as a way of coping with an internal crisis. One of the most developed accounts of the social depletion of the individual is to be found in Marxism and its analysis of the appropriation and reification of parts of the self in the processes of capitalist production and commodity exchange. Hinshelwood points to the homologies between this account and the Kleinian one he has been using. Schematic but suggestive, his conclusion invites a further consideration of the case material he has presented: what pathogenic contributions might the wider social environment have made to the processes observed, whether in the institutional set-up or elsewhere in the life-worlds of the individuals concerned?

Karl Figlio's discussion of some unconscious aspects of our thinking about health and disease, and its relation to the notion of a 'public sphere', builds on the paper by Hinshelwood in that it brings the concept of projective identification to bear upon the widest social processes. Figlio suggests that disease, as a category of thought and a range of bodily states, is something into which we project split-off aspects of ourselves – damaged and damaging fragments. This projective tendency has a long and deep history as part of our general construction of and relationship to 'nature', some of the complexities of which are explored here.

However, it is not a changeless feature of mental life but a tendency which can be shaped into particular forms by particular social relations. Drawing on his previous work in medical sociology, Figlio shows how the actuarial construction of risk groups is the basis for an intensification of the projection and its crystallization into a class-based 'loop' of projective identification. High-risk (usually lower-class) groups become identified with the threat of disease, and so the imagery of class (which continues, though in changing ways, to structure much of our social experience) becomes infused with phantasies surrounding disease: phantasies of the destructiveness and badness represented by disease itself, and of the omnipotent, idealized self which has purged itself of badness. Interactionist sociology, in its conception of illness as 'deviance', had some grasp of this intergroup element in our experience of health and disease, but in pointing to the content and strength of the unconscious processes involved Figlio provides a crucial interdisciplinary link between interactionist and psychoanalytic sociologies.

Figlio argues that 'public' represents an unconscious phantasy of ampleness, of a common wealth not depleted by primitive conflictual anxieties. But 'public' is often degraded into a residual 'public sector', the remains of a privileged access to an idealized breast, which leaves it exhausted and feared. The projections that help to locate disease in the working classes animate the demand for private health care, that is, for an alternative breast which will not be drained by the demands of others. The National Health Service in Britain is now widely felt to be drained, and although those who protest its depletion usually see the cause of this in a withholding, depriving mother-government, the 'cause' is arguably of secondary importance to the effect: the breast is deserted for a better (idealized) one. The solution to a psychic crisis produces a public one.

In grounding his discussion of health in the major cultural categories of nature, culture and the 'public', Figlio offers more than a focused analysis of the phantasies surrounding disease. He considers in the same way the kinds of paranoid and catastrophist phantasies that have been postulated as lying near the core of the scientific world-view, of which some attitudes to nuclear technology are particularly clear examples. His paper is a deep contribution to the whole project of integrating a psychoanalytic understanding into the study of cultural history.

Another example from institutional life, again developing Hinshelwood's theme, is the centre-piece of the next chapter, by Sheila Ernst. Drawing upon her experience as a consultant to a social services department, she links a particular example of managerial heavy-handedness to some wide theoretical concerns. Central to

10

these is the concept of omnipotence as a normal state of mind in infancy, when it is required in order to protect the infant from the terrors of confronting its real helplessness. Inside the protection of this developmentally necessary reversal the early delicate growth of more realistic ways of confronting the world, neither helpless nor omnipotent, may be sheltered. In adulthood, however, when these competences have hopefully developed to the point where the individual can meet the demands of others, and responsibility is required, the reappearance of omnipotent illusion as the implicit basis for action is a pathological retreat from reality.

Here lies one of the major contributions of contemporary psychoanalytic thinking to the understanding of social life. Ernst examines that aspect of bureaucratic culture in which there lives a phantasy of achieving absolute control over the business of the organization through the application of ever more formal procedural controls and specifications. While acknowledging the real gains in accountability and efficiency which may result from such rational procedures, she points to the kind of falsehood which they may also promote, and the distress they may cause, if they are employed in the service of an omnipotent defence. In this case the appearance within the organization of an admission of inadequacy was the occasion for a punitive intensification of managerial controls and a conspicuous failure to listen, either to the worker concerned or to the consultant. Inadequacy, especially in the explosive area of child abuse, could not be tolerated, even though it was a realistic response to the emotional complexities of the situation and its admission was an opportunity for further learning. An illusion of professional omnipotence had to be preserved.

Ernst compares this 'masculine' form of omnipotence, characterized by a striving for technical mastery over the chaos of feeling, with a 'feminine' form characterized by a belief in a redemptive maternal figure, who can still the troubled waters of organizational life through an infinite capacity to nurture. She found her own role as consultant to be a ready vehicle for this phantasy, despite (and to some degree because of) her lack of real power. The two forms may coexist, and men and women may participate in both – as in other areas, forms of experience which may characterize a key issue in the psychological development of one gender are none the less available to most members of the other. The omnipotent defences employed so damagingly by the women in the therapy group reported here can be found in identical as well as analogous forms in the lives of men.

11

Again, the reader is invited to consider the wider societal context for these pervasive phantasies of omnipotence and their gendered expression. Crises of self-confidence reaching far into emotional life are dealt with by actions which are rooted deeply in the traditions of professional and administrative life. What forces in a society may promote or discourage this use of ignorant and potentially destructive ways of solving problems? Reflecting on the current British political scene, Ernst suggests that a leadership style which both represents and offers omnipotence can call upon some powerful emotional support.

In organizational settings, drawing people's attention to the irrational, phantasy elements in their behaviour may help to change things for the better. It is not clear though if this kind of intervention is likely to be of equivalent usefulness in the wider political process.

A similar concern with the expulsion of unmanageable parts of the self is found in Marie Maguire's paper, though in a somewhat different theoretical context. Here Chasseguet-Smirgel's conceptualization of perversion as the attempt to assert omnipotent control over reality is deployed in a comparison of two clinical cases, the one a bulimic woman and the other a man committed to pornography. Taking these two cases as examples of an important difference between the sexes in characteristic psychopathology, she explores the differences in their transference relationships, the woman's dominated by guilt and the man's by eroticized aggression. These differences can be partly attributed to the specific tragedies of their individual life histories and partly, argues Maguire, to the different developmental tasks faced by boys and girls in the process of early psychological separation from the mother.

However, there is an important common element in their early experiences, that of the absence of a parental figure able to contain their most painful feelings. Neither mother was able to acknowledge or to sustain her child in its agonies, whether of guilt at the death of a sibling or of rage at a premature and abrupt weaning. Yet both mothers were intrusive, seductive and controlling, at the same time as they were closed to the child's most urgent demands for a space in their minds. In neither case was a father or other adult on hand to mitigate this problem. These two individuals were thus prevented in similar ways from contending with their – and everyone's – deepest and most shared problem, the acceptance of reality. The external realities of actual losses and inevitable disappointments and the internal realities of need and guilt can only be borne, it seems,

12

through the agency of a responsive and containing parent in helping to establish the child's capacity to tolerate reality.

(The reader may notice a potentially confusing variation in spelling, in that the word 'fantasy' is found throughout this paper, while in the previous chapters the spelling has been 'phantasy'. We are trying here to follow the usage common in British psychoanalytical writing, whereby the 'ph' spelling is applied to mental activity of an *unconscious* kind, with 'fantasy' reserved for daydreams and other products of the conscious imagination. It may be that in particular areas such as pornography this distinction is not one that can be made very firmly.)

Moving between these two cases Maguire thus shows how gender both is and is not constitutive of the deeper levels of subjectivity. The brute fact of our separate and to some degree helpless existence in an intransigent world of others and other-ness owes nothing to gender. But from the first our efforts both to accept and to avoid this fact will be mediated by another brute fact (albeit one that can only speak in the languages of culture), that of our gender, itself one of the most powerful signs of other-ness.

In addition this paper refers to the questions that can be asked about the societal provision for perverse strategies for avoiding reality, most obviously the output of the pornography industry, and less clearly the complex of cultural imagery and consumption practices which must underpin the choice of eating as the site of the symptom. Given the strength as described here of the intrapsychic dispositions towards these strategies, we must ask anew how the social means for their expression may be related to other aspects of the social whole. Is perversion necessarily as dominant in capitalist consumer societies as it is in the minds of some individuals, or can more containing forms of response to crises of the self also be found or developed outside the consulting room, in public imagery of the body?

Amal Treacher's report on changes over time in the contents of *Woman* magazine takes some similar theoretical concerns with the psychoanalysis of gender into a very large and important area of life outside the consulting room – the domain of popular culture. Focusing on some short stories and on the contents of the 'problem page', she shows how from the 1950s to the 1980s there was a change in the representation of womanhood. Broadly speaking this change is from a preoccupation with the duty of supporting the husband and anchoring the family to one with opportunities for expressing and fulfilling the self. In some of today's conventional wisdom this change is seen as an uncomplicated change for the better, as one of the achievements of feminism. While not arguing with the very substantial gains for many women with which this shift in representations might be associated, Treacher considers some of its complications and possible costs.

There are moreover some important continuities between the earlier image of familial service and the newer one of truthfulness to the self. While the latter is not construed as a form of duty, it may in practice be as moralizing and coercive as the former. Where there are discontinuities, it is not always the later, 'free' woman whom one would rather see as representing the future. A selfish and individualistic trend can clearly be seen, amid some welcome plain-speaking about sexuality and the generally greater sensitivity to emotional needs. It is not difficult to see links between the trajectory of *Woman* and a simultaneous shift in British society as a whole, from a welfarist ethos of support for others to a more individualistic one of self-reliance. However, Treacher goes beyond these more manifest levels to look at the unconscious meaning of the image of the new independent woman, and sees it in terms of the defence against disappointment, against the possibility that the pain of the earliest loss of the mother might be repeated in later relationships. She thus provides an empirical demonstration of the controversial theory that our culture is now a predominantly narcissistic one, in which last-ditch illusions of autonomy and control have become a frequent mode of psychic survival.

In the immediate post-war period the crisis contemplated by the woman of *Woman* (agony aunt and correspondent alike) was a crisis of commitment: could she sustain her love for her husband, while around and inside her she felt the instabilities to be growing? Now, the crisis is one of independence: can she keep herself free of debilitating emotional attachments, and affirm her independent selfhood? As Treacher remarks, 'dependency' is now seen as a poison: it threatens us with the loss of self. It is a tendency within the self which has to be vanquished. While falling out of love used to be the problem, now falling *in* love is a threat, in so far as it evokes the malign force of dependency. Our need for others is felt to have grown to crisis proportions.

However, in many areas of popular culture this crisis has not yet been felt. In much popular music and romantic fiction, for example, happiness and fulfilment are still to be found in merger with another rather than in some hard-won 'independence'. And in a particular genre of film, as Jed Sekoff shows in the next chapter, a woman's love of and commitment to a man is still a healing force, and not a form of incarceration. Of course, we move here to a set of cultural products made very much more from the man's point of view; and also, the romantic ideal of fusion with the loved one is – in broad diagnostic terms – as defensive a strategy as self-proclaimed independence. In both cases the other-ness of reality, and the reality of others and of our needs for them, are denied. However, the different inflections and mediations which these strategies have in different cultural contexts, and thereby their different potentials for modification, are an important area for detailed psychosocial analysis.

The 1987 'Psychoanalysis and the Public Sphere' conference closed with a showing of John Huston's film *Freud*, which was prefaced by a talk by Jed Sekoff on 'Freud in the movies', in which he gave a review of some of the most important cultural themes in the relationship of the cinema to psychoanalysis. For this collection Sekoff has extended his study of certain representative films and the stories they have to tell about our inner worlds and about the psychiatric and psychoanalytic technicians of interiority. In this long but entertaining paper he examines closely three examples (*Spellbound, Random Harvest* and *Return of the Soldier*) of what he calls the 'mind-doctor' genre, that is, films in which the figure of a psychiatrist or psychoanalyst is an important element in the film's staging of a 'conversation' (within itself and with its audience) about the social bases of order and rationality. In the three films focused upon, the plot concerns the amnesia of the male lead, and the question of whether it can be cured through the love of a woman (who in *Spellbound* is also the psychoanalyst).

Amnesia is a crisis of identity; Sekoff's suggestion is that we can understand the amnesia films to be expressing a feeling that personal identity is in crisis in some wider way, beyond the specific traumas suffered by the heroes. For the amnesiac, the sense of order and identity derived from time, continuity and tradition has been lost. Yet, as such, his predicament is no worse than that of any modern individual, who also finds himself dropped as if from nowhere into a new situation. The social skills necessary to negotiate a superficial adjustment are there, but lacking are any deeper feeling and knowledge of connectedness and belonging.

A cure for the amnesiac is however possible, by a recovery of the real and coherent self which has been buried under the debris of fragmented experience, heaped upon it by explosions of violence occurring at random in this dangerous world. The cure is basically an act of remembrance, and its vehicle is a passionate relationship with

15

a woman (as is also the case, we might note, in Woody Allen's *Zelig*, where the hero has a more 'post-modern' complaint in his involuntary adoption of the characteristics of the people with whom he is in immediate contact). This often involves a restoration of desire as well as memory, since either or both parties may have been suffering from another modern complaint, the inhibition or dissipation of desire.

Sekoff links this interpretation of the films to a basically Kleinian account of the development of the self, and thus shows how psychoanalysis can elaborate our understanding of the dislocation of the self (as well as, in this case, providing part of the cultural scenery for dramatizations of that dislocation). Both his essay and Treacher's demonstrate the value of close, empirical considerations, guided by psychoanalytic ideas, of specific artefacts in popular culture, and both highlight the importance of romantic love as one of our major cultural provisions – in the absence of more therapeutic forms of containment and recovery – for stabilizing the agitated and rootless self.

The power of projective defences against intolerable inner states, particularly against phantasies of death and annihilation, when these become embedded in relations between different social groups, is returned to as the subject of Les Levidow's paper on 'moral panics', a synthesis of two papers he gave in successive years at the conferences. He examines two recent examples from Britain of a sustained campaign in the press about a particular issue.

The first case study is of some of the invective and fear that was both reported and produced by newspaper coverage of the introduction of a 'positive images' policy in the schools of a London borough. This policy was intended to combat 'heterosexism' by presenting affirmative images of gays and lesbians. What it might actually have amounted to in the classrooms (and how much it might have served to overcome fearful prejudice against homosexuals) became impossible to discern in the storm of hatred that ensued. Many local activists (most prominently but by no means only on the political Right) took stands against the policy, clearly feeling themselves to be threatened in a most profound way. Levidow traces some of the contours of this fear, and is able to make some striking observations on its apparent unconscious significance. He notes the irrational fears of epidemic (loosely connected with concerns about AIDS) and of violence that are manifest, but also goes on to postulate an underlying configuration of unconscious phantasy in which homosexuality is equated with death. The precise contents and determinants of this phantasy

16

remain to be explored, and some of the imagery is obscurely condensed or displaced; scenarios of the dissolution and death of society
and of the family are mixed with references to the death of the
species. Overall though, the clear implication of this study is that
political debate on this issue is likely – especially where, as in this
case, children are involved – to be heavily influenced by urgent
phantasies of psychic death. These are only tangentially related to
any realistic concern about physical death through AIDS, and result
in violent projections of annihilating and annihilated elements of the
self on to political opponents.

In the second case one national newspaper in particular attacked
the medical and social services in one region for the very high
number of children removed from their homes on the grounds of
suspected sexual abuse. What had been a growing national consensus of opinion that child sexual abuse was far more common than
previously assumed (a consensus that had itself reached at times the
proportions of a panic) was, within a period of days, punctured by
anger at these allegedly unjustified separations of children from their
parents. Something of a panic developed at the possibility that
malevolent professionals were attacking innocent families. Levidow
shows that, whatever the rights and wrongs of the situation might
have been (and at the time of writing it is still not clear how many of
the children had been abused), the feelings of outrage expressed and
orchestrated by the *Daily Mail* were of a primitive and irrational
kind. An explosive reserve of guilt about sexuality in the family,
displaced on to the enforced separations and projected on to the
professionals, lay behind many of their headlines and pronounce-
ments. This response obstructed the necessary, complex task of evaluating the responsibilities and competences of professionals concerned with child abuse.

Another kind of local government policy, involving an attempt at a
deliberate reversal of what are taken to be oppressive social practices,
is the starting-point of the next chapter. Valerie Sinason confronts
head-on the lack of emotional understanding at work in some 'positive discrimination' practices. She points out that the rehabilitation of
the outcast which is sometimes undertaken, however understand-
able it may be as a response to external realities, is in danger of being
blind to internal realities, to crucial questions of inner resources and
competences. Some forms of positive discrimination are perhaps not
discrimination at all, despite the endless preoccupation with the
discriminating factors of race, gender and sexual orientation. At root

they express the belief that there are no differences, that achievements as well as opportunities must be shared equally among all. As an immediate programme for social action, this owes less to an empathic respect for the struggles of disadvantaged and disabled people to develop their talents and better their lot than it does to a compulsive need to abolish the pains of differences as these are most powerfully felt, in differences of competence. By projective identification with the outcast, that is, by identifying with the outcast as the repository of our own feelings of impotence in the face of difference, we create a situation in which we can attempt to cancel out those feelings by turning the outcast into the ideal.

Sinason's complex essay goes on to explore capacities for discrimination in the mind of the outcast, showing how the perception of reality which depends on it may have only a fragile basis in the inner world. It may either be shattered completely by what is culturally presented to the self, or, by appropriate intervention, be strengthened. This can happen only on the basis of a greater capacity for tolerating difference, which is harder to develop the more that the experience of difference is grounded in persecutory fears. Language, as Sinason shows, is a route into understanding the simultaneously social and psychic origins of these fears. She suggests many valuable insights into the unconscious dimensions of psycholinguistics, using the analogy of linguistic habits as symptoms. She shows how our choices of words can helpfully be read and heard as symptoms, both as crystallizations of unconscious irresolution and as expressions of narcissistic omnipotence. At the same time language is of course a product of cultural tradition. Her case material shows how national history and the current political scene can reverberate powerfully in the minds of young people whose inner worlds are desolate or unstable, and can provide the means for the outward expression of those inner troubles. Some of it also points up the deeply parental meanings with which the institutions of welfare and education are invested, an issue with which the leftist advocates of autonomy and self-determination for client-groups, as much as the neo-liberal deconstructors of the welfare apparatus, have failed to come to grips.

The most pernicious and permanent form of 'moral panic' is racism, where difference is experienced in the most persecutory way. Stephen Frosh reviews some of the established psychoanalytically influenced theorizing about racism, particularly in *The Authoritarian Personality* research and in the writing of Frantz Fanon. He sets out a framework within which some of the insights of this work can be deepened, by linking them to some post-Freudian theory and to

18

INTRODUCTION

recent analyses of the experiential qualities of contemporary culture. The rigidity of the authoritarian is in the last analysis a defence against psychotic disintegration rather than – as social psychology has tended to interpret it – against some loss of self-esteem or a forbidden sexual pleasure. And at a social level, as we have already noted in discussing Chapter 3, the experience of disintegration is emblematic of modernity.

Racism in its leading present-day forms is therefore grounded in an intolerance of the psychic fluidity demanded by the culture of advanced capitalism. Where a lack of sufficiently stable internal good objects, which might enable the individual to negotiate the external flux from some position of inner stability, occurs in a social context of inter-ethnic relations, then racism is a likely outcome. Other conditions must also be fulfilled: one group must somewhere feel itself to be powerless, and so need to resort to the omnipotent phantasies typical of racism. And the pattern of social or economic life must somehow have given grounds for the ethnic difference to represent the break-up of an idealized world of order and security. An example of this would be the appearance of black people in many British towns and cities simultaneously with the dislocations of redevelopment and economic restructuring. The former was related to but not causal of the latter; the racist mind seizes upon the association, but is incapable of analysing it.

Here, however, Frosh's focus is on the sexual factor, which – following Fanon, or rather adopting a Lacan-influenced reading of Fanon – he argues must continue to be seen as central. Although in Fanon's analysis it is an image of the black *man* that is at the hub of the racist's sexualized fear, envy and hatred, the realm of uncontrollable other-ness which the racist struggles to obliterate is seen by some as the expression of the feminine, and as the negation of a 'masculine' principle of order and stasis. There are many objections that can be raised against this argument, but Frosh's presentation of it establishes that perverse eroticism in some form is vital to racism. He shows that this perversion must be understood as arising in desperate response to psychic crises of a historically specific kind, and reminds us furthermore that psychoanalysis and its associates have not always stood squarely against the most destructive expressions of those crises.

Frosh's theoretical essay is followed by an extract from the work of Philip Cohen, who has presented papers at both conferences on psychoanalytically informed work with schoolchildren around the problem of racism. In the account given here of a particular kind of

19

anti-racism work, Cohen illustrates how a psychoanalytic under-standing of the 'racist imagination' prescribes a very different sort of approach to education from that taken by the more didactic or confrontational approaches recently popular.

The starting-point of this work is an appreciation of the function of racist images of the alien in containing hated parts of the self, and a recognition that psychologically real progress towards a reduction of racist feeling can be achieved only on the basis of some recovery of those parts. As Frosh's argument suggests, racism institutionalizes a crisis of the self, and dismantling it as one of our key cultural formations can proceed only if there is some active attempt to address this crisis, and to recover or reorganize the projections which are its psychic basis. Cohen's work shows some of the important practical possibilities that may be opened up when recent bodies of work on popular culture are harnessed with a psychoanalytically informed sensitivity to inner needs.

The central theme in this approach is the uses that children make of 'Monster' imagery. A vital distinction is made between the Mon-ster as a repository of projected and disowned feelings, and thereby as a hated and persecutory figure, and the Monster with whom some identification is made and who can therefore be the vehicle for some confrontation with and integration of those feelings. Cohen links the first kind of use to the history of medieval and colonial represen-tations of the non-white Other, and to the present-day racist imagi-nation. The second, therapeutic use of the Monster, involving the creative aspect of projective identification, is explored in a selection of children's books. A number of these demonstrate how through stories and play some acceptance of the internal realities of rage and envy, and the external realities of difference, can be built up, and how the crisis of self-recognition at the heart of racist murderousness can be averted.

To this end it is necessary that the Monster does not become too tame, which is a danger in some of the books reviewed. There are also problems, as Cohen points out, in that some of their scenarios reproduce elements of colonial or romantic world-views that may impede the work of integration. And when that work is undertaken in the classroom, there are a number of anxieties among the adults involved which need to be dealt with. This is perhaps not surprising, since the change in approach signified here has implications not only for anti-racism but for the educational process in all spheres. Again, the aim is no less than a reconstruction of rationality and of the 'civilizing process', and it depends on the persistence and subtlety of practical undertakings of this sort.

The final chapter is a statement by Jane Temperley about the thinking that lay behind the formation in Britain of Psychoanalysts for the Prevention of Nuclear War (PPNW), a group including members of all three streams of the British Psycho-Analytical Society. As she points out, this was a highly significant development, not only for the helpful influence which this body may be able to exercise but also because it was the first organized entry of psychoanalysts into the public sphere. This is a measure of the impact, in the early 1980s, upon the imagination of many sections of British society of a new wave of imagery and propaganda about the effects of nuclear war. Whether and how this mobilization can be sustained and adapted in the new conditions of the Gorbachev era remains to be seen. None the less there is a lasting achievement in the preparedness of many psychoanalysts to affirm the political dimension of their work.

Temperley outlines the basic Kleinian concepts which provide one underpinning of this affirmation. These may be seen as coming in two parts. The first is the analysis of the processes at work in international relations, in military strategy-making, and in popular perceptions of the enemy. These can clearly be understood as heavily influenced by primitive fears of persecution, as belonging in large part to the 'paranoid-schizoid' position. Many of the other chapters in this book have told similar stories of social processes dominated by splitting, projection and projective identification, of psychic crises caused by intolerable feeling-states and managed, however disastrously, by the violent evacuation of the unbearable mental contents into a social space that is usually in some way receptive to these projections. Here it is most obviously impulses towards rampant aggression which are split off from national self-consciousness and attributed to the enemy.

The second is the hypothesis about what the ultimate source of this uncontainable aggressivity is. As is well known, Klein here adhered to Freud's notion of the death instinct. In Chapter 3 is offered a translation of this concept into the social relations of the modern world – the death instinct is the reflection in theory of the nightmare of dissolution and disintegration with which the extremes of modern, fragmented experience confront us. This social reading of the death instinct can be no more than a partial translation, however, an apprehension of just one strand of meaning in this contentious

21

and at times obscure concept. It does not grasp the 'Nirvana princi-ple' element of the death instinct concept, the urge to return to some state of zero tension, nor does the translation seem able to express the strength of the annihilatory force at work in the arms race. The concept of the death instinct conveys, enigmatically, the ultimate crisis of the self, and will retain some currency until some other and better way can be found of registering, with equal starkness, the sort of clinical and social phenomena which led Freud to formulate it.

The papers collected here represent quite a wide range, both in their ways of using psychoanalytic ideas and in their social concerns, and moreover in the conference programmes from which they are der-ived there was much greater diversity. None the less there is a growing basis – in the contents of this volume, and its predecessor, and in many articles published in *Free Associations* – for claiming that a broad but distinctive body of work is being generated. A set of theoretical and political concerns with culture (the influence of Ray-mond Williams is to be found in a number of the papers here), especially with the destructiveness at large in political culture, is coupled with modes of understanding derived from contemporary psychoanalytic work in the Kleinian and object-relational traditions. The progeny of this coupling will have a lot to contribute, we hope, in the work of reconstituting and enriching the public sphere.

NOTES

1. In two papers (those by Stephen Frosh and myself) use is made of a notion of 'modernity' (drawing in both cases on the work of Marshall Berman, 1982), seen as a very broad set of societal arrangements and as a concomi-tant type of individual experience, both characterized by high degrees of flux, discontinuity, secularization and rationalization. Both social forms and their subjective registration seem to reach back in time to the rise of capitalism, although a clear consciousness of them did not emerge until the nineteenth century. Moreover, both the forms and the experience of modernity have undergone various extensions and intensifications in more recent periods, a process still under way. Within this perspective, the idea of a post-modernity, of a post-modern *world*, makes little sense; crises of the self are crises within modernity, and on their resolution the success of the 'project of modernity', as Habermas, Berman and others call it, depends. However this perspective does not necessarily prescribe any particular use of the terms 'modern*ism*' and 'post-modern*ism*' to refer to specific aesthetic modes (unless a 'post-modernist' sensibility presents itself as a reflection of the passing of modern*ity*, in which case it would be

seen as based on a false understanding). For some discussions of the complex debates in this area see, for example, Anderson (1984), Appignanesi (1989), Eagleton (1985), Richters (1988) and Schulte-Sasse (1986) and *Theory, Culture & Society* 2(3), 1985, a special issue on 'The Fate of Modernity'.

REFERENCES

All books are published in London unless otherwise stated.

Anderson, P. (1984) 'Modernity and revolution', New Left Review 144: 96–113.
Appignanesi, L., ed. (1989) *Postmodernism. ICA Documents.* Free Association Books.
Berman, M. (1982) *All That is Solid Melts into Air.* Verso, 1983.
Bion, W.R. (1970) *Attention and Interpretation.* Tavistock.
Chasseguet-Smirgel, J. (1984) *Creativity and Perversion.* Free Association Books.
Eagleton, T. (1985) 'Capitalism, modernism and post-modernism', *New Left Review* 152: 60–73.
Gramsci, A. (1977) *The Prison Notebooks.* Lawrence & Wishart.
Klein, M. (1975) *Envy and Gratitude.* Hogarth.
Richards, B., ed. (1984) *Capitalism and Infancy: Essays on Psychoanalysis and Politics.* Free Association Books.
Richters, A. (1988) 'Modernity–postmodernity controversies: Habermas and Foucault', *Theory, Culture & Society* 6(4): 611–43.
Rustin, M. (1989) 'Post-Kleinian analysis and the post-modern', *New Left Review* 173: 109–28.
Schulte-Sasse, J. (1986) 'Modernity and modernism, postmodernity and post-modernism: framing the issue', *Cultural Critique* 5: 5–18.
Williams, R. (1973) *The Country and the City.* Chatto.
Williams, R. (1977) *Marxism and Literature.* Oxford: Oxford University Press.
Winnicott, D. (1982) *Through Paediatrics to Psycho-Analysis.* Hogarth.

PART 1
CONTEXT

2   THE CULTURE OF UNCERTAINTY

Paul Hoggett

> The crisis consists precisely in the fact that the old is dying and
> the new cannot be born; in this interregnum a great variety of
> morbid symptoms appear . . . The death of the old ideologies
> takes the form of scepticism with regards to all theories and
> general formulae . . . and to a form of politics which is not simply
> realistic in fact (this is always the case) but which is cynical in its
> immediate manifestation.
> ANTONIO GRAMSCI, *The Prison Notebooks*

> The recurrent configuration is of an explosive force within a res-
> training framework.
> WILFRED BION, *Attention and Interpretation*

THE GREAT WAVES of capitalist development, sometimes
referred to as Kondratiev waves, which have punctuated the
last two hundred years of world history have resulted in the
continuous construction, destruction and reconstruction of the world
we live in. Each new wave of development amounts to a qualitatively
distinct form of capitalist society. To compare the form of the industrial corporation, the family or the state during the classical period of
imperialism at the beginning of the twentieth century with the new
forms which developed after the Second World War is to compare
two sets of quite distinct phenomena. We cannot predict what new
forms will emerge if capitalism manages to come through its present
profound crisis to a new wave of development. We can however
agree with Carlotta Peres (1983) that the social and institutional
innovations which facilitated the post-war boom constitute 'a list of
obsolete mechanisms as regards the effective institutions required to
unleash the upswing of the fifth Kondratiev based on microelectro-
nics'. The Keynesian Welfare State, the traditional bureaucratic organizational form, monopoly capitalism, neo-colonialism and many
other institutional arrangements which were central to the development of the post-war boom now confront us as problems and
obstacles rather than as solutions.

If we can agree that successive mutations in the form of capitalism
have profound effects upon our ways of life then a history of cultural

forms tracing the interrelationship between waves of capitalist development and trends within literature, art, philosophy and politics would seem to be possible.[1]

My impression is that such an analysis has yet to be undertaken. What I would like to examine here is something slightly different. Rather than focus upon cultural discontinuities I would like to consider the possibility of cultural continuity or, more accurately, recursivity within culture. Irrespective of the different embryonic social forms that were incubating within them, each successive 'great recession' has etched a similar pattern upon the grain of collective human sentiment. In other words, there have been repeated themes in the way in which culture has performed its working through of economic and social crisis. To this extent one can speak of recurring 'cultures of uncertainty' marked by a number of essential ideas, emotions and orientations bound up with a complex we might usefully describe as being one of failed dependency. It is to an exploration of such sentiments that I would now like to turn.

To live through a deep-seated crisis within capitalist society is to participate in a period of uncertainty where all existing answers have ceased to serve. We are used to speaking of 'the economic crisis' but the sense of crisis I am reaching for goes beyond this. All of our certainties – economic, moral, political and aesthetic – are presently shaken. Moreover, not only do the old solutions no longer work. Worse than this, they now seem positively to contribute to the straits we find ourselves in. For those who, in the past, always considered themselves to be 'part of the solution' this is perplexing indeed.

The situation we are in affects each one of us personally and deeply. I say this in the full realization that some will disagree. The 'fundamentalist Left' will argue that there is indeed a crisis 'out there', in society, but it is not one that affects them. They will argue that objectively things are ripe for change, the problem is in the 'subjective factor', the absence of a political party capable of bringing about a revolutionary transformation. Closer inspection however reveals that this is not a prescient piece of self-criticism. No, the party exists, the problem is that the people won't come to it! The fact that this so-called 'crisis of the subjective factor'[2] appears to have existed since the destruction of revolutionary Marxism by Fascism and Stalinism fifty years ago doesn't appear to have shaken their belief that the problem lies with the people (and their present leaders) and not with the party. I think this kind of attitude is clearly 'part of the problem' we now face. It is indicative of a process of splitting 'out there' from 'in here', the 'objective' from the 'subjective', external from internal.

The truth, that we no longer have answers, hurts. And the pain is greatest for those who've striven the most conscientiously to use a system of thought as an instrument for turning a barren existence into one rich with meaning. Where, on the other hand, ideas are clung to as a badge of faith, as a way of erasing the nagging search for understanding, then no uncertainty will be felt. If crises are always, potentially, turning points – for economy, culture and politics – then the problem for Marxism has been its traditional reluctance to turn. To this extent it has taken on the form of a 'restraining framework', a form of consolation to be adhered to in face of the explosive force of truth. But the more we cling the more we betray our own deep anxiety. So we see that the crisis does affect us all internally, the difference being that some cannot contain this anxiety and work on it but adhere all the more desperately to that which, in the past, provided comfort.

This is the dilemma at the heart of truth-seeking. Our language betrays our predicament. As Balint (1959) noted, when we speak of 'understanding' we speak in terms of 'grasping' something. The best we can ever hope for is to have a grip on things which is 'good enough', one adequate to the tasks facing us but never complete or perfect. For the problem soon becomes one of relaxing our grip sufficiently for the journey of truth to begin again. This then is the problem of depressive anxiety, of 'letting go' and 'leaving behind' sufficiently for development to proceed while holding on to the feeling that what had been arrived at was basically good and valuable. Failure to adopt this depressive state of mind forces us to cling rigidly to a framework which no longer guides but traps and the more the force of truth threatens to explode this understanding, the more desperately we idealize it.

However, my impression is that the resurgence of fundamentalism is not the main problem we on the Left face at the moment. There has been a far more striking development than this, noticeable particularly within what were once 'progressive' sections of the intelligentsia. I would link it to a failure to maintain the depressive position in the context of failed dependency; as a result old attachments cannot be left with any dignity. Rather, they must be attacked and spoiled, for only in that way can their grip be relinquished. The perceived failure of existing totalizing systems such as psychoanalysis and Marxism leads to an attack upon the idea that the construction of

organizing systems of thought is possible, that is, upon the possibility of what Bion would call 'the selected fact'.[3]

The basis for such a development lies in a crisis of the very idea of
progress. This in itself is not unique. As Gramsci's comments suggest, the idea of progress was no less subject to doubt in the 1920s
than it is today. Of course, since then man has proved capable of acts
of cold savagery and impersonal destruction which to us seem
unprecedented. How can one be optimistic with this kind of legacy?
Yet reality itself, even the most stark and horrific, never leaves a
simple imprint upon consciousness. The bomb, the camps, the liqui-
dation of the Soviet peasantry and opposition, all of these things had
occurred by the 1950s and 1960s, yet hardly for a moment did they
dent our confidence in the idea that 'we'd never had it so good'.
Though I fear that to some this may sound crude, periods of economic development and economic crisis do produce contrasting,
popular, barely conscious sentiments. I would not wish to call them
optimism and pessimism for I feel these describe very particular and
vital human attitudes that I will investigate later. Rather, I suggest we
use the term 'contentment', the attitude of the infant feeding at the
bountiful breast – which, as we know, is a temporary illusion – to
describe those sentiments bound up with economic development
and 'resentment' to describe the sentiments evoked by crisis. Such
sentiments, then, mediate our perception of reality, its triumphs and
its catastrophes.[4]

Let us probe a little deeper into this disbelief in progress, for
though at one level it concerns itself with the real world problems of
unemployment or warfare, at another level it reveals quite primitive
and catastrophist assumptions. Consider the following extracts. The
first comes from Oswald Spengler's work *Decline of the West* which
was published just after the end of the First World War, at the
beginning of the last great world recession. Then come two extracts
from contemporary writers speaking on the issue of 'post-
modernism'.

First Spengler:

> We are civilized people; we have to reckon with the hard cold facts
> of *late* life, to which the parallel is to be found not in Pericles's
> Athens but in Caesar's Rome. Of great painting or great music
> there can no longer be, for Western people, any question. Their
> architectural possibilities have been exhausted these hundred
> years. Only *extensive* possibilities are left to them . . . It has been
> the convention hitherto to admit to no limits of any sort in these

30

matters . . . now, nobody but a pure romantic would take this way out. What are we to think of the individual who, standing before an *exhausted* quarry, would rather be told that a new vein will be struck tomorrow . . . than be shown a rich and virgin clay-bed near by? (1926, p. 40)

Note here the references to ancient Rome, the cold and weary realism and its antipathy to romanticism, but above all savour the repeated reference to 'exhaustion'. Now to Jameson:

there is another sense in which the writers and artists of the present day will no longer be able to invent new styles and worlds – they've already been invented; only a limited number of combinations are possible; the most unique ones have been thought of already . . . all that is left is to imitate dead styles. (1983, p. 115)

and to Baudrillard,

space is so saturated, the pressure so great from all who want to make themselves heard . . . (1983, p. 132)

We see then how the crisis in the idea of progress recurrently evokes the idea of the end of human development – all forms, all ideas, all aesthetics, all moralities have been exhausted. It is the phantasy of an exhausted breast with nothing left to give and, at this deeper level, the abandonment of hope. Here we have the intellectual's nightmare, that the thing he or she has been labouring over for months or years is also about to be produced by someone else. The intelligentsia's world has become peopled by doppelgängers, the possibility of transcendence has gone. No one can any longer leave their mark. No more Nietzsches, Freuds, Joyces or, for that matter, Presleys. The seam has been exhausted. An army of cultural miners fights over scraps and flotsam left by predecessors who still had a real job to do.

The end of thought invokes an era of intellectual petty commodity production in which we scrape a living like the street boys once did in Saigon, selling single cigarettes to passers-by. Enter an era of anti-thought in which the intelligentsia's only role is to pour scorn on those misguided fools who still speak of commitment . . . 'really, darling, how naïve, it's all been tried before.'

This is not pessimism, but hatred and despair. Having been caught once in an embrace with something which was good but then failed, one resolves firmly never to be caught again. The only future for culture lies in 'debunking' and pastiche, either the merciless stripping bare of tired systems or a corporophilic fiddling with, and

31

agglomeration of, cultural antiques. This is a pre-depressive attitude, one without the grace or courage to acknowledge past dependencies. This is not scepticism but cynicism, a crucial difference as we shall see.

Some describe this as 'going relativist' (D'Amico, 1986). But if 'anything' goes, this is not the sentiment of the 1960s (for whom today's relativists have the utmost scorn). In the 1960s this was emancipation from the rule of the father, from the law of restraint and unquestioning 'responsibility'. For the relativists of the 1980s those who once opened our prison gates (Freud, Marcuse, Laing, Marx, Luxemburg, Mao) are the real authority from whom they now promise liberation. Not surprisingly, the more they cry 'anything goes', the more others cling to their systems, to their consolations. A cultural nihilism feeds off and reproduces a set of petrified totalities. More importantly, each of these orientations emerges from a fundamental incapacity to bear frustration. Thus cynicism, despite its stylish garb, and fundamentalism share the same emotionally primitive foundation.

Both orientations are forms of thoughtlessness, that is, they are primarily positions from which meaning is attacked rather than nurtured. The difference, however, is this: the fundamentalist considers an event and, refusing to be fooled by appearances, reads into it only what he has evacuated from his own constipated mental system – no dialogue occurs, events provide no food for thought, such systems can only feed off their own (waste) products (Robinson, 1984). The cynic, on the other hand, refuses to be fooled by the idea that there is any depth to events at all. There is nothing more to behold than meets the eye; it is as if 'general laws were only meant for the stupid' (Sloterdijk, 1984). Whereas the one sees some meaning (if only the meaning of its own reflection), the other refuses the idea of meaning altogether. Bion calls this latter 'anti-thought'; it is something more radically pathological than simple thoughtlessness.

> it shows itself as a superior object asserting its superiority by finding fault with everything. The most important characteristic is its hatred of any new development . . . as if the new development were a rival to be destroyed. The emergence therefore of any tendency to search for the truth, to establish contact with reality and in short be scientific in no matter how rudimentary a fashion is met by destructive attacks on the tendency and the reassertion of the 'moral' superiority. (Bion, 1962, p. 98)

32

So, whereas fundamentalism is a form of ideological secondary narcissism (scientific but in the most primitive fashion), cynicism's only purpose lies in the collection of meaningful elements 'so that these elements can be stripped of their meaning and only the worthless residue retained . . . denudation not abstraction is the end product' (Bion, 1962, pp. 98–9). This, I fear, is where Lyotard's (1984) 'pragmatics of language particles' takes us. As such, far from constituting any kind of critique of the society of the fragmentary image, postmodernism stands as its champion and exemplar. The task of culture, to go beneath the surface of things, is abandoned for the celebration of surface-itiality (to borrow from this fashionable form of expression). We are by now used to the way in which the misfortune of some becomes 'high fashion' for others; we can only gasp when this is done to the ultimate nightmare of psychosis.

So far I have used a restricted sense of terms like 'culture' and 'intelligentsia' as if in some way this referred to a class of opinion-leaders. It is important to extend this sense to one that includes the general category of intellectual labourers in our society, in other words to those privileged enough to have a training and education to be in a position to know better. For my perception is that such cynicism is becoming a popular sentiment within this social layer; one encounters it, for instance, in many varieties of public servant – educators, planners, accountants – and in general in 'the professional classes'. I have found the writing of Peter Sloterdijk (1984) provocative in this context.

He speaks of cynicism being no longer an individual attribute, more a diffuse cultural phenomenon. For the educated, cynicism is the price to be paid for survival during a recession in which justice appears to have been defeated. Sloterdijk calls this an accommodation which knows about itself, one in which 'we see a detached negativity which scarcely allows itself any hope, at most a little irony and self-pity' (p. 194). He uses the term 'enlightened false consciousness' to describe an inward-looking fatalism which is nevertheless subliminally aware of its own retreat. It is an attitude which accepts the rewards of the system through a little self-parody. For example, one jokingly speaks of 'selling out' when personally laying out 'thousands' on a new car. The witticism here is meant to signal one's detachment from the career planning, home developing, consumption-orientated lifestyle that one's behaviour might otherwise suggest. It is not easy for 'progressives' to become 'normals' without much self-consciousness. In place of a broad moral and historical perspective life becomes filled with little projects – word processors to be bought and mastered, research in some urgent (but localized) social problem, a shift into freelance work and out of the oppressiveness of public institutions. These developments can be rationalized as contributing to some grander, longer-term transformative goal. But all the time, in the background, other thoughts keep breaking in, fuelling this uneasy humour.

Because of our background we should know better, and indeed a part of us does know better. A small, split-off part knows that we have become complicit in a broader sentiment of hopelessness through which the forcefulness of our enemies has been allowed to assume the majesty of fate. We know that late twentieth-century politics is all about dancing on the edge, and that if the odds are not quite against us surviving, then what of our children and our children's children? We know of the ruination of the Amazon basin and its peoples; we know that others starve while we eat, and in style; we know of the results of the application of science to torture so that victims cannot prematurely die; we have heard that arms are necessary to keep the peace, greed to feed the hungry, secrecy to preserve freedom. We know these and a thousand other things, being educated types, but it no longer arouses our passion except perhaps when in moments of impotent fury we fantasize acts of political murder. 'To be intelligent and to perform one's work in spite of it, that is the unhappy consciousness in its modernized form' (Sloterdijk, 1984, p. 194). One is reminded of Sartre's concept of 'bad faith'.

Yet we also know that others do fight, do continue to commit themselves to what seems like an unequal struggle. However, the problem for a renewed politics today is how to be hopeful without recourse to faith. The cynic would say that 'to hope' in these times is to find salvation in calculated naïvety; better not to kid ourselves again than embark upon another self-deceiving commitment. Well, in times like these, when it seems that defeat gets piled upon defeat, at least the cynic doesn't run the risk of being proved wrong yet again. But of course this is the hidden basis of the cynic's own consolation. By never putting oneself in a position where one has to take sides, let alone take action on the basis of such judgements, one can retain what Bion called an attitude of 'moral superiority'.

As Meltzer et al. note (1975, p. 241), political action can only ever proceed from an imperfect basis. Effective action is always based upon an incomplete understanding. If one were to wait until one had really studied a situation, was convinced that the evidence available really did point to certain conclusions, had consciously striven to explore and entertain the opposite point of view before rejecting it, if one did all those things then one would never take action until it was too late.[5] This makes it difficult for thoughtful people to become active (I'm sure many of them end up being analysts or psychotherapists where a sustained capacity to be 'in doubt and uncertainty' is perceived as the only helpful attitude), as difficult indeed as it is for active people to become thoughtful. How to combine decisiveness with thoughtfulness, a 'visionary consciousness' with a 'questioning consciousness', are the issues we must resolve.

Meltzer's argument is that action can only take place on the basis of a splitting process. To act decisively one must have some sense of being right. Given that there are no absolute truths we can be sure of, we have to temporarily suspend doubt in order to act upon what seems like the most justified position. Of course, we may have backed the wrong horse but in taking action we have to assume that we are right, the other wrong. Thus good is on our side, the bad on theirs. A certain idealization and projection is inevitable but, as we know, such processes can equally be in the service of development as of regression. The problem then is how to act decisively, with the passion that stems from feeling right and good, yet preserve the capacity to be proved wrong. For this is what distinguishes an intervention from an 'act of faith', and a starting point must be the consciousness of risk. To know risk is to know that one might be wrong but to act in spite of this. It is, then, to toy in public with the possibility of one's moral and intellectual imperfection, it is to hand over one's narcissism as if it were a hostage voluntarily given to an opposing position. An intervention is, to use Balint's (1959) formulation, inherently philobatic,[6] a step into the unknown which may result in one being brought roughly down to earth.

To know risk is to realize the necessity of toleration. To know that one might be wrong is to know that one has no monopoly on the truth. On the other hand, we know that a key characteristic of fundamentalism is its intolerance. In this way it reveals the regressive and paranoid foundation of its splitting between right and wrong. It is a basically ungenerous attitude where others are refused 'the benefit of the doubt'. There are no grey areas, the fissure between the ideal and the rotten is complete. As Meltzer (1978, p. 105) notes, this is an attitude of 'Those who are not with me must be against me'. It is an attitude which assumes the worst in others, unlike the contrary *New Testament* attitude which presumes that 'Those who are not against me must be with me'. Within the latter the will is still optimistic; it is optimism based on a benign view of human and group development, of people's capacity to struggle through to find answers which, even if not identical with one's own, are certainly no less just and truthful.

In writing these passages I'm trying to develop my own understanding of Gramsci's phrase 'pessimism of the intellect, optimism of the will', a phrase which has proved extremely irritating to some recent commentators on the Left, like Ralph Miliband (1985) but which I've always found profoundly pleasing. 'Pessimism of the intellect' has been the easiest to comprehend – then as now the problem was to develop forms of political practice which were not reliant upon a background teleology, to develop a Marxism which could face reality without crutches. But how can we concretely understand something which seems so voluntaristic as 'optimism of the will'? I feel Gramsci provides a clue when elsewhere in the *Prison Notebooks* he talks about the relationship between action and passion.

I feel that there may exist two paths towards truth. For Bion the appearance of truth is akin to the birth of meaning – an 'immaculate conception', though in this case one with a proper parentage. We know the centrality of Keats's phrase 'when a man is capable of being in doubt and uncertainty without irritable reaching after fact or reason' to Bion's sense of the truth-seeker. This is a quietistic path, equivalent to a period of confinement in which eros achieves its task of synthesis, binding and bringing together fragments of previous understandings to give birth to a new whole.

But there is another path, the active one of experimental action. Here reality is not a 'given' to be deciphered, but a process of becoming to be engaged with. For Gramsci this is the difference between a 'political scientist' and a 'politician'. In his essay 'The modern prince', Gramsci notes 'the political scientist has to keep within the bounds of effective reality in so far as he is merely a scientist. But Machiavelli is not merely a scientist: he is a *partisan*, a man of powerful *passions*, an active politician, who wishes to create a new balance of forces . . .' (1977, p. 172). Whereas the former understands reality, the latter creates it. Who is closer to the truth?

And if we think on this, is not the psychoanalyst partisan? Does he or she not 'take sides' with the forces of life? Do we not hear of the 'analytical intervention', of the importance of 'timing'? I wonder then if Bion has told us just one side of the story, the side with the 'purer' form. For although the other side is undoubtedly messy, there seems little point in understanding a patient or group only after the encounter has ceased. No, we have to grasp at fragments and live with the risk this necessarily involves.

Perhaps the difference between the political and the analytic partisan lies in the nature of their passion. For, as Gramsci notes, the politican bases passion on a sense of 'what ought to be'. But this is not necessarily a regressive yearning for an idealized system. As he notes, 'the attribute "utopian" does not apply to political will in general, but to specific wills which are incapable of relating means to an end and hence are not even wills, but idle whims, dreams, longings, etc.' (1977, p. 175).

This is faith, 'nothing other than the clothing worn by real and active will when in a weak position' (p. 337); it is not passion. This passion is a fusion of anger and love. It is an anger which comes from 'one's own better knowledge' harnessed constructively, not split off in murderous fantasy, to fuel an attention which can be directed violently towards the present, 'that pathological itch to scratch surfaces for concealed depths' (Eagleton, 1985, p. 70). This is what Gramsci means by 'pessimism of the intelligence'. But it is a love also, a love based upon a deep identification with a benign object; not perfect, but 'good enough' to keep alive an inner conviction that things can be different, indeed that people have in them the capacity to make a difference. This then is what perhaps both Gramsci and Winnicott in their different ways meant by 'optimism', the experience of hope in object relating.

NOTES

1. Over sixty years ago Trotsky (1923) speculated upon this very possibility.
2. The use of the terms 'subjective' and 'objective' factors has been a characteristic of Leninist and Trotskyist thought since the formation of the Third International in 1919. The significance of these concepts to the revolutionary movement lay in their intimate connection with a world view which assumed that European capitalism was 'objectively' disintegrating under the weight of its own contradictions and hence the revolutionary transformation was not only immanent but also imminent. The only factor missing was the revolutionary party, that is, the 'subjective' factor. The crude and simple counterposition of these two terms can be criticized in many ways – for instance, the prolonged absence of a revolutionary party surely in itself constitutes an element of the 'objective factor'. Moreover, in orthodox style 'the subjective' is made equivalent to 'the party' as if only the latter were capable of bringing about a change in the given.

37

3. Bion uses the term 'selected fact' to refer to a particular form of thought which has the property of giving organization to incoherent and fragmented experience. It is a property which enables the subject to emerge from a state in which psychotic anxiety, that is, persecution by doubt and the chaos of experience, predominates (Bion, 1962).

4. I could not, at this moment, give much more meaning to these two collective sentiments. Suffice it to say that contentment would appear to carry with it a strong element of what one might call 'omniscient complacency' whereas 'resentment' carries with it much irritability, the kind of irritability experienced when one is abruptly ejected from a state of grace.

5. In political as well as group and therapeutic settings, the issue of 'timing' is essential – an 'intervention' is a particular form of action in which the issue of 'when' is as important as 'what'. Moreover, there is but a short step from a 'questioning consciousness' to a fear of learning from experience. To say that all action necessarily proceeds from an uncertain basis means that in taking action we must live with the fear of an experience which can't be anticipated.

6. In *Thrills and Regressions* Balint develops a theorization of two essentially contrasting object-relational configurations resembling Fairbairn's notion of the phobic and counter-phobic orientations. For Balint the ocnophile is one who finds excitement and security by staying close to objects of desire. The philobat (based upon the Greek word for acrobat), on the other hand, derives excitement and security from inhabiting the wide open spaces between objects (though the philobat may need objects, typically instruments of one kind or another, to maintain his or her balance).

REFERENCES

Balint, M. (1959) *Thrills and Regressions*. Hogarth.

Baudrillard, J. (1983) 'The ecstasy of communication', in H. Foster, ed. *The Anti-Aesthetic*. Port Townsend, WA: Bay Press, pp. 126–34.

Bion, W.R. (1962) *Learning from Experience*. Heinemann.

—— (1970) *Attention and Interpretation*. Tavistock.

D'Amico, R. (1986) 'Going relativist', *Telos* 67: 135–46.

Eagleton, T. (1985) 'Capitalism, modernism and post-modernism', *New Left Review* 152: 60–73.

Gramsci, A. (1977) *The Prison Notebooks*. Lawrence & Wishart.

Jameson, F. (1983) 'Postmodernism and consumer society', in H. Foster, ed. *The Anti-Aesthetic*. Port Townsend, WA: Bay Press, pp. 111–25.

Lyotard, J.-F. (1984) *The Postmodern Condition*. Minneapolis: University of Minnesota Press.

Meltzer, D. (1978) *The Kleinian Development Part III: The Clinical Significance of the Work of W.R. Bion*. Strath Tay, Perthshire: Clunie Press.

Meltzer, D., Bremmer, J., Hoxter, S., Weddell, D. and Wittenberg, I. (1975) *Explorations in Autism*. Strath Tay, Perthshire: Clunie Press.

Miliband, R. (1985) 'The new revisionist spectrum', *New Left Review* 150: 5–26.

Peres, C. (1983) 'Structural change and the assimilation of new technologies in the economic and social system', *Futures* 15.4.83.

Robinson, S. (1984) 'The parent to the child', in B. Richards, ed. *Capitalism and Infancy: Essays on Psychoanalysis and Politics*. Free Association Books, pp. 167–206.

Sloterdijk, P. (1984) 'Cynicism – the twilight of false consciousness', *New German Critique* 33: 190–206.

Spengler, O. (1926) *The Decline of the West, Vol. I*. Allen & Unwin.

Trotsky, L. (1923) 'The curve of capitalist development', in *Fourth International*, May 1941.

3 PSYCHOANALYSIS IN REVERSE

Barry Richards

ONE OF THE FEW THINGS about the practice of psychoanalysis which has remained unchanged from its early days to the present is what is known as the 'fundamental rule'. This is the instruction given to analysands at the beginning of their psycho-analysis that they must speak about whatever comes into their minds, however trivial, irrelevant or unpleasant it seems. This is the *only* instruction given; no agenda is provided for the analysand. The aim of the 'free association' which will hopefully ensue is, according to one recent writer on the subject (Kris, 1987), nothing more than simply to extend itself; the process has no specific aim outside itself. As Zilboorg (1952) pointed out, free association is not free in the sense of being without determinants, but it is free (or largely so) from externally imposed determinants and from conscious direction, and it proceeds with minimal unconscious restriction.

The analysand's speech and thought during the analytic session may then consist in significant part of the tracing out of complex networks of words and images, each one leading to another or others. The work of the analyst, of course, is to try to interpret this flow of material, to suggest to the analysand what certain sequences of images and ideas may mean, to find the threads of meaning which link together what may initially appear to be disconnected thoughts and feelings. Over the years of an analysis, through a long and in essence hopefully co-operative effort, analyst and analysand try to generate frameworks of meaning, within which diverse aspects of the analysand's life experience may be situated. Through this excava-tion of unconscious meaning, significance may be found in many apparently trivial or accidental experiences and actions. Thus the mean-ingfulness of *conscious* experience can be recomposed and enlarged.

41

This is a familiar conception of the nature of psychoanalytic work. A number of observers have noted Freud's commitment to meaning, and some (e.g., Bakan, 1958) have seen it as in part a product of his Jewishness, that is, as a secularized expression of the Judaic mystical belief in the meaningful connectedness of things. Others, notably Rycroft (e.g., 1985), have suggested that psychoanalysis is *basically* a semantic activity, an exercise in the creative production of meaning rather than an empirical investigation. There is probably no need to pose such a hermeneutic account of psychoanalysis against *all* claims that it is concerned with establishing causes, or with a verifiable reality. We can see psychoanalysis as both an investigation of what is causing what in someone's internal world, and as a practice of producing meaning. The former implies the latter.[2]

The meaning-generating work of free association is what the 'fundamental rule' is about; it is the basis of clinical psychoanalysis. If then we explore the social meanings of free association, we are likely to find something of importance to the understanding of the social meanings of psychoanalysis as a whole. This paper aims to do this by looking historically at the emergence of free association as a specific technique, and asking some questions about why it emerged when it did and in the way that it did. The basic question is this: what is the *social* meaning of the psychoanalytic project of recovering *personal* meaning through associations and their interpretation? Answers to such a question should tell us something about what kind of enterprise psychoanalysis is, socially speaking, both in its emergent phase and today.

I will present a case for seeing its emergence partly as a response to the simultaneously developing culture of the modern city. Freud spent nearly his whole working life, relieved by long country holidays, in Vienna, and when psychoanalysis began to appear elsewhere it was in some of the other great cities of the world – Berlin, New York, London and so on. This is a most unsurprising observation: obviously psychoanalysis could emerge only where there were established high degrees of professional specialization and vanguardism, and where there was a potential market for psychoanalytic therapy. These conditions were unlikely to be met outside the great cities. However, we might ask whether specific features of life in these cities are reflected in, and may in some way have helped to shape, the particular directions which psychoanalysis took.

A positive answer to this question does not have to be another version of the clichéd notion that psychoanalysis is a product of *fin-de-siècle* Vienna. Peter Gay (1978) has pointed out the absurdity of

42

the argument that Freud's theories were all based on neurotic, middle-class Viennese women, which they weren't. He suggests that the idea that Freud's thinking was simply determined by something homogeneous called 'Viennese culture' is a myth constructed by cultural historians (or rather, I think we can say, by anti-Freudian psychologists playing at being cultural historians). He notes that some versions of this myth are mutually contradictory: both the hypocritical sexual repressiveness and the sexual permissiveness of Vienna have been blamed for Freud's preoccupations.[3] Gay rather overstates the case, proposing that 'Freud lived far less in Vienna than in his own mind'. Sociologically we cannot take that to be the whole truth, and the inconsistency of the 'Viennese culture' theories may point to the complexity of the relationships between Vienna and Freud's work, not to the absence of any relationship (Zanuso, 1986).

However, it is not Vienna as a unique city which is of relevance here, but rather the fact that the environment of psychoanalysis is the urban one, and specifically the most developed and intensive form of urban environment, the administrative and commercial metropolis of advanced capitalism. Lewis Mumford, the theorist of the city, contends that after 1890 there was a shift in the centre of gravity of the advanced nations. The industrial cities, the Coketowns, declined in political, cultural and to some extent economic significance, he argues (Mumford, 1938), as they became increasingly overshadowed by the metropolitan centres, the cities of administration, finance and consumption, which were the growth points of what sociologists were soon to call 'mass society'. These modern cities were not organic communities organized around a military or religious authority, or around a common industrial enterprise; rather they were shifting aggregations called into being by national and international forces outside themselves.

By 1900 there were eleven cities in the world with populations of over one million, including Vienna, Berlin, New York and London. In what Mumford described as their 'shapeless giantism' and their 'overpowering congestion' (pp. 233 and 240), these megalopolitan growths on the frontiers of cultural development brought new qualities of experience to everyday life, or at least dramatically intensified certain aspects of the experience of inhabitants of earlier cities.

Among the new or intensified qualities was that of the discontinuity and fragmentation of experience. There were many literary testimonies to this, some of them celebrating the exciting variety and 'feverish joys' which were now at hand, but most recoiling in anxiety or confusion from the bombardment of the senses.[4] In the city one is continually confronted by, and is part of, a motley human traffic in which the only unity usually experienced is that of a physical mass; people succeed one another in each other's experience in a disconnected stream, their purposes unknown. Faces, bodies and vehicles are adjacent in time and space, but apparently not linked by anything else. Images, goods and information are presented simultaneously or in rapid sequence, each perhaps with a powerful appeal but with no intrinsic relation to the next.

It is very difficult not to be clichéd when trying to specify this disintegative quality of city life, because complaints about the pace, impersonality and chaos of the city have become routinized in popular discourse. It helps therefore to go back to the earlier statements of distress about the quality of the metropolitan experience, to the attempts of commentators at the turn of the century to articulate what were perceived as the new pressures and costs brought by these unprecedented human settlements.

We can do this by taking not a literary example, but one from early sociology. In an interesting coincidence, Freud's *The Interpretation of Dreams*, though it actually appeared in 1899, bore the publication date of 1900, as did a book entitled *The Philosophy of Money* by the sociologist Georg Simmel. Simmel lived and worked in Berlin, and in this book he set out some observations about the phenomenology of city life. He extended these three years later in his classic essay of urban sociology, 'The metropolis and mental life'. Simmel states very clearly some points which have since been endlessly repeated, usually less clearly, in the everyday critique of the city: the intensity of stimulation and the 'crowding of impressions', the anonymity and the matter-of-fact soullessness. The number and variety of human contacts, he suggested, are such that no individual can respond to them all and remain inwardly coherent. The options for the city-dweller are therefore to become unresponsive or to disintegrate psychically. In more recent psychoanalytic thinking, a worse scenario than Simmel imagined is described, in which both these alternatives are combined: in the schizoid condition a degree of inner disintegration is characteristically masked by a degree of outward indifference. Simmel's diagnostic framework did not comprehend such ironies of the unconscious, but his analysis of urban subjectivity is none the less a rich one.

He described the conditions of life to which, I am suggesting, the technique of free association, and indeed psychoanalysis as a whole, can be seen as a response. At the same time that Simmel and others were charting the fragmenting impact of metropolitan life, Freud was

44

tracing configurations of meaning beneath the senseless fragments of dreams. These tend to be collections, as Freud (1900, p. 18) put it, of the 'indifferent and insignificant' elements of waking experience. Looking beneath the imagery of the dream, which multiplies the bizarre juxtapositions and disconnections of waking life in the city, he found patterns of personal meaning, threads of association which could be woven together into a restored fabric of experience. Freud saw dreams as stemming partly from the need to work out ideas, and work through feelings, that had been provoked by some aspect of the previous day's experience, and which there had been no opportunity to deal with during the day. Perhaps this has always been one function of dreaming, but how much more urgent and burdensome a task it must have become in a world where even a few minutes of waking experience in a city centre can generate a mass of unfinished business – desires and fears evoked by passing faces in the street, memories and wishes associated with an advertisement glimpsed on a hoarding or vehicle, and so on.

In his major publication of the following year (*The Psychopathology of Everyday Life*), Freud applied the same method to a range of common phenomena in waking life, especially to lapses of memory. Through these trivial gaps in consciousness he pulled scraps of experience from the pre-conscious, where they had been deposited by everyday life in a literate, metropolitan culture – place names, newspaper headlines, snippets of historical knowledge, literary and artistic references, and so on. Like a broken vase expertly made whole, these bits were then fashioned into a shape that was – to the person concerned – a recognizable part of himself, usually linked to some quite urgent feelings. From the outwardly unconnected precipitants of daily experience in the public sphere, a private knowledge of inner connections could be formed, and some part of the subject restored to a wholeness.

Why was and is the modern environment so fragmenting in its effect upon subjectivity? Beneath the urban flux Simmel saw the money economy and the dominance of social relations by impersonal calculation. His voice is one among a number to be heard in classical sociology according to which the major source of modern dislocation is the capitalist market. By driving out all considerations except ones of profit, market forces tend to dissolve those frameworks of meaning and community which can provide for the deeper coherence of experience. As Erich Fromm (1947, p. 77) was to put it in his description of the dominant psychic orientation of the modern era, 'the premise of the marketing orientation is emptiness, the lack of any specific quality which could not be subject to change.' The problem with the city is therefore not only nor even mainly one of the sheer quantity of stimulation. Its disorganizing impact is not primarily a matter of its scale, though that is important, but of its soul. It is a problem of the moral quality of interpersonal contacts and of relationships with the physical environment.

To these sociological analyses we can add a psychoanalytic dimension, drawing upon recent debates about the possibility of deep changes in psychic structure having occurred as a consequence of the socio-economic development of capitalism. It has been argued (most forcefully in the works of American cultural critics Philip Rieff and Christopher Lasch) that the dissolution of traditional frameworks of meaning and authority, including and especially those organizing family relationships, has led to crises of superego formation and ego-integration. The miscellaneous and atomized nature of the external world is thus impressed upon a psychic apparatus itself beset by internal disintegrative pressures.

Since the initial formulations of this problem, around the turn of the century, it has arguably got a great deal worse. People everywhere in the advanced industrial and post-industrial nations, whether or not they live in the metropolis, live increasingly in the metropolitan mode. Moreover, the business of consumption has assumed an increasingly dominant place in the everyday life of the city and its extending hinterland. Social membership and personal identity are increasingly defined in terms of consumership. Marketing, retail, leisure and service industries absorb larger proportions of the work-force. Advertising comes to dominate the iconics of everyday life. Public space becomes more saturated with the imagery and the practices of consumption, and 'commodification' – treating people and things only in terms of their market value – becomes a powerful trend in all social spheres. All these effects are felt most acutely in the city, where the frontiers of consumption are pushed out furthest.

The variegated tradition of critique of the 'consumer society' is then relevant here, in so far as it is concerned with the corrosive effects upon psychic integrity of a culture in which the pleasures of consumption have displaced more substantive and ethical codes. Consumption knows no values outside itself. A malign spiral effect can be discerned,[5] in that the world of consumer goods does offer some kind of integration to the disoriented, disenchanted modern self: an integration into and through the rituals of consumption, and ways to hold the self together in membership of the community of consumers, in a largely spurious sense of agency through the exercise of 'consumer choice', and in omnipotent psychic satisfactions in fusion with or possession of needed objects. However, the citizen-turned-consumer is then even further removed, as a result of immersion in the fragmentary imagery of advertising and consumer culture, from any possibility of more authentic integration. There is little basis in successive acts of consumption for an individual's experience to cohere around stable configurations of feeling and value, and for the painful, affective interchanges with other people upon which the development and sustenance of selfhood depends.

Through these psychoanalytic reflections on the experiential effects of the growing city and of the culture of consumption, we are able to complement the social-historical analysis of free association with a psychoanalytic perspective on socio-historical change, and so move towards a thoroughly two-way strategy for interdisciplinary work.

The related critique of 'mass society' is another tradition of social analysis of relevance here, in that it has often included reference to the experiential qualities of life in the city, which is the primary stage on which the 'masses' and 'mass culture' make their appearance. In the classic writings of the Frankfurt School (e.g., Horkheimer, 1947) a major theme is the 'decline of the individual', by which was meant the erosion in mass society of an autonomous, rational, integrated individual who occupied a coherent moral space and was therefore capable of moral choice and spontaneous authenticity. The individual is increasingly a passive, de-centred consumer manipulated by the 'culture industry', and is easily seduced, through the process of 'repressive desublimation' (as Marcuse termed the cultural liberalization of late capitalism), into the consumption of commodified pleasures.

However, we are by now in some very deep waters of social theory and face some serious terminological difficulties and problems in periodization. Take, for instance, the historical account offered by Jameson (1984). Under the heading of *post*-modernism, he describes – and locates within the last thirty years – a number of the cultural tendencies which I have been referring to: the fragmentation of the subject, the superficiality of affect, the break-up of stylistic norms. I have been describing such developments as 'modern' (in a sociological if not in a literary or history-of-art sense), and locating their emergence at the turn of the century. Among the questions which then suggest themselves are these. Are there different phases to these psychosocial developments? Are they best described as characteristics of 'modernity' or of 'post-modernity'? And how in *today*'s experience do the tendencies towards fragmentation appear? What is the utility in this context of the terms 'consumer culture' and 'mass society'? Both terms are often used in ways that lack precision, and the latter term is for some discredited by its associations with highbrow distaste for anything popular.

Without going further into these issues, I will try to clarify the assumptions which are involved in the broad historical perspective on psychoanalysis being offered here, and which I think remain tenable whatever answers are given to the foregoing questions. I am assuming that, although our contemporary world has been in the process of formation for many centuries, a particularly rapid and profound phase of its establishment can be seen to have occurred in a period of thirty years or so across the turn of this century. Some of the cultural phenomena and qualities of social experience which came to prominence in that period, and which were particularly characteristic of the emergent metropolitan environments, are still central to everyday life. (This though is not to overlook the profound changes in the 'cultural logic of capital', as Jameson calls it, that have taken place since, especially in the post-Second World War 'settlement' and again in the 1980s.) A particular range of psychosocial phenomena are in focus here, all characterized by the fragmentation of experience and the decomposition of meaning. This focus invokes a central theme in a wide and long tradition of modern lament, for which present-day society (whether defined as capitalist, as market society, consumer society or mass society) has destroyed the old values and regularities. This tradition shades on one side into reactionary or empty cliché, but also it incorporates some of the most profound sources of social and moral critique, from Marx through Weber to a number of contemporary positions. It is a tradition of some melancholy, but not necessarily of élitist hauteur or of nostalgic reaction.

Accordingly, the reader can appropriately place this argument within that tradition, providing that it is borne in mind that we are not talking about a total description of modern society, but rather about one trend or one set of elements within it, and one important way of evaluating those elements. Nor is it even an adequate account of the principal features of the metropolitan experience, which like the society of which it is a part is a much more mixed phenomenon than the foregoing discussion might suggest. Simmel, though unsparing in his critique of it, was in many ways an enthusiast for

48

the city, for the real gains it could provide in individual freedom. Alongside the reaction against the modern metropolis, there has been a contrary tradition of appreciation, following Baudelaire, which has influenced social thought about the city, as in the work of Sennett (1970), for whom the disorder of the turn-of-the-century city offered rich new possibilities for psychological growth in the diversity of contacts with others it made possible. Clearly any one-dimensional jeremiad about the ills of consumption and the megalopolis will poorly match the lived experience of modernity, with the real as well as the illusory possibilities it has brought for individual freedom, expression and satisfaction. Berman (1982) offers an eloquent exploration of the complexity of modern experience, while in Saunders's (1986) contribution to a 'new sociology of consumption' there is an example of the argument that consumption can provide a legitimate sphere of choice, control and self-expression, and a genuinely therapeutic way of contending with contemporary disorientation.

Here I am concentrating on just one aspect of metropolitan culture, and the main argument will probably by now be clear. It is that the practice of psychoanalysis, following the fundamental rule of free association, is concerned with the integration of experience and the generation of meaning, and as such constitutes a potential opposition to the psychologically disintegrative tendency in metropolitan experience. To some degree this opposition is of the kind that was offered by Romanticism and its defence of feeling in the age of rationality, but what is distinctive about psychoanalysis is its translation of this defence into a programme of rational enquiry, and into interventions which depend on the capacity to think. There are of course different views about this; some neo-Romantic readings of Freud, and some versions of Lacanian theory, celebrate psychoanalysis as the voice of disorder in an age of repressive order. From the position taken here, psychoanalysis is commended more for its role in the production of subjective order in an age of oppressive disorder.

This is not a novel idea, but what may be added to it here is the suggestion that it can be given a concrete grounding in the historical sociology of everyday life. I am suggesting that as well as seeing the clinical application of free association as the outcome of complex developments in the history of psychology, most obviously in the history of associationism, and as a Romantically influenced challenge to modernity, we can also see it as a response to more mundane features of the culture in which it originated, as a response to the day-to-day interactions and experiences of people in the milieux of its development. It offered to restore meaning to subjectivities which were increasingly being constructed and maintained in environments of impaired meaning.

'Meaning' is to be understood more in the senses of affective and moral meaning than those of cognitive or perceptual meaning. The issue is not whether people can make logical statements, perceive physical objects correctly, understand messages, and generally perform cognitive processing of information; on the whole they can. It is more a question of whether they can feel that their whole life experience can be contextualized within some encompassing framework of meaning, whether this be in the terms of an explicit ethical code, at a more implicit level of felt values, or is simply a matter of their capacity to give coherent accounts of their lives and conduct.

The contemporary crisis of the self is then rooted in the psychic costs of modernity. These are felt most acutely in the metropolitan environment, where meaning is most under attack and where consumption is at its most intense – and where accordingly phantasies of omnipotence are most persistently excited. This environment is also that in which the reality of the Other is most pressed upon us – in all the myriad complaints about the city there is inevitably a complaint about the very fact of other people. *They* are the problem – the ostensibly inhuman 'stresses' and 'pressures' of the city can be nothing other than the bodies and noises and needs of others as they too go about their business. Yet the city is also said to be the place where we are most separated from others and least able to make abiding commitments to them. Given this contradiction, the city is likely to pose particular problems for the integration of the self around a renunciation of omnipotence, a toleration of others and a loving internalization of the Other.

Having at last arrived at the nub of its argument, I should now explain the title of this chapter. One of my starting-points for this line of thought was a statement attributed to the literary critic Leo Lowenthal.[6] It is a very rich statement: 'Mass culture is psychoanalysis in reverse'. What Lowenthal probably had in mind here was the inter-war experience of Fascism, and to a lesser extent Stalinism, which led the Frankfurt thinkers to the idea that modern mass society inevitably generates authoritarianism: authoritarian systems of government and authoritarian personalities in its individual members. Psychoanalysis, on the other hand (he presumably implied), is concerned with trying to free the individual from the compulsions and illusions produced by repressive authoritarian socialization, and with developing a rational ego in place of a cruel, irrational authoritarian superego. This is a valid and important statement, both about mass society and psychoanalysis, though it lends itself to simplifications by libertarian rhetoric.

However, the statement can be understood in a different way, as a comment on the vicissitudes of meaning in human experience – an observation that in important ways mass culture acts to destroy meaning, while psychoanalysis is about the recovery and construction of meaning. This is one of the most important *social* meanings of the psychoanalytic pursuit of unconscious meaning. What Freud and psychoanalysts since have sought to do, through the arduous process of free association and interpretation, is to sift through the chaotic debris which necessarily constitutes a large part of modern experience, uncovering its abiding emotional content and trying, where necessary and possible, to reorder it around a core of meaningful selfhood – in other words, to act in a reverse fashion to the cultural tendency towards the *dis*sociation of experiences, thoughts and feelings from each other. Moreover, it provides a number of ways to theorize the dissociative trend, such that we can talk both of the social meaning of psychoanalysis and of the psychic meaning of the social trends which elicited the development of psychoanalysis.

Freud's own way of theorizing disintegration emerged in the controversial concept of the death instinct, which he conceptualized as a force at work in living matter seeking 'to disintegrate the cellular organism' (1924, p. 163), to dissolve the complex structures of life and return matter to inorganic stillness. This speculative concept failed to establish itself in much post-Freudian theory, yet we can see it as an indirect expression in Freud's thought of actual social trends (characteristically transmuted by him into philosophical absolutes). The strand of post-Freudian theory which has given greatest credence to the notion of a death instinct, namely Kleinian psychoanalysis, has also been the one to explore states of psychic disintegration most fully, and so to provide the most useful vocabulary for describing both the fragmentational and the reparative tendencies in contemporary experience.

It would be pleasing to report that, in addition to his oblique theoretical grasp of modernity, Freud's own experience of the city of Vienna was consistent with the features stressed here, that he too felt overwhelmed and fragmented by the clamour of anonymous persons going disconnectedly about their unknown business outside the windows of his home and consulting room at number 19 Berggasse. Promisingly, Freud is known to have disliked Vienna; in letters to

Fliess he spoke of his 'loathing' and 'hate' for it, and described it as 'repulsive' and 'extremely disgusting' (Masson, 1985, pp. 314, 403, 336 and 409 respectively). However, he did not enlarge on the grounds for these strong feelings, and the quality of his comments suggests more of an obsessional, libidinal involvement with the city than any fear that it threatened him and others with psychic disintegration. (This is also borne out by Freud admitting to an ambivalence about Vienna: after arriving in London, he spoke of his love for the prison he had finally escaped (Jones, 1957, p. 245). This points away from the theme of this chapter towards another theme in the psycho-history of the modern city: the significance for anally dominated phantasies of the new problems in sewage and rubbish disposal posed by the dense squalor of the inner cities and the greedy sprawl of the suburbs. That is another story though (see Schoenwald, 1973). Moreover, Jones suggests that the main source of Freud's feelings about Vienna may have been its illiberal, anti-Semitic atmosphere, and the opposition to his work and the progress of his career which he encountered there. Nor is there much sign in the self-reports given by the early patients of psychoanalysis that they were particularly preoccupied with the problems of living in Vienna. So we must conclude there is no evidence that Freud explicitly or personally registered the disintegrating qualities of urban life, but it is fortunately not necessary for the argument that he should.

This is because the argument is not about the conscious intentions of theorists and practitioners to address their work to problems they were aware of. My case for the social significance of free association is rather based on the notion, commonplace in the history of science, that developments in theory and technique can be related to aspects of the social context unbeknown to those responsible for them. It may clarify the case, or make it more plausible, briefly to compare psychoanalysis with other roughly contemporaneous developments in psychological theory seen as different kinds of responses to metropolitan disorientation.

Let us turn to Chicago, another of Mumford's eleven monsters of 1900, in the early years of this century. Here American urban sociology was about to emerge, and another very different and influential response to the mass urban experience was being elaborated within psychological theory, one with enormous subsequent influence in socio-psychological thought. This is the tradition of symbolic interactionism, which grew around the notion of the self developed by Cooley and Mead. They theorized the self as consisting *only* of the myriad reflections it saw of itself in interactions with others – the 'looking-glass self' in Cooley's famous though not entirely appropriate phrase. Here, and in the subsequent elaboration of the concept of 'role' in social psychology, the shifting, discontinuous nature of the new subjectivity, continually interrupted or intruded upon by others, came to dominate completely the theoretical attempt to grasp the essence of the self. Freud in comparison strove to find the constant interior of the self, the durable and autonomous patterns that lay beneath the kaleidoscope contents of the urban consciousness. In other words, Freud's response was more to *contest* the exigencies of the new order, while symbolic interactionism tended more to *reflect* them, uncritically, in its theoretical formulations.

A similar comparison can be made between psychoanalysis and behaviourism, and again between a Viennese and a Chicagoan response. In an interesting paper on the origins of behaviourism, Bakan (1966) has suggested that John Watson, the founder of behaviourism, was profoundly influenced by his experience of Chicago when he arrived there to study at the university, also in 1900. Watson was a raw youth from the rural South, and a refugee from a powerful Baptist upbringing. He was ill-equipped emotionally to deal with the new world of the city, where it seemed as if one's very survival depended upon acquiring a dissociated, mobile and instrumental self. His way of coping with this was not, like Freud, to *challenge* the atomization of experience but to embrace it, theoretically – to posit that human mental life was everywhere nothing other than a morally meaningless aggregation of responses to isolated stimuli. This response to the problem of urban alienation could at least help Watson, and those who adopted his theory, avoid the pain of feeling that there is something better in life that they have missed out on.

Thus, at least in this context, psychoanalysis can be favourably contrasted with interactionism and behaviourism, which are the main sources of most of today's non-psychoanalytic theories of the person. We should beware though of heroizing Freud as a lone fighter for meaning in an age of meaninglessness. There is for example another John Watson who is closely linked with another contemporary of Freud's – someone probably more famous than Freud himself and certainly more clearly understood as someone who could put together the pieces in the shattered life-worlds of troubled individuals. This was of course Sherlock Holmes, who has been likened to Freud by a number of writers. Raymond Williams, whose *The City and the Country* is the source of a number of my generalizations about responses to the urban experience, has suggested that one aspect of

the Holmes phenomenon is the capacity of his intelligence to pene-
trate beneath the bewildering surface detail of life in the city, and to
understand a state of affairs by revealing the motivated human
action which has brought it about. Freud had to find his way through
a different sort of fog, but had – in this respect – a similar project.

Hyman (1962) claims that the dramatic, revelatory construction of
Conan Doyle's stories was a clear stylistic influence on Freud. Ginzburg (1980) has discussed the way in which both Holmes and Freud
worked by the close examination of detail, apparently trivial, disconnected or incidental fragments which prove to be parts of an important whole. And Shepherd's essay (1985) hints at a similarity of the
content of their discoveries, in that the two were both centrally
concerned with guilt. We should not get carried away with these
homologies, striking and significant though they are; Holmes was
concerned with the social prosecution of material guilt, and Freud
with the psychic management of irrational guilt. As Marcus (1984,
p. 248) suggests, the shift in the location of meaning from Holmes to
Freud, from external to internal worlds, 'marks a great historical
transformation'. None the less, Conan Doyle's readers may well be in
pursuit of more than a good story on their vicarious visits to the
consulting room in Baker Street.

This leaves us on the brink of some crucial questions about the
Holmes/Freud method. Both Conan Doyle and Freud were medical
men, transposing techniques developed in medical diagnosis to
other spheres. Why should we believe their conclusions? Holmes
was fortunate: the culprit, when accused, often admitted the deed.
Unconscious wishes are rarely so helpful. The truth value and the
healing power of psychoanalysis cannot be so clearly attested. And
while the dramatic impact of some psychoanalytic interventions may
be considerable, in most cases the only means at our disposal for
supporting the claims of psychoanalytic knowledge are those of
rational argument about concepts and observations. Freud's rationa-
lism was as much an element of modernity as were the problems of
personal identity which his work has helped us to identify and to
mitigate. We have to distinguish between different kinds of
approach to crises of the self, between the inevitably spurious resolu-
tions offered by many other psychological approaches, and the
Freudian counsel of endurance. For although the disintegrative effect
of much social experience may to some extent be made good, the
psychoanalytic insight which is the instrument of repair insists that a
substrate of chaos and terror must remain. And our internal
resources for the management of disintegrative tendencies are as

much a part of modernity as are the external forces which evoke them.

NOTES

1. An extended version of this paper forms Chapter 2 of my *Images of Freud: Cultural Responses to Psychoanalysis* (Weidenfeld Dent, 1989). In addition to the broad psycho-social analysis summarized here, I discussed there the origins of free association in the philosophical traditions of associationism and Romanticism.
2. For analyses of these issues from the perspective of philosophical realism, see Rustin (1987) and Will (1986).
3. Compare Esslin (1972) on Vienna's commitment to hedonism with Trosman's (1973) rebuttal of the argument that a Viennese looseness of conduct helped to produce psychoanalysis.
4. Baudelaire (see Williams, 1973, p. 234) was an influential enthusiast for the modern 'fever'. Williams also discusses the dark and horrendous visions of the city in nineteenth-century literature, as in Gissing's 'Nether World'. Jennings's *Pandaemonium* documents how some contemporary observers recorded their experiences of the emergent metropolitan environment. For example, in the late nineteenth century the metaphor of a mass of molecules was used by a number of writers to capture the atomized, dissociated quality of pedestrian crowds in the cities (Jennings, 1985, pp. 347–8).
5. A fuller discussion of this hypothesis can be found in Richards (1985).
6. Martin Jay quotes it, without reference, in his book on the Frankfurt School (Jay, 1973).

REFERENCES

Bakan, D. (1958) *Sigmund Freud and the Jewish Mystical Tradition*. Boston: Beacon Press, 1975.
—— (1966) 'Behaviorism and American urbanization', *Journal for the History of the Behavioral Sciences* 2: 5–28.
Berman, M. (1982) *All That is Solid Melts into Air*. Verso, 1983.
Esslin, M. (1972) 'Freud's Vienna', in J. Miller, ed. *Freud: The Man, his World, his Influence*. Weidenfeld, pp 41–54.
Freud, S. (1900) *The Interpretation of Dreams*, in James Strachey, ed. *The Standard Edition of the Complete Works of Sigmund Freud*, 24 vols. Hogarth, 1953–73, vols 4 and 5, pp. 339–627.
—— (1901) *The Psychopathology of Everyday Life*. S.E. 6.
—— (1924) 'The economic problem of masochism'. *S.E.* 19, pp. 155–70.
Fromm, E. (1947) *Man for Himself*. Ark, 1986.
Gay, P. (1978) *Freud, Jews and Other Germans*. New York: Oxford University Press.

Ginzburg, C. (1980) 'Morelli, Freud and Sherlock Holmes: clues and scientific method', *History Workshop* 9: 5–36.

Horkheimer, M. (1947) 'Rise and decline of the individual', in *The Eclipse of Reason*. New York: Seabury Press, 1974, pp. 128–61.

Hyman, S. (1962) 'On *The Interpretation of Dreams*', in P. Meisel, ed. *Freud: A Collection of Critical Essays*. Englewood Cliffs, NJ: Prentice-Hall, 1981, pp. 121–44.

Jameson, F. (1984) 'Postmodernism, or the cultural logic of late capitalism', *New Left Review* 146: 53–91.

Jay, M. (1973) *The Dialectical Imagination*. Heinemann.

Jennings, H. (1985) *Pandaemonium*. Pan, 1987.

Jones, E. (1957) *Sigmund Freud: Life and Work. Vol. 3: The Last Phase*. Hogarth.

Kris, A. (1987) *Free Association – Method and Process*. New Haven, CT: Yale University Press.

Marcus, S. (1984) *Freud and the Culture of Psychoanalysis*. Boston: Allen & Unwin.

Masson, J., ed. (1985) *The Complete Letters of Sigmund Freud to Wilhelm Fliess 1887–1904*. Cambridge, MA: Harvard University Press.

Mumford, L. (1938) *The Culture of Cities*. Secker.

Richards, B. (1985) 'The politics of the self', *Free Assns* 3: 42–64.

Rustin, M. (1987) 'Psychoanalysis, philosophical realism and the new sociology of science', *Free Assns* 9: 102–36.

Rycroft, C. (1985) *Psychoanalysis and Beyond*. Chatto/Hogarth.

Saunders, P. (1986) *Social Theory and the Urban Question*. Hutchinson, second edition.

Schoenwald, R. (1973) 'Training urban man: a hypothesis about the sanitary movement', in H. Dyos and M. Wolff, eds *The Victorian City, Vol. 2*. Routledge & Kegan Paul, pp. 669–92.

Sennett, R. (1970) *Uses of Disorder: Personal Identity and City Life*. Allen Lane, 1971.

Shepherd, M. (1985) *Sherlock Holmes and the Case of Dr. Freud*. Tavistock.

Simmel, G. (1900) *The Philosophy of Money*. Routledge & Kegan Paul, 1978.

Simmel, G. (1903) 'The metropolis and mental life', in K. Wolff, ed. *The Sociology of Georg Simmel*. Glencoe: Free Press, 1950, pp. 409–24.

Trosman, H. (1973) 'Freud's cultural background', in J. Gedo and G. Pollock, eds *Freud: The Fusion of Science and Humanism*. New York: International Universities Press (Psychological Issues Monograph 34/35), pp. 46–70.

Will, D. (1986) 'Psychoanalysis and the new philosophy of science', *Int. Rev. Psycho-Anal.* 13: 163–73.

Williams, R. (1973) *The Country and the City*. Chatto.

Zanuso, B. (1986) *The Young Freud*. Oxford: Blackwell.

Zilboorg, G. (1952) 'Some sidelights on free association,' *Int. J. Psycho-Anal.* 33: 489–95.

4 TRANSITIONAL PHENOMENA

Production and Consumption

Robert M. Young

T HIS IS an exploratory essay, designed to illustrate a mode of analysis. At its roots lie the ideas of D.W. Winnicott on transitional objects and transitional phenomena and of Wilfred Bion on the alimentary basis of all knowing. Winnicott argued that the child's first 'not me' – neither subjective nor objective but partaking of both – was the basis of all culture, all religion, all play, all scientific creativity. Bion argued that the process of knowing never transcends its primitive origins in the alimentary canal and that all of the senses and all of thought continue to function according to primitive mechanisms, whatever else they are doing at the same time. Hence, emotion lies at the heart of the thinking process (Meltzer, 1986, p. 301). My point in this and in a previous paper (Young, 1986) is to begin to see what it would be like to take these thoughts seriously when applied to scientific knowledge, to culture, to leisure and to the rest of life.

I want to make a beginning at relating production, consumption and psychoanalysis – large topics. In particular, I am interested in the bearing of psychoanalysis on the origin and production of scientific ideas and on the creation and consumption of culture. But these merge easily, since I think of science as part of culture, not above it and certainly not its arbiter. This is not a particularly eccentric view, since it has become commonplace in recent research in the history, philosophy and social studies of science. I also think of culture-as-consumed as increasingly mediated by science, technology and medicine. This is also a fairly commonplace thought, if one considers satellite communications, high-fidelity, health fads and the drug industry.

If we look at the philosophy of science and technology through

Kleinian and Winnicottian lenses, we are left with no 'conflict-free sphere of the ego'. If we consider the theory of knowledge in this light, the Enlightenment project of objective, value-free rationality becomes a will-o-the-wisp. We are then empowered to embark upon exploration of the emotional origins and the ideological determinations of knowledge.

In recent work in the philosophy of science, it has become uncontroversial to say that all facts are theory-laden, that all theories are value-laden and that all values are constituted by ideological frameworks. Another fashionable way of putting that is that truth is made, not found. Since the sociology and anthropology of knowledge have been fully extended into science, it was thought that the relativists, contextualists and constitutivists had touched bottom. Relativists eschewed objectivity; contextualists broke down the conventional separation of science from its socio-economic and ideological contexts; constitutivists argued that truth is socially constructed and that its criteria are constituted by the forces that evoke enquiry.

Once the special status of science above culture was undermined, some of us came along and treated the history of ideas, including scientific ideas, as culture – as a moving army of metaphors. This approach included the deepest ideas of the greatest scientists – gravity, affinity, natural selection, that is, physics, chemistry and biology in their most profound and basic theoretical assumptions. Could there be more? Apparently so. Psychoanalysis holds out the hope of transcending the positivism of the *origins* of knowledge, just as various radical approaches to knowledge – going beyond the sociology of knowledge to its anthropology – have transcended the positivism of *context*. Traditional positivism separated fact from value. Psychoanalysis can help us to overcome the separation of fact from meaning and motive.

Turning from the origin and production of ideas to the creation and consumption of culture, my recent experience is that high-tech consumption has become ubiquitous. For my generation this meant records, radio, movies and hi-fi. For my children it has meant video and Walkmans and will one day include implants in the ears and receivers inside the skull. But technology, like all else, is historically relative, just as the concept of culture is, so we must not be too imaginatively impoverished and forget to notice what it felt like for my grandfather to be able to buy a dime novel or his grandfather to buy a penny magazine, and so on back to Gutenberg and medieval illuminated manuscripts, ancient scrolls and prehistoric cave paintings. Each seemed remarkable when it was new. Each seemed the epitome of technology. Each was treated as a comfort, a source of deep satisfaction. Each was neither subjective nor objective but partook of both.

An analogous point can be made about epistemology. The idea that symbolism and metaphor lay at the heart of science was not new to Charles Darwin when he spoke of 'natural selection' as a metaphor or to recent philosophers who have treated science as culture, for example, Richard Rorty. This insight was commonplace in Renaissance philosophy, just as was the shaping of nature into gardens in which the microcosm reflected the macrocosm. I once made a film in which the historicity of nature was illustrated in successive periods by a series of gardens, culminating in a garden city and an urban garden centre. That is, every period had its own conception of a garden, offering a highly condensed version of how nature was conceived at that time (Young and Gold, 1982). Nature has never been raw: for humankind it has always been symbolic, metaphorical, anthropomorphic, shaped, cooked.

How does all this bring us to psychoanalysis at the heart of experience – either in creating or consuming? It does so by way of the debate about transitional objects and transitional phenomena. I say debate, because no sooner do we invoke Winnicott's ideas about the primitive and persistent roots of culture, than we discover that it was on this very point that he and Melanie Klein fell out, so that a modern-day Kleinian would say that there are no transitional objects – only failed primary object relations. But just so. Is there such a gap between the theory of trying to recover the object via creativity and play, on the one hand, and that of trying to reconstitute it via reparation, on the other? I don't see the rift, but I haven't persuaded any of the Winnicottian or Kleinian sectarians to help me to sort it out, either. Nor have I been able to fathom it in my own reading.

Until we get some illumination on this point, I shall persist in saying that no matter how it is solved, both Kleinians and Winnicottians (though not Freudians) will agree that both the epistemology of science and that of cultural studies cry out for integration with each other and with psychoanalytic epistemology. It's obvious once you think of it.

Once we move off a positivist philosophy of science and accept that knowledge never severs its links with its genesis or its context – that, on the contrary, it is constituted by them – then how can primitive psychogenesis be left out? Or rather, how can it not be fundamental? The Habermasian hermeneuticists have argued that psychoanalysis – as reflexive knowledge – is the paradigm for all the rest. Interpersonal knowledge, including the moment of self-reflection, becomes the norm: I/thou rather than I/it. Introspection and interpersonal knowledge are not ways of knowing that fall short of scientific objectivity. Rather, scientific knowledge becomes a highly abstracted and rather worrying special case – an impoverishment of deeper, fuller knowing. Psychoanalytic knowledge is not only the model, i.e., the formal exemplar: it is the foundation.

Similarly, in the sphere of consumption, once we grasp the persistence of transitional objects and transitional phenomena into adult life, can we fail to see how perfectly stereo, surround sound, indwelling earphones and deeply textured music and video enfold one? In my view this sensuous recovery of the infantile idyll extends to Porsches, BMWs (cars and motorbikes), Muddy Fox and Claud Butler bicycles, Sony Professional Walkmans, Dolby C noise reduction, Video 8 cameras, instant cassette reverse with only 0.3 second delay at the end of the tape before the continuous music is resumed, digital insert earphones, stereo enhancers for videos, compact discs, digital audio tape, and more to come, so as to enrich the resonance and texture of cultural consumption.

When I built a special pair of speakers to do justice to the base notes in the Rolling Stones' 'Sympathy for the Devil' in the 1960s, I had no idea that in two decades I'd be made newly orgasmic by a pair of earphones smaller than a sixpence or that I would gladly pay all I had for a car system more powerful, moving and reverberative than the one in my sitting room. Or that I would get greater solace from these than from practically any other experience I've ever had. Breast, womb, object – near-perfect reunion. The sensuous satisfactions of these comforts seemed to me at least as pleasurable as a child's blanket or teddy bear.

But the pleasures and comforts do not stop here. They extend to food, clothing, bedding, saunas and jacuzzis, training shoes, luxuriant bathing, massage, the representation of art. There is no end to comfort, to the savouring of design, to the delights of the technologies of relaxation and the Body Shop. Think of all those oils and fragrances, all those soaps and conditioners, all that solace. Who ever said that socialism was the enemy of prosperity? Not Neil Kinnock, nor the editor of *Marxism Today*. Left rhetoric is no longer a language of abstention, of an asceticism in the name of class struggle or sacrifice for the cause. The anhedonic model of the hard Left is played out. Consumption is for now, not after 'the victory is ours'. Lest this seem a strange perspective on politics, I should mention that one of the most potent objects of debate in Britain is the personal organizer or Filofax. It is reviled by the Old Left President of the National Union of Mineworkers, Arthur Scargill. It is extolled and indeed sold by the Eurocommunist journal of the British Communist Party, *Marxism Today*. Filofaxes are attractive, sensuous and offer at least the illusion of containment of one's life. They are transitional objects.

I say that it behoves us to try to think about these private phenomena of the public sphere and their role in the organization of consent. For all her radicalism, when Isadora Duncan's scarf got too long, it strangled her. That is, Left asceticism asked too much; Left consumerism may take too much of the moral edge off political work.

On the other hand, there is subversive potential in popular culture. Think of the role of music in 1960s, in the 1930s and in the nineteenth century. Think of radical video, pirate radio, agitational films, strength in banners and tracts. The cynical slogan at the end of the 1960s about how subversion gets domesticated into mere fashion – 'revolt into style' – captured only one moment of the dialectic. Both need our scrutiny.

Returning now to the philosophy of science, technology and medicine, I believe that we should fight decontextualization and the idea that to think of the genesis of knowledge is to commit 'the genetic fallacy'. If we refuse to separate what was once called (by followers of Karl Popper) the context of discovery from the context of justification, then we will *know* how societies constitute their knowledge. We will achieve this by knowing the forces that evoke them and get them researched and developed. This occurs through patronage, education, careers and, above all, reification and fetishization. In reification relations between people are treated as if they were relations between things. In fetishization, things are treated as if they have magical, human qualities. These two mechanisms disconnect primitive processes, passions and values from products and the processes of production, from theories and things, from commodities and therapies.

One of the consequences of the comfort given by transitional phenomena is that they can become more real and intimate than human relations *per se*. One of the consequences of the fetishism of commodities is that the products of human hands 'appear as inadequate beings endowed with life and entering into relations both with one another and the human race'. This arises not only from the commodity form but also from the formation of character in the image of the commodity. As Victor Wolfenstein and Michael

61

Schneider note, 'The objectively inverted reality of "material relations between persons and social relations between things" is thus
subjectively reflected in a "perverse displacement of libidinous energies from the world of reified persons into the world of personified
objects" ' (Wolfenstein, n.d., p. 39, quoting Schneider, 1975, p. 251).
The relations become inverted so that my best friend is my Walkman
or my personal computer. Some people are so attached to computers
that they sever other relationships and become 'computer hacks'.
This touches more than a few weird people. Think of the vogue of
Herbie Volkswagen films, the children's film *Dirt Bike* about a motor-
cycle with its own personality, the personalities R2D2 and C3PO in
the *Star Wars* films, the android knights in *Aliens 2*, the computer in
War Games, ads for Renault cars which ask 'What's yours called?',
highly personalized telephones and earphones, and so on and on in
the realm of toys for boys and girls of all ages.

The task for a critique of science and of consumption becomes the
tracing of the threads and the seeking out of the connections or
articulations so that the more abstract the knowledge, the more
dedicated the research task – be it in mathematics, fifth-generation
computers, fundamental physical particles or genetic engineering.
The same kind of questions needs to be asked of consumer objects
and phenomena. Whence? *Cui bono*?

Moreover, the task of psychoanalytic epistemology, like the psychoanalytic theory of cultural consumption, is that of demystification
as well as the subversive development of counter-hegemonic uses,
products and processes. If we can reconnect things with motives,
uses and values, we can keep our eyes on the emotional resources
and social consequences. I have in mind, for example, shared rather
than isolating music and radio, community radio, low budget and
open access TV and video, organic farming, community computer
memory. All of these have proud histories in various settings in
Europe and America and, in some cases, Latin America (see Radical
Science Collective, 1985). Other developments – especially genetic
engineering – should be halted until their primitive roots become
clear and amenable to a more democratic form of social control. At
the moment the sequestration of the passions and values involved
from the material and efficient causes makes this an alienated and
alarming technology.

My text for all of these reflections is the ideas of Winnicott and of
Klein, Bion and post-Kleinians on the persistence of the alimentary
basis for knowledge, the failure in development *ever* to transcend
primitive assimilative, ruminative and projective mechanisms. If a

62

Kleinian theory of thinking is to be elaborated – and it is in the process of so being – then it will also be a theory of culture, including scientific and technological thinking and linked to what uses we make of science, technology and medicine. The most abstruse solid state physics can be so interpreted, along with fantastic fifth-generation computer technologies, the digital watch, the personal computer, the ever more sophisticated camera, sound system and technologies for encoding and decoding both video and audio tapes, as well as systems for pacing, surveillance and control in the work-place and for body scanning and washing clothes. They are of a piece: amino acid sequencers, Star Wars technologies and ways of listening to Tchaikovsky, Talking Heads and Willie Nelson.

Similarly, Winnicott's diagrams in which he tries to convey some of the meanings of transitional objects and phenomena encompass, as he says, 'the whole cultural field'. In a paper on 'Psychoses and child care', given nine months after the one on 'Transitional objects and transitional phenomena', he provides very helpful diagrams about this cultural envelope in relation to external and subjective reality and to instinct, dreaming, fantasy, play and work.

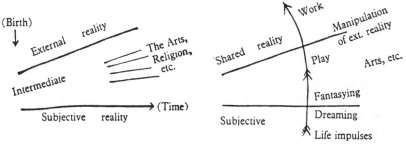

(from Winnicott, 1952)

In the text, he sketches the imbalances that lead to psychosis, hyper-intellectuality and a false life based on splitting. He also refers to the desire to do intellectual work: 'Intellectual understanding converts the not-good-enough environmental adaptation to the good-enough adaptation' (Winnicott, 1952, p. 225).

It seems to me that here we have some of the elements of a psycho-sexual developmental psychology as well as an epistemology of science, technology and medicine, that is, of expert knowledge and creativity. One of the tasks of an understanding of psychoanalysis and the public sphere is to trace the deepest roots of both alienated and integrated production and consumption – of both knowledge and of culture.

The idea of a genetic epistemology is not new. Kant put his schemata into the head, and Hegel made the realization of the universal an *historical* process, while Marx and Engels stressed the historicity of all concepts, including those of science. Piaget rendered this a developmental science, but his research parameters were confined to those of shape and other concepts drawn from physics.

A psycho-sexual genetic epistemology is still a desideratum, while a critical (in the sense of critique, i.e., questioning the terms of reference, assumptions and concepts) psychosexual genetic epistemology is but a gleam in one unreconstructed libertarian socialist's eye/mind. The crucial – the utterly fundamental – reunion lies in the reintegration of that which the scientific revolution and rationalist and empiricist traditions did all they could to abrogate, that is, emotion, value, aim, purpose, use value – the final cause or *telos* of the Aristotelian causal framework, which found its way into the Marxist concept of the labour process. The labour process perspective was importantly Aristotelian in stressing the means of production, the raw materials, purposive human activity – loosely recalling the Aristotelian material, formal and efficient causes. This leads, of course, to a use value, a purpose or final cause (for further elaboration see Young, 1985). My hope is that this analysis can retain the primitive while examining the utilitarian.

If we look at the efforts to think anew about nature, human nature, farming and industry associated with the feminist, environmental, ecology and Green movements, the aim is to heal the splits that lie at the heart of the scientific revolution. Modern knowledge is founded on a separation of body and mind, primary and secondary qualities, outer and inner, object and subject (see Burtt, 1932; Whitehead, 1985). The aim is to reconstitute the totality, the organism. This approach has been arrived at by looking much more closely at the articulations of knowledge and its production – the patronage, funding, hidden motives.

One dimension of all this has been afoot – only partly self-consciously – in the growing interests in the psychobiographies of intellectuals. I have in mind Frank Manuel on Newton; Ralph Colp, Howard Gruber, Jim Moore and myself on Darwin; Steve Heims on Norbert Weiner and John Von Neumann; Evelyn Fox Keller on Barbara McClintock; Andrew Hodges on Alan Turing. In J.D. Sutherland's psychobiography of Ronald Fairbairn, we have a psychoanalyst's careful reflections on psychoanalytic creativity, based on

Fairbairn's own intimate notes about his inner world. If we look at group processes, we get some insights from J.D. Watson on *The Double Helix* and the recent play about the discovery of DNA, *Life Story*, as well as the work of Latour and Woolgar on *Laboratory Life*.

Among the above, only Sutherland provides a full-blooded psychobiography in the way that Victor Wolfenstein's biography of Malcolm X is. The others are insufficiently object relational and insufficiently historical. But they make the project I am sketching less implausible. They fill in contexts and motives, life and thought. They help us to understand the intimate determinations and the social processes of intellectual research.

The connections between scientific creativity, on the one hand, and transitional objects and transitional phenomena, on the other, are manifold. An obvious relationship is inside science in the feelings of researchers about their equipment. These are often themselves of the kind to which I am referring – a kind of aestheticism of gear. Who has got the latest computer or amino acid sequencer? At the beginnings of the epoch in biology which is bearing such alarming fruits in genetic engineering, a patron – the Rockefeller Foundation – would give you a fancy ultracentrifuge if you would approach biology according to the parameters of physics. Second, the paradigm case of the great scientist, at the frontiers of knowledge doing research in a university laboratory and free from commercial pressures, has been getting out of date at least since Lord Rothschild outlined a more commercial, customer-contract basis of research in the 1970s. The goals of research now come directly from a particular vested interest.

The old view of the disinterested researcher is thus almost wholly out of date in the universities. Beyond that, the majority of funding for research and development is for military work, and more than half of all research funding and nearly half of all researchers in Britain are engaged in this military research work. Of the rest, most scientists and technologists work for commercial firms, for example, ICI and Unilever, and a huge contingent works to make the very same transitional objects and phenomena with which I began this paper, that is, the people that work in the cosmetics, hi-fi, computer and office-equipment industries. The loop is closed for the technical employees at an automated firm when they spend their earnings on the products of that firm. I well remember the longing of Ford workers when I worked in an assembly plant in the early 1950s to own their own Ford.

I am aware throughout this analysis that drawing the boundaries in particular cases and at particular times between transitional objects and phenomena, on the one hand, and clinical fetishism and narcissism, on the other, is not easy. I am not really talking about true fetishism, where the object of desire becomes the fetish object, or of true narcissism, where mature object relations do not occur. I am trying to broaden our concept of the transitional area and its central role in production and consumption – all production, even of the most abstruse theories, and all consumption, even of the most primitive forms of pleasure.

I have often wondered how it is that people can work in certain jobs, for example, manufacturing and assembling nuclear weapons. We know that the armaments industry pays a lot of mortgages, but how do its workers think of themselves? Some of the answer lies, of course, in splitting and projection, in scapegoating, in rationalization and denial. But some of it also lies in traditional analysis of alienation as eloquently spelled out in Marx's *Economic and Philosophic Manuscripts of 1844*. He speaks there of alienation from the means of production, from the product, from fellow workers and fellow humans and from one's own species being. A writer on the labour process among computer workers in the armaments industry has given details of how programmers have little or no idea of the use to which their sub-routine will be put in the larger program (Hayes, 1989, Chapter 6). No idea at all. A civilian computer consultant who read a draft of the book said that exactly the same rules apply in non-military programming for reasons of commercial secrecy, in order to avoid competitors pirating the program. Only a small number of senior staff know what a program is *for*. The final cause is split off in the structure of the research.

I know someone who works in optics, a field which you might imagine is a safely obscure branch of physics. He says that it is no longer possible to have any certainty of successfully avoiding military research and funding. You go to a conference, and it turns out to be NATO-sponsored. You get grant money, and it turns out to be at only one remove from questions the military wants answered. You are fascinated with a problem, and the seductions of funding for it or for general lab purposes are very great, if only you will keep the military informed. Magazines in this field have many adverts for big, high-tech firms. The adverts stress skiing, water sports, tramping and other utterly wholesome activities in the region of, say, Boeing or Rockwell. Bell Labs, where transistors, microprocessors and hundreds of radar and surveillance and encoding techniques were invented in the Second World War and since, is the largest research institution in the world, with nonpareil of facilities. The joys of working for a given firm are stressed. The military purposes of the work are not even mentioned.

All – I say all – of this blinkering is made possible by emotional as well as formal alienation and the separation of use value and *telos* from the labour process and the metaphysical foundations of modern science. This process of splitting lies at the heart of modern epistemology.

The understanding of the process by which we introject this splitting with the world view of science, technology and industry, and are socialized into it, could not be more important. At one level it is perfectly well understood and certainly not confined to high-tech business. One of my closest childhood friends who was almost as hard up as I was when we were children tells me that he is not yet rich by local standards. That is he has not yet got $50,000,000. He is an entrepreneur with the basis of his fortune in oil leases. He says that the norm in his peer group is to get money any way you can. He described a mutual friend with whom I've lost touch who is 'in the real estate business'. He sells graveyard plots to poor blacks for $400, at $5 a week. My friend asked what happened if they pay it off. The reply was that nobody has done that yet; all default at some time during the eighty weeks. However, if anyone did make it to the finish line, there is a clause in the contract saying that another plot could be substituted for the lovely one that the customer was shown. The norm, as I say, is to make money – to compete from Little League baseball at age six to near the grave and *then* to endow a hospital wing, a university chair or a clinic for handicapped children with your name on it. I am, and my friend was, perfectly serious. The getting of money is utterly split off from doing good, though that is an ostensive long-term goal. This is an extreme, though true, example. I chose it to illuminate the norm.

When I talk about the reintegration of emotions, primitive motives, use values and final causes with other dimensions of work, I am after very large changes. But let us not be too sanguine. One of the things post-Reichian psychoanalysis has taught us is that it is not the case that de-repression opens up good motives. It opens Pandora's Box – motives all mixed up. However, if pursued judiciously, the reintegration of the primitive with the efficient and rational leavesus with the hope of working on these matters rather than having their effects occur only through unconscious processes.

67

ACKNOWLEDGEMENTS

The publishers would like to thank the Hogarth Press for permission to use the diagram from D.W. Winnicott, 'Psychoses and child care' in *Through Paediatrics to Psycho-Analysis* (1982).

REFERENCES AND FURTHER READING

Barnes, B. and Edge, D., eds (1982) *Science in Context: Readings in the Sociology of Science*. Milton Keynes: Open University Press.

Berger, P.L. and Luckmann, T. (1987) *The Social Construction of Reality: A Treatise on the Sociology of Knowledge*. Garden City: Anchor Books.

Bion, W.R. (1977) *Seven Servants*. New York: Aronson.

—— (1984) *Second Thoughts: Selected Papers in Psychoanalysis*. Maresfield Reprints.

Brody, S. (1980) 'Transitional objects: idealization of a phenomenon', *Psychoanal. Q.* 49: 561–605.

Brown, E.R. (1979) 'He who pays the piper: foundations, the medical profession and medical education', in S. Reverby and D. Rosner, eds *Health Care in America: Essays in Social History*. Philadelphia: Temple University Press, pp. 132–54.

—— (1979a) *Rockefeller Medicine Men: Medicine and Capitalism in America*. Berkeley: University of California Press.

Burtt, A. (1932) *The Metaphysical Foundations of Modern Physical Science*. Routledge, second edition.

Colp, R.H., Jr. (1977) *To Be an Invalid: The Illness of Charles Darwin*. Chicago: University of Chicago Press.

Douglas, M. (1970) *Purity and Danger: An Analysis of Concepts of Pollution and Taboo*. Harmondsworth: Penguin.

—— ed. (1973) *Rules and Meaning: The Anthropology of Everyday Knowledge*. Harmondsworth: Penguin Education.

—— (1975) *Implicit Meanings: Essays in Anthropology*. Routledge.

Fagen, M., ed. (1975, 1978) *A History of Engineering and Science in the Bell System*. 2 vols. Bell Telephone Laboratories.

Feyerabend, P. (1978) *Farewell to Reason*. Verso.

Fisher, D. (1978) 'The Rockefeller Foundation and the development of scientific medicine in Great Britain', *Minerva* 16: 20–41.

Fosdick, R.B. (1952) *The Story of the Rockefeller Foundation*. New York: Harper & Row.

Grolnick, S.A. *et al.* eds *Between Reality and Fantasy: Transitional Objects and Phenomena*. New York: Aronson.

Gruber, H.E. (1974) *Darwin on Man: A Psychological Study of Scientific Creativity*. Wildwood House.

Habermas, J. (1972) *Knowledge and Human Interests*. Heinemann, chs 10–12.

Hales, M. (1986) *Science or Society? The Politics of the Work of Scientists*. Free Association Books.

Hayes, D. (1989) *Behind the Silicon Curtain*. Free Association Books.

Heims, J. (1980) *John von Neumann and Norbert Wiener: From Mathematics to the Technologies of Life and Death*. Cambridge, MA: MIT Press.

Hodges, A. (1983) *Alan Turing: The Enigma*. Burnett Books.

Horton, A. (1967) 'African traditional thought and Western science', *Africa* 37, Part I: 'From tradition to science', pp. 50–71; Part II: 'The "closed" and "open" predicaments', pp. 155–87.

Kahne, M.J. (1967) 'On the persistence of transitional phenomena into adult life', *Int. J. Psycho-Anal.* 48: 247–58.

Keller, E.F. (1983) *A Feeling for the Organism: The Life and Work of Barbara McClintock*. New York: Freeman.

Klein, M. (1988) *Envy and Gratitude and Other Works 1946–1963*. Virago.

Knorr-Cetina, D. (1982) 'The constructivist programme in the sociology of science: retreats or advances?', *Social Studies of Science* 12: 320–8.

—— and Mulkay, M., eds (1983) *Science Observed: Perspectives on the Social Study of Science*. Sage. (Critique by Tim Rowse, 'Sociology pulls its punches', in L. Levidow, ed (1986) *Science as Politics*. Free Association Books, pp. 139–49.)

Kohn, D., ed. (1985) *The Darwinian Heritage*. Princeton, NJ: Princeton University Press.

Kolakowski, L. (1972) *Positivist Philosophy from Hume to the Vienna Circle*. Harmondsworth: Penguin.

Kovel, J. (1986) *Against the State of Nuclear Terror*. Free Association Books.

Latour, B. and Woolgar, S. (1979) *Laboratory Life: The Social Construction of Scientific Facts*. Sage.

Levidow, L., ed. (1986) *Radical Science Essays*. Free Association Books.

—— and Young, R.M., eds (1983, 1985) *Science, Technology and the Labour Process: Marxist Studies*. 2 vols. Free Association Books.

Lichtheim, G. (1967) *The Concept of Ideology and Other Essays*. New York: Vintage.

Lukács, G. (1971) 'Reification and the consciousness of the proletariat', in *History and Class Consciousness*. Merlin, pp. 83–222.

Mannheim, K. (1960) *Ideology and Utopia: An Introduction to the Sociology of Knowledge*. Routledge.

Manuel, F.E. (1968) *A Portrait of Isaac Newton*. Cambridge, MA: Harvard University Press.

Marcuse, H. (1968) *One Dimensional Man: The Ideology of Industrial Society*. Sphere.

Marx, K. (1961) *Economic and Philosophical Manuscripts of 1844*. Moscow: Foreign Languages Publishing House.

—— (1976) 'The fetishism of the commodity and its secret', *Capital*, vol. I. Harmondsworth: Penguin, pp. 163–77.

Mattelart, A. (1985) 'Infoteck and the third world', in Radical Science Collective, eds *Making Waves: The Politics of Communications/Radical Science* 16: 27–35.

Melly, G. (1970) *Revolt into Style*. Allen Lane.

Meltzer, D. (1985) *The Kleinian Development*. Strath Tay, Perthshire: Clunie Press.

—— (1986) 'Discussion of Ester Bick's paper "Further considerations on the function of the skin in early object relations" ', *Br. J. Psychother.* 2: 300–1.

Moore, J.R. (1985) 'Darwin of Down: the evolutionist as squarson-naturalist', in Kohn, pp. 435–81.

Nicolson, W. (1987) *Life Story* (television play). BBC2.

Radical Science Collective, (1985) *Making Waves: The Politics of Communications*. Free Association Books.

Radical Science Journal Collective (1981) 'Science, technology, medicine and the socialist movement', *Radical Science Journal* 11: 3–70.

Reich, W. (1972) *Sex-Pol: Essays 1929–1934*. New York: Vintage.

Rifkin, J. (1983) *Algeny*. New York: Viking.

Rorty, R. (1980) *Philosophy and the Mirror of Nature*. Oxford: Blackwell.

—— (1982) *Consequences of Pragmatism (Essays: 1972–1980)*. Minneapolis, MN: University of Minnesota Press.

—— (1989) *Contingency, Irony and Solidarity*. Cambridge: Cambridge University Press.

Rothschild, Lord (1971) *A Framework for Government Research and Development*. HMSO, CMND4814.

Rustin, M. (1982) 'A socialist consideration of Kleinian psychoanalysis', *New Left Review* 131: 71–96.

—— (1989) 'Post-Kleinian psychoanalysis and the post-modern', *New Left Review* 173: 109–28.

Schneider, M. (1975) *Neurosis and Civilization*. New York: Seabury Press.

Stocking, W., Jr. (1985) 'Philanthropoids and vanishing cultures: Rockefeller funding and the end of the museum era', in W. Stocking, ed. *Objects and Others: Essays on Museums and Material Culture, History of Anthropology* vol. 3. Madison, WI: University of Wisconsin Press, pp. 112–45.

Sutherland, J.D. (1989) *Fairbairn's Journey into the Interior*. Free Association Books.

Watson, J.D. (1968) *The Double Helix*. New York: Atheneum.

Whitehead, A.N. (1985) *Science and the Modern World*, with an introduction by R.M. Young. Free Association Books.

Wiener, N. (1989) *The Human Use of Human Beings: Cybernetics and Society*. Free Association Books.

Winnicott, D.W. (1951) 'Transitional objects and transitional phenomena', in Winnicott (1982a), pp. 224–42.

—— (1952) 'Psychoses and child care', in Winnicott (1982a), pp. 219–28.

—— (1982) *Playing and Reality*. Harmondsworth: Penguin.

—— (1982a) *Through Paediatrics to Psycho-Analysis*. Hogarth.
Wolfenstein, E.V. (1988) *The Victims of Democracy: Malcolm X and the Black Revolution*. Berkeley: University of California Press.
—— (no date) 'Groundwork for a Marxist psychoanalysis', unpublished manuscript.
Wulff, M. (1946) 'Fetishism and object choice in early childhood', *Psychoanal. Q.* 15: 450–71.
Young, R.M. (1971) 'Evolutionary biology and ideology: then and now', *Science Studies* 1: 177–206, revised in W. Fuller, ed. *The Biological Revolution*. New York: Anchor (1972), pp. 241–82.
—— (1973) 'The human limits of nature', in J. Benthall, ed. *The Limits of Human Nature*. Allen Lane, pp. 235–74.
—— (1977) 'Reconstituting technology: chips, genes, spares', Conference of Socialist Economists, *Conference Papers*, pp. 119–27.
—— (1977a) 'Science *is* social relations', *Radical Science* 5: 65–129.
—— (1979) 'How societies constitute their knowledge', unpublished manuscript.
—— (1979a) 'Interpreting the production of science', *New Scientist* (29 March): 1026–8.
—— (1979b) 'Science as culture', *Quarto* (2 December): 8.
—— (1979c) 'Science is a labour process', *Science for People* 43 : 31–7.
—— (1979d) 'Why are figures so significant? The role and the critique of quantification', in J. Irvine and I. Miles, eds *Demystifying Social Statistics*. Pluto, pp. 63–75.
—— (1981) 'The naturalization of value systems in the human sciences', in *Problems in the Biological and Human Sciences*, Block VI of Open University Course on Science and Belief from Darwin to Einstein. Milton Keynes: Open University Press, pp. 63–110.
—— (1985) 'Darwinism *is* social', in Kohn (1985), pp. 609–38.
—— (1985a) *Darwin's Metaphor: Nature's Place in Victorian Culture*. Cambridge: Cambridge University Press.
—— (1985b) 'Is nature a labour process?', in L. Levidow and R.M. Young, vol. 2, pp. 206–32.
—— (1986) 'The dense medium: television as technology', *Political Papers* 13: 3–5.
—— (1986a) 'Introduction' in L. Levidow, ed. *Radical Science Essays*. Free Association Books, pp. 1–15.
—— (1987) 'Darwin and the genre of biography', in G. Levine, ed. *One Culture: Essays in Science and Literature*. Madison, WI: University of Wisconsin Press, pp. 203–24.
—— (1988) 'Biography: the basic discipline for human science', *Free Assns* 11: 108–30.
—— (1988a) 'Darwin', in D. Herman, ed. *Late Great Britains: A Series of Six Historical Reappraisals*. BBC/Brook Productions, pp. 42–54, revised and reprinted in *Science as Culture* 5: 71–86.

———— (1989) 'Psychoanalytic critique of productivism', talk delivered to Cambridge Labour Students, 18 February.

———— (1989) 'The role of psychoanalysis and psychotherapy in the human sciences', talk delivered to Department of Experimental Psychology, University of Cambridge, 17 February.

———— (1989a) 'The mind-body problem', in G. N. Cantor *et al.* eds *Companion to the History of Science*. Croom Helm.

———— (1989b) 'Persons, organisms and primary qualities', in J. Moore, ed. *The Humanity of Evolution: Essays in Honour of John C. Greene*. Cambridge: Cambridge University Press.

———— and Gold, M. (1982) *A History of Nature* (film). Crucible: Science in Society, Central Television to Channel 4.

Yoxen, E. (1983) 'Life as a productive force: capitalizing upon research in molecular biology', in L. Levidow and R.M. Young, eds *Science, Technology and the Labour Process*, vol. I, pp. 66–122.

———— (1986) *The Gene Business: Who Should Control Biotechnology?* Free Association Books.

PART 2
CASE STUDIES IN HEALTH AND WELFARE

5 SOCIAL POSSESSION

OF IDENTITY

R.D. Hinshelwood

T HE PSYCHOANALYTIC CONCEPT of projective identification is a mechanism of intrapsychic defence (Klein, 1946). It is also an element in interpersonal relatedness (Ashbach and Sharmer, 1987). It is therefore one of the bridging concepts that we have between the intrapsychic and the social. There are other bridging concepts between the individual and the social, ones which come from the social sciences; in particular I will deal with 'role' (Miller and Rice, 1967; Agazarian and Peters, 1981) and 'alienation' (Geyer and Schweitzer, 1981; Meszaros, 1970).

I shall describe a process that consists of a sequence of repeated projective identification that proceeds through a network of relationships (Hinshelwood, 1982). It is as though a path can be traced from one person to another; I shall illustrate with material first from a small therapy group and then from a working institution. This process throws light on the difficult and alienating experience of being in large institutions. I shall then examine the general properties of this process and its relationship with the concepts of 'role' and 'alienation'.

A SMALL-GROUP EXAMPLE

It is a quite ordinary session of a group with five members and atherapist. At the beginning of the session it had been announced that a new member would be joining the group. After an initial half an hour of discussion about one member's domineering manner of talking, she (Mrs A) became quite angry at what felt to her

75

like criticism. She turned to Mr B, a reticent man, who had been less involved than the others and said 'Well, at least I do more than you.'

In this interaction Mrs A was justifying herself and passing on her sense of being criticized to Mr B. The insertion of her own feeling-state into Mr B is a projective identification by Mrs A.

Mr B looked up rather surprised and awkwardly said that he had been thinking over, since the session last week, what had been said by Mr C who had told Mr B that his silence was a kind of dishonesty because it kept people mystified about what he was thinking and made them uncomfortable. He continued that he thought Mr C was wrong, and that there was nothing wrong with being fairly quiet. It was a question of keeping one's own privacy; one was entitled to do that. Mr C, he complained, was now pestering Mrs A in an equally unkind way. He asked, rhetorically, why could Mr C not stop getting at people.

Mr B in turn was passing on the sense of being in the wrong to Mr C.

Mr C looked around him rather startled, as he had not really been the only one tackling Mrs A on her intrusiveness. He went a little red in the face and started to justify himself on the grounds that someone in the group had to confront difficult things, but this defensiveness abruptly changed to a more hectoring quality as he began to complain that the therapist did not do these things which were so difficult for the members of the group. The therapist should control things if they went wrong. At this point the therapist suddenly felt on the spot and that he was letting the group down. He felt he had to do something to stop the nasty atmosphere that was developing in the group. Provoked in this way to do something, he came in quickly to say that Mr C was clearly seeing him (the therapist) as irresponsible. He rather clumsily related this to what the group knew about Mr C. Mr C was a rather direct man from an unsophisticated background who had come to treatment because of repeated violent episodes in pubs and finally once at work with a customer. The therapist explained that Mr C felt bad because it played on his feeling that he was a violent man.

I hope it is clear that so far there is an uncomfortable interchange going on in which Mrs A's sense of guilt or blame was transmitted first to Mr B who then tried to put Mr C in the wrong. Mr C in turn made the therapist feel guilty and irresponsible.

76

The therapist's hasty intervention did not alter the atmosphere significantly as it returned the focus to Mr C. Mrs A made a pun on Mr C's name (Vic) suggesting he had a violent need always to be the victor. There was laughter that relieved some tension for the members of the group, apart from Mr C who erupted with rage in a punitive outburst against the whole group. The smiles faded rapidly as an atmosphere of fear gripped the group, and Mrs D, a depressed woman, began to cry. Her crying seemed to make Mr C feel reproached even more. He seemed to be torn between hitting her and leaving the group. His control was sufficient for him to stand up and turn slowly towards the door. At this point the therapist intervened more thoughtfully and said that Mr C was needed by the rest of the group to take away from the group everybody's anger and rage at being let down. Mr C remained standing at the door for some ten minutes while the group, in fear, began slowly to pick its way consciously through what had happened. As some of the other members of the group became aware of what Mr C represented for them he was able rather sullenly to return to his place and remain a brooding presence silently reproaching the group.

The whole sequence has five steps. (1) Firstly Mrs A was put on the spot by the members of the group in order to examine an aspect of her relationship with them, her domineeringness. She began to feel to blame for what she does. (2) She then made the point that she was not as bad as someone like Mr B and thus passed on her sense of being blamed to Mr B. (3) He adeptly managed to pass it on again, this time to Mr C, blaming him for what Mr C had said the week before. (4) Mr C managed to control himself by, in turn, passing on this sense of blame to the therapist. (5) The therapist then tried to make an interpretation but was filled with the blame put into him, and succeeded only in passing the sense of blame back to Mr C. And there it rested for a while, as Mr C acted in such a way as to accrue more blame for his explosive outburst.

I am drawing attention to the way that a *feeling-state*, in this case a sense of blame, is passed on from one member of this group to the next. The process halted when one person, Mr C, came to be established as the blameworthy culprit – a scapegoat.

My thesis is that an essential ingredient of a social network is that bits of experience, affects, emotions, feeling-states, are moved around. These channels of unconscious, non-symbolic communication are separate from, but intertwined with, the verbal and cognitive communication. I will term this aspect of the network, the *affective network*.

AN INSTITUTION'S NETWORK

The other example[1] is a set of observations from a day hospital. It shows a chain of similar emotional events (projective identifications) taking place in the affective network of an institution.

1   Dr A had advised one of his patients, Mr B, to leave the hospital and return to work, and was thus pushing him to accept that he had failed at his university career.
2   Mr B's symptoms intensified. He believed one of the occupational therapists, Miss C, was in love with him. Delusionally, a failure at university had become a success in love. When Miss C did not admit she was in love with Mr B he became abusive and threatening towards her. It was an intimidating attempt to make Miss C feel a failure – i.e., a projective identification of part of his feelings into Miss C.
3   Miss C sought support from a fellow occupational therapist, Mrs D, against the abuse from Mr B. She passed on part of her fear and intimidation to her colleague.
4   Mrs D then tackled Dr A and attacked him for not giving sufficient support to the non-medical clinical staff. Failure and blame had come around full circle to be put back to Dr A.
5   Dr A then had a further discussion with Mr B about leaving and about his abusiveness towards Miss C.
6   Following this Mr B became aggressive with other patients, throwing a piece of wood across the workshop in one of the OT sessions.
7   The effect on the patients was a paradoxical one. Mr B's violent event was a very concrete form of projecting his state of mind at the rest of the patients and occupational therapists. He frightened the others and they turned to each other for support. This took the form of another delusion intended to reassure everybody. It was asserted that the hospital was a peaceful and tranquil paradise.

   The patients' view of the hospital as a soft option, a peaceful, untroubled paradise, had been a recent topic of discussion among the staff; and it seemed to them that consequently patients stayed there too long and became chronic. As a result the staff believed they should challenge the view of the hospital as paradise and introduce a stricter regime.
8   The staff then reacted by increasing their resolve to toughen up

the hospital regime and new energy was put into discussing and shaping this new policy.

The affective network 'contained' the initial traumatizing of Mr B by passing on the emotional element or piece of identity (in this instance Mr B as a failed student) from one person to another. As it flowed through the network it changed – from failure, to aggression, to fear, to delusional peace, and to instituting new policies. It is of considerable interest that the initial quantum of personal experience or identity was eventually disposed of as the energy for a piece of work of the organization as a whole. It is possible to show that institutional actions are frequently driven by energy derived from the split-off parts of personal experience and personal identity.

THE PROJECTIVE LIFE OF INSTITUTIONS

There are a number of general properties of affective networks that can be seen in these two illustrations:

(1) Individuals use the context of the social network as a means of passing on to others certain feeling-states, elements of identity, which they wish to disown – a form of psychological *defence by projection.*

(2) Personal affects of the individuals come to be possessed by the social network to form the energy for institutional activity.

And as a result of the above two properties:

(3) There is a depersonalization of the individuals' experiences and feelings.

(4) The individual becomes deeply fused to the group or institution since the social network, to a degree, *is* the individual.

The individual becomes raw material for the developing culture, its structure and activity. His unconscious investment in it is based on primitive mechanisms involving splitting. A split piece of experience comes adrift from one member and is projected as if it were a package, a discrete quantum of experience which, in the unconscious minds of the individual members, can be taken in and given out.

The individual actually loses his own experience in the ramifications of the network and with it some of his sense of self or identity. A large institution feels inhuman because individuals literally lose themselves (or parts of themselves) in it.

79

Because these processes are based on the *unconscious* mechanisms of individuals, the institution comes to be felt unconsciously as alien, split from the individuals who make it up – 'the faceless bureaucracy', 'the monolithic organization', terms we use to convey the way institutions reduce the sense of identity of the individuals. At the same time the process binds the individual into an identification from which the individual has great difficulty in extricating himself whole.

ROLES AND THE UNCONSCIOUS

In the field of social science, roles are the collections of functions performed by the individual for the social group. Typically these roles belong to the institution but are voluntarily adopted by individuals. They can be thought about rationally and altered or adhered to for rational and conscious purposes.

However, it is not necessarily like that, since a role can be felt to be imprisoning or alienating. One reason for the imprisoning experience was shown in the example of the small therapy group arising, at the unconscious level, from projective identification. One individual came to play a specific part for the others. In that case it was a scapegoat, a well-known phenomenon that goes back to biblical times. Its relationship to widely held feelings of guilt in the group was always known too.

The precise means by which this unconscious role for the group was established is the process I have drawn attention to – a quantum of emotion, of a feeling-state or of an identity was passed around by projective identifications and finally localized in one individual who was subjected to an 'enforced introjection' (as Menzies, 1959, called it). Such a process causes the individual a distortion of his identity. Greatly enhancing certain aspects of his personality will obliterate others. At the same time, it also distorts the identity of others, depleting them of certain aspects (Hinshelwood, 1982; 1987). This unconscious function of carrying the guilt (or some other emotional aspect of identity) for the other members of a group needs to be carefully distinguished from performance of conscious, rational roles.

We need, at this point, to make some careful distinctions. A role entered into may be congenial or it may be uncongenial. Acceptance of a role may be voluntary but that does not exclude the occurrence of the processes I have discussed, in which the person in addition to his conscious role is also unconsciously elected to a position that distorts his own personal identity. A role within an identified institution may acquire specific personality characteristics through the social projective system; Menzies (1959) showed, for instance, that student nurses were regarded and treated as irresponsible without regard to their actual individual personalities, so much so, in fact, that it worked to the detriment of recruitment to the nursing service.

Also, many roles that are consciously entered into are alienating because of a specific impoverishment due to socio-economic exploitation, for example many work roles, or the role of 'mother' for some women. And many, being alienated already, may attract psychological exploitation as well: blacks may not only be correctly identified as different from whites but become stereotyped 'blacks' with anal and faecal connotations that are attributed socially but unconsciously.

The question arises of the relation between the role that is alienating because of socio-economic exploitation, and those that are so because of the psychological exploitation. In my view alienation in socially exploited roles invariably attracts exploitation for projective purposes as well, giving rise to a state of affairs in which economic exploitation and psychological exploitation go hand in hand.

Carrying a socially projected emotional identity that turns a social role into a highly restricted personality is usually felt as an alienating experience and destructive of personal development. Yet some people will take up such places that will seriously hinder their own identity development; perhaps we all do to some extent. However, it is not always consciously experienced in this way: Turquet (1975) has described advantages, as well as the threats, of a group-defined identity. Compliance with the unconscious projected identity is, at the level of the individual, akin to 'false consciousness' at the class level (Lukács, 1971). The invitation for projective exploitation is clear in the small group example, in which Mr C's emotional role, that the group needed to exploit, was close to one aspect of his personality – into which he was restricted by the group.

ALIENATION

The depersonalizing effect of projective identification at the psychoanalytic level of the individual becomes *alienation* at the level of the group network (Hinshelwood, 1983), a depersonalization of the individual actually within the institution which, to an extent, *is* him. Expropriation of a particle of his own experience comes about through transformations that occur and the individual actually loses some of his experience as it passes away through the ramifications of the network.

In our own culture the affective networks of institutions have come to be remarkably efficient at exploiting individuals' feeling-states and experiences, reifying bits of human beings and estranging them from the human world.

The affective network is an exchange system of human emotions and identity, of reified bits of human beings. In this sense affective networks parallel the exchange systems of commodities which are also reified bits of human relations. And it is possible that economic exploitation is a concrete precipitate of projective exploitation; that is to say, the projective processes are the special medium by which economic exploitation takes a hold on individuals. Capitalism has learned to accurately reflect and exploit the potential in human beings to alienate and reify qualities and identities. The way the capitalist system aligns the psychological potential for projective identification in groups and commodity fetishism in the economic system is a powerful union. To dismantle such a system requires attention to the psychology of institutions as well as the economics and politics of the capitalist system.

The losing of parts of human emotions and identity in the affective network compares with the expropriation of surplus value in the labour of economic production. Both are alienated from the individual to be exploited by the (capitalist) institution. It is likely that both 'surplus identity' and surplus value are needed in the oiling of the wheels of capital accumulation.

NOTE

1. This illustration was used elsewhere to demonstrate general characteristics of affective networks (Hinshelwood, 1982).

REFERENCES

Agazarian, Y. and Peters, R. (1981) *The Visible and Invisible Group*. Routledge.

Ashbach, C. and Sharmer, V. (1987) 'Interactive and group dimensions of Kleinian theory', *Journal of the Melanie Klein Society* 5: 43–68.

Geyer, F. and Schweitzer, D. (1981) *Alienation: Problems of Meanings, Theory and Method*. Routledge.

Hinshelwood, R.D. (1982) 'The individual in the social network', in M. Pines and J. Raphaelson, eds *The Individual and the Group. Volume 1: Theory.* New York: Plenum Press, pp. 469–77.

———— (1983) 'Projective identification and Marx's concept of man', *Int. Rev. Psycho-Anal.* 10: 221–6.

———— (1985) 'Projective identification, alienation and society', *Group Analysis* 18(3): 241–54.

———— (1987) 'Social dynamics and individual symptoms', *International Journal of Therapeutic Communities* 8: 265–72.

Klein, M. (1946) 'Notes on some schizoid mechanisms', in *The Writings of Melanie Klein, Volume III.* Hogarth, pp. 1–24.

Lukács, G. (1971) *History and Class Consciousness.* Merlin.

Menzies, I. (1959) 'The functioning of social systems as a defence against anxiety', *Human Relations* 13: 95–121.

Meszaros, I. (1970) *Marx's Theory of Alienation.* Merlin.

Miller, E. and Rice, A.K. (1967) *Systems of Organization.* Tavistock.

Turquet, P. (1975) 'Threats to identity in the large group', in L. Kreeger, ed. *The Large Group,* Constable, pp. 87–144.

6   UNCONSCIOUS ASPECTS OF HEALTH AND THE PUBLIC SPHERE

Karl Figlio

THE WORD 'PUBLIC' is unusual in the vocabulary of social life. It evokes little of the grandiosity that 'nation' or 'people' attract; little of the snugness of 'community'; little of the implied profoundity of 'culture' or of the lawfulness of complex organization conveyed by 'social'; and none of the tyranny just under the surface of 'collective' or of 'democracy'. Its blandness suits it for uses such as 'public utilities'. It doesn't suggest membership, because anyone can belong: one need only be where the public gathers to be automatically included. Public seems to be a word without energy, lacking affect, drive, quality and intensity.

And yet it is an important word. It refers to the life of a group as a commonwealth, rather than to a structure held together defensively. Its usage in the Middle Ages, as today, defines it partly by contrast with private: what is withdrawn from public is private; and the severance can lead either to privation or to privilege (Williams, 1984, pp. 242–3). In contrast with privation, public means a source of nourishment; with privilege, an attack on wealth, both literal and metaphorical. But the word flourishes without these polarizations, and does not suggest either bountifulness, as nature might, or insatiability, as 'crowd' or even 'people' might. That is its strength.

The word public identifies a phantasy of a group in which people can participate without cost to others: without privilege or deprivation. I will develop this theme further, but first I want to put 'health' with public in order to propose that it shares the same qualities. If one speaks of the privation of health, as in illness, then one can picture the aggressive encroachment of disease upon the person. But health is not the opposite of disease: to inject a countervailing quality into the word health, we have to say something like 'perfect health' or to use another word altogether, such as fitness or robustness. On its own, health does not refer to an active defence against disease, but to a kind of commonweal of the person, as public is a commonweal of the group.[1]

As reservoirs[2] of group phantasies of participation – psychic representatives of the commonweal – 'public' and 'health' are different from other reservoirs of group phantasy such as 'nature' and 'culture'. The latter terms are used as oppositional pairs, unlike public and private, where private is defined as something withdrawn from the public, rather than complementary to, or standing against, it. Psychoanalytically speaking, oppositional pairs give evidence of splitting and projection, and are, therefore, terms of psychic defence.

Nature and culture, as they are used today, convey their oppositional quality in dominant imaginative constructs or metaphors, such as the brutal nature of Darwinian natural selection or as the redemptive nature of pastoral ideologies, against which stands culture: abstract and aloof, perhaps as high or intellectual culture, or as a master bringing nature under cultivation. At this level, they are imbued with mythical themes (as in Bion's row C) and contain aspects of a sexual couple, as in creation myths or in the Oedipus myth. In imagination, such notions, informed by mythic themes, are founded upon an introjection of a phantasized relationship, genital or pregenital, a union or a form of domination. To this extent one could speak of the relationship of culture to nature as an unresolved oedipal conflict: (mother) nature brought under (father) cultivation, and the human children identifying with each of them, as well as internalizing their relationship.

The unresolved oedipal conflict of nature and culture provides reservoirs for destructive and idealized phantasies. 'Public' does not: by contrast, it is a reservoir of sublimated phantasy. What appeared in our first acquaintance to be without energy might better be seen as desexualized and available for common endeavour.

The public is easily endangered. There are two forms of danger that I will examine in this paper. The first lies in the way western civilization has, historically, produced an objective view of nature. As I shall illustrate below, this process has also stimulated primitive phantasies which it manages through omnipotent defences that degrade the public from commonweal into battleground.

The second danger lies in specific historical and political conflicts, such as private vs. public health care, which draw upon these underlying phantasies and push them in one direction or the other. When there is an overall attack on the public, the private – including private health care – adds force to it. It undermines the commonweal and exaggerates primitive defences, such as splitting and projection. That sort of process, once going, spirals out of control. Once the public is undermined, only more private action seems tenable – a feature of the degradation of the public that I will spell out below. The power of these particular assaults on the public derives from their capacity to tap the underlying structure and dynamics of primitive phantasy.

A brief example might help at this point, before looking at these reservoirs of phantasy in more detail. I have elsewhere related the development of contract law, and of insurance provision for injury and illness within labour contracts, to modern scientific theories of natural events, including accidents and disease (Figlio, 1985). I argued that the notion of a contract, especially the modern one that included penalties for *not* doing something (non-feasance), rather than for doing it wrongly (malfeasance), established a social basis for perceiving events – including natural events – simply to have happened. I wanted to show that the notion of 'simply happening' represented an achievement in the modification of phantasy, which informed and underpinned the consciously held view of causation in the natural world: an event might not be motivated, but could simply occur. Here was a new model of social relations – in this case, among employers and workers in a period when a market in labour was replacing the relationship of master and servant – crystallized in contract law and projected into nature in the form of a perception of injury and illness as an event occurring in the absence of intention.

Such a contractual arrangement among people and with nature is unstable, and needs constant reinforcement. The belief that illness or injury could just happen gives way easily to a primitive talionic belief that injury and illness express a sense of social disharmony or retribution for unavenged arrogance (as in Thebes under Oedipus). Recent anthropological work has shown how near the surface this sort of thinking remains today in small rural communities (Wilke, 1984). It remains in large metropolitan societies as well, but mediated by institutional structures.

Insurance-based financing in health policy gives us an example of institutionally mediated phantasy. Insurance is a major institution in modern culture, not just as a means of financing the consequences of risks of all sorts, including the risk of illness, but as the socio-economic foundation of an actuarial way of thinking; and this way of thinking reinforces a projective dynamics at the same time as it promotes an objective view of both natural and social phenomena.

Insurance divides people into groups according to the risk that members will fall ill. In addition to reinforcing a view of illness as a law-like event, such an actuarially based division implies that a healthier social group can remove the burden arising from a less healthy group. Not only can members of a low-risk group feel safely different from those of a high-risk group, but the projective relationship between them pushes them both to look inside the latter group for the cause of its poor health record. In this way, the social glue of shared experience and responsibility is weakened. The burden of disease may then be experienced – perhaps in the cost of treatment as well as in the sense of threat of disease – as an attack on the health of the society. And the source of the attack can be displaced from the social centre into the marginalized group.

Differentiating itself from the unhealthy group, the healthier group can experience itself as free of the causes of disease, indeed freed of them by the availability of higher-risk groups to act as depositories for projective phantasies. We find this stratification of 'goodness' in studies of social-class-linked illness, especially where behaviours, such as smoking and dietary preference, are implicated. This sort of structure reinforces projective identification across the groups, lodging destructive parts in other groups whose behaviour can then be regulated.

Let me provide a concrete illustration of these dynamics, using a brief historical example. In the nineteenth century, these destructive parts might have included incestuous sexual phantasies, or the apparently self-satisfied display of an ostentatious diet, such as in tea- and coffee-drinking, or other 'luxurious' habits. An upwardly mobile middle-class fraction, as part of its self-definition, lodged phantasies of this sort in sectors of the working class and of the aristocracy; and certain clinical entities served to objectify and condense them and their dynamics. In another paper (Figlio, 1978) I have analysed one disease in particular, a common illness of young women during this period, called chlorosis. These girls of different backgrounds were joined into one group with respect to their bad habits and their susceptibility to chlorosis. The epidemiology of chlorosis gave evidence to a rising professional middle-class stratum, including doctors, of the danger of idle and fantasy-charged habits, both of working-class and of aristocratic girls. Thus this upwardly mobile class fraction perceived a common disease to be 'in' the social groups from which this fraction was differentiating itself.

I won't look at specific examples of the projective relationships of today, beyond suggesting that they will probably include the same search for the point of entry of disease into society. Let us instead apply this perspective to private medicine, as a particular case in which actuarial thinking is intensified. Private medicine is withdrawn from the public. Its insurance basis separates the private group from the public which can thereby be degraded into a residual 'public sector' by absorbing the private sector's projectively identified destructive parts. The very meaning of public as a commonweal is lost in such a transformation, and a relationship between private and public sectors, driven by the dynamics of primitive defences, takes over.

When the sense of public is lost, public sector expenditure in support of health services can generate phantasies of greediness of psychotic proportions; and these can be projected into a theoretical structure, such as, in health economics, the notion of health demand. Even the word 'demand' in economic thinking – a drive which must be frustrated by price – conveys its psychic history. Health undergoes a transformation into a frustrated – and therefore angry and destructive – need to be disease-free, and the demanding, frustrated child is additionally forced to recognize that greed itself is the problem, thereby cementing in place a successful projective transfer. Only private health care could, in this way of thinking, sort out the declining health of the public, by containing demandingness and rewarding goodness.

Health care has broad implications for the dynamics of social groups, in particular for the way in which deviance functions to secure the boundaries of 'normal' society. It is a way of thinking that, in the sociology of deviance, is associated with the work of Emile Durkheim (1895). In the Durkheimian tradition, deviant groups are essential to the stability of a society. The continuous process of labelling, ostracizing, punishing and rehabilitating them is part of the equally continuous process of self-definition of the society as a whole. A society knows what it is by where it draws its boundaries, and it sets these limits in the course of refusing to include particular subcultures. The dynamics of the relationship of dominant to deviant cultures are therefore at the heart of social formation and stability.

Durkheim sought a view of social life in which social 'facts' and the laws of their relationships could be discovered. Facts and laws as the objects of sociological enquiry replaced moral evaluation of social life and distinguished a scientific from an ideological approach to the social world. Crime, like illness, was for him a pathology, and the relationship of illness to health and crime to legitimate social behaviour was that of the pathological to the normal – a deviation from the expected – as one might find in anatomical structures and physiological functions of living organisms.

Talcott Parsons explored this view of illness extensively in a work that has become a classic in sociology, and particularly in medical sociology (Parsons, 1951). Although Parsons did not use the language of projective identification, he clearly had something like it in mind when he spoke of illness as a form of deviance – the main channel for deviance in modern society (Parsons, 1958). The health-care system, for Parsons, benignly brought the patient into line with healthy values, and by encouraging deviants to present as ill people, it took over from more retributive systems of justice the task of re-integrating the deviant. Deviance as illness, in a Durkheimian formulation, could be observed and treated as a natural fact – a lawful, if pathological, variation of the organismic properties of a society.

Extending the kind of case I made for chlorosis, one could speculate that the discovery of discrete pathology in a distinct group of patients externalizes – in an attempt to master – primitive terrors for a society, and that this externalization is facilitated by subdivision of a population into actuarially based risk groups. These groupings are part of the more general gathering of social 'facts' in census and other statistics, which in the aggregate reflect back to society a picture of itself as an articulated structure. The fact of this form of social structure and the fact of the distribution of illness in its subgroups promote the projective dynamics that I have described.

Perhaps, then, disease itself has a projective aspect, in that its localization suggests a projective placing of an attacking agent in particular sectors of the body and the body politic. The insurance-driven intensification and projection of blame for being at risk of poor health, therefore, also suggests phantasies of nature, in which nature is destructive – makes people ill. But before exploring these phantasies, let us remember our path. I have referred to 'nature' and 'culture' as reservoirs filled with and supplying primitive phantasies associated with an unresolved Oedipus complex, and I have proposed that 'public' and 'health' stood apart by providing reservoirs of non-conflictual phantasy. According to this argument, disease represents a phantasy of diviseness and danger, perhaps with paranoid overtones. Next to these, such reservoirs as are provided by 'public' and 'health' are essential to any society, regardless of how they are degraded and their existence is replaced by conflicts invested with primitive idealizing and denigrating phantasies.

90

I argued earlier that the modern scientific world-view has left primitive phantasies of nature and nature's scourges, especially disease, intact. Scholarship in the history of science makes this less unexpected, by criticizing the earlier notion that scientific development in the modern period produced a radical new attitude towards nature and by subjecting simplistic notions of the scientific conquest of irrationality and prejudice to detailed historical inquiry (Teich and Young, 1973; Webster, 1975).

Socially and politically oriented work in this field has linked the mechanical world-view, with its disenchantment of nature, its reductive drive to replace sensuous qualities with matter-in-motion and its equation of knowledge with technological mastery, with the transformation from feudal to capitalist economy and of labour to abstract labour power (Levidow and Young, 1981; 1985). And what of the unconscious? If, from the point of view of social history of science, the empiricist character of modern science expresses the division of nature as an aspect of the division of labour – both broken into units of matter in motion that can be quantified, controlled and costed – then what of its unconscious dimension? This line of thinking suggests that the empiricist relationship to nature and the naturalistic conception of disease have been achieved, not just by passive, naïve looking, but by an act of violence – a deed of the same sort as the primitive phantasies that it sought to replace. And if that is so, then its continuation rests, at least in part, upon a continuous repression of an awareness of that violence and of nature's retribution.

Brian Easlea (1981) has made such a case, in which masculine science has suppressed and violated feminine nature. Gustav Bovensiepen (forthcoming) has uncovered a language of violence and aggression in German parliamentary debates on peace and the environment, and argues that the German power-élite is organized as a male homosexual band, defending itself against a matriarchal retaliation by nature for her violation by patriarchal society. Bovensiepen's work shows the continuous struggle to deny the violence wrought by science and to defend against its emergence into consciousness.

Another version of the repression of awareness of a primal act of violence, and of the unconscious control that the act continues to exert, is given in Freud's thesis on Jewish monotheism. For Freud, monotheism represented a delayed re-emergence of a fragment of an archaic experience of parricide, enacted in the murder of the scientifically minded Egyptian king, Akhenaten, and of an Egyptian Moses,

91

who stood for monotheism and against magic (Freud, 1939). For Freud, the murder of Akhenaten was a rebellion against the stringency of the authoritarian father. In the resurfacing of this theme of monotheism, Freud sees the return of the repressed in a repeated denial of parricide: there is no room for ambivalence towards the father, and patriarchy owes its power to the continual return and denial of the primal murder. Thus, whether one emphasizes the violation of mother earth by father science, or the denial by the mother-loving sons of their parricide, the dominance of science over magic, animism and sensuous relating to nature appears to be maintained by continuous denial and repression.

In a psychoanalytic age, it is no surprise to hear that beneath a fear of retribution lies an attack on the object whose retaliation is feared. What might stand out and might be relevant to the fragile hold of a scientific world view, as we look at the modern period, is the way the non-human – especially inanimate – world can enter into these phantasies. Thus, mother earth is no longer simply the repository of maternal phantasies, but a power of a grotesque and overwhelming sort, which can be released by co-operation with human agency. Identification with the non-human world implies a projection of a non-human part of ourselves into it. The identification with the non-human world, about which Harold Searles has written extensively, includes a terror of absorption into it, a comforting merger with it and a sharing in its immense power (Searles, 1960).

This identification adds another dimension to the relationship between nature and humanity. In addition to phantasies connected with generation or with retaliation, there are those connected with the ego-alien sense of pure force – a theme which shows again the confusion of scientific objectivity and primitive phantasy. One of our immediate experiences of an ego-alien force is disease, the terror of which is processed projectively, as I've described above. Let me develop this point further.

On the benign side, children identify with the human operators of machines, but in addition with the machines themselves – perhaps with their power, or invulnerability, or even the ease with which they can be repaired. Similarly, the testing of atomic weapons does more than provide an occasion for the release of sadistic phantasies patterned on an attack on the mother's body; it releases a non-human force with which we identify. In a malignant way, perhaps nuclear winter refers to something deeper than the destruction of internal objects projected into future generations, which is a phantasy that relies on depressive anxiety – and hence on life, even if lost – in order to exist as a phantasy. The nuclear winter scenario evokes a world wholly without life: not killed, but without life, inanimate. Perhaps identifying with this form of non-human environment touches on the death instinct (cf. Segal, 1987).

Non-human identification also includes submission to nature's machinery, that is, to its uncompassionate, inevitable lawfulness (on extreme forms of identification with machines in narcissistic conditions see Ledermann, 1981). When we speak of events taking their course, we submit ourselves to such an identification, sometimes with a thrill at the power and destructiveness that such an inevitable sequence of events will entail. Perhaps this is because it is difficult – probably impossible – to get to a psychic level in which extinction itself could be represented. Freud refers the instinctual satisfaction of the death instinct back to narcissistic satisfaction, a phantasy of the ego's old wish for omnipotence. The extinction is therefore displaced on to an object, while the ego experiences a moment of completion.[3]

Such narcissistic satisfaction can take the form of identifying with the absolute quality of relentless processes or even with destructiveness itself. Freud ranges beasts of prey among the objects which, because of the narcissism displayed to us by their completeness in themselves, we tend to envy (Freud, 1914, p. 83). His reference to beasts of prey suggests that we extend that urge to any object or process that represents relentlessness. Perhaps we could extend it even further: *not* using ultimate weapons offers a similar narcissistic gratification. Their very existence, even with their use held in abeyance, fuels a narcissistic phantasy of omnipotence which might be more immediately experienced than the dread of ultimate extinction. And perhaps this reactive omnipotence is a different axis from that of triumph over an internal persecutory attack or the fear of using them, with which we might identify.[4] This sort of phantasy is in line with the Biblical accounts of the sacrifice of children – and the decision not to sacrifice them. Not killing might be seen as a form of omnipotent control over the duration of life, which in phantasy could extend indefinitely, towards immortality; the sacrifice of future generations – and the restraint upon it – might activate a similar phantasy (Bakan, 1968; 1979).[5]

Thus there is a primitive relationship with nature, which includes human and non-human aspects. The denial of that relationship, which is more characteristic of the scientific world view, signals a primitive level of the psychic transaction, rather than a secure sense of having taken control of it. In the 1950s, American schoolchildren were shown films of atomic testing. The enormous destruction of nature and human construction by nature's own power was presented with a benign overlay: the awe that it conveyed could have been mistaken for a moral lesson about humility, while viewers secretly indulged in the thrill of joining forces with such relentless power. The films also showed troops moved in very close to 'ground zero', as if to negate the very destructiveness that was demonstrated; and peaceful violence added another layer to the denial of the primitive phantasies, in that raw atomic explosions were touted as a new technique of excavation. As powerful as a lion, but as tame as a kitten, atomic power could also be as reliable a friend as the farmer's draft horse.

Following Searles, I have argued that nature is an 'other' with whom we have a complex relationship which, especially with respect to our dependency, is denied. A scientific relationship to nature, which denies that dependency, requires continual defendedness. The destructiveness inherent in this denied relationship surfaces in both idealization and in disregard. Returning to health and disease, one can see the violence of the underlying relationship to nature and to the body as a natural object in the understanding of the causes of disease. In both the idealized imagery of holistic attitudes towards health and the fragmentation of society into health-risk groups, a sense of healthiness is achieved, in part, through projection of the persecutory anxieties connected with the body as hostile nature: into high-risk groups and into one's own body, to be experienced as an enemy in orthodox medicine and idealized into a mirroring of perfection in holistic medicine.

The charged phantasies of nature allow this divisiveness; so does the notion of disease as an alien entity, composed of projected sadistic and non-human fragments. When medicine discovers and treats illness, it also localizes in externalized forms these terrorizing bits. Sectionalization of society allows them to circulate in closed loops, spreading out the fear of nature and her diseases into social groupings, with their destructive relationships to their bodies. It thereby reduces the terror and cements the projections into these external structures.

The projection of destructiveness into parts of both the body and society localizes it and allows it to be separated from the centre of selfhood, whether individual or cultural. David Bakan (1968) calls this distancing of the source of the sense of threat 'telic decentralization', and he links it with the mythical theme of sacrifice. In nearly

slaying his own son, Abraham came close to acting out an infantici-
dal impulse and to losing the symbolic dimension of sacrifice, which
also included the omnipotence of satisfying this impulse by replacing a child by an animal. Job recognized the helplessness that is the
other face of omnipotence, in that sacrifice became pointless. The
mythical theme of sacrifice can thus be seen as an attempt both
omnipotently to control existential dread and to put omnipotence
aside. Similarly, the modern organization of health care, including
the epidemiological perception of the distribution of diseases in
relation to nature and to society, reinforces the omnipotence of
sacrifice in institutionalizing a form of telic decentralization; it also
seeks knowledge of the reality of disease and limited but effective
action against it.

The distribution of diseases, related to natural factors such as
disease vectors, and to naturalistic social factors, such as class-related
behaviours, sets up projective systems operating between social
groups, such as social classes, mediated by non-human nature. We
can only speculate that, when a sector of society suffers at the hands
of nature, some part of society also identifies with nature's power,
and that this mechanism achieves by an alternative route some of the
discharge of aggression that, since *Group Psychology and the Analysis
of the Ego*, we have assumed must occur for group solidarity.

From this point of view, a naturalistic notion of disease as consisting of attacking, alien, non-human entities externalizes and anchors,
in closed projective loops, terrorizing split-off fragments, perhaps
including non-human identifications. Without such a process,
members of a group would be subject to a sense of internal dissolution. But aggression turned outwards acts to externalize the dread
and lodge it elsewhere. This is similar to Freud's notion of the
'narcissism of minor differences', by which he referred to the way
groups fasten upon small differences between themselves, in order to
establish an essential distinguishing characteristic that would then
bear the weight of aggression.

Freud used this concept a small number of times, once haltingly
basing it upon men's hostility towards women, whose phantasied
castration bore the weight of aggression aimed at them as a defence
against the narcissistic injury that women reflected back to men; he
seemed to imply a narcissistic rage that could be externalized and
anchored through detecting small but highly significant occasions for
massive projective systems in defence of narcissistic intactness
(Freud, 1918). This theme is consistent with the notion above that the

anxiety of extinction exists in phantasy in the form of narcissistic satisfaction and identification with relentless forces, and that minor differences mark out a group to absorb a massive projective transfer of 'bad' internal objects.

That the anxiety of extinction occasioned by illness can be replaced by a group phantasy, in which another group is attacked for minor differences that reflect back a narcissistically injured condition, serves a similar function. The cases to which I have referred are the social-class correlations of illness proneness and the insurance-based grouping of people into risk categories. The social-class ranking brings out features that deserve public attention, but which also focus relentlessly on class-related behaviour.

But let us return to the original theme. 'Public' and 'health' are reservoirs of phantasies of a commonweal. They are easily deprived of this unique character, however, and degraded into defensively structured systems in which projective loops disperse and encase the primitive phantasies that such systems evoke in the very process of seeking to be 'objective'.

As a counterpoise to such systems, proper notions of public and of public health eliminate at least the actuarial ideology; and institutions founded upon them at least establish a setting in which this ideology has no place in practice. In so doing, they give weight to the commonweal and resist its degradation.

A young doctor once said that the National Health Service, whatever its failings, had a precious feature – actuarial notions were completely foreign to it. What he said about the NHS I would say about the notions of public, of health and of public health, as notions that tap a level of unconscious life that has only limited opportunities for expression. Public is not the same as state, class or culture. Health is a public word; disease is a private one, which stands as a challenge to it, and relies on mastering anxiety by externalization. Public and health provide reservoirs of group phantasy of a particular sort, in that they are removed from contributing to the projective loops that I have described. They receive and supply phantasies that cannot be absorbed into cycles of idealization and contempt.

Our vocabulary is depleted of valuable reservoirs of participation in communal – public – life, which are not given over to primitive group phantasies. We need to attend to 'mature' phantasies, and in studying the history and ideology of institutions, we benefit from listening carefully to the symbolic overtones of words like public and health.

ACKNOWLEDGEMENTS

I would like to thank Ludmilla Jordanova and Barry Richards for their very helpful comments on an earlier draft of this paper.

NOTES

1. Roger Cooter (1982) has shown for Britain an interesting convergence of social sentiment with notions of health and its privation in the urbanized and mobile situation of the latter part of the nineteenth century. Speaking of public health and medical officers of health, he noted the predominance of theories that treated disease as endemic (of the nature of a place) rather than epidemic (spread by contagion). And the matrix of endemic disease was the air, a medium of social as well as physical life – in a sense, the common element of the new urban mass groupings.

2. I use 'reservoir' frequently in this paper. I mean by it both a depositary – a place in which phantasies can be lodged – and a source – a place from which they can be introjected.

3. Freud formulated this replacement of narcissistic injury by narcissistic satisfaction through projecting the injury into an object, in his description of the 'fort–da' game. With it, he drew attention to the child's mastery of catastrophic loss by projecting his or her helplessness into an object that could be lost and retrieved – an early adumbration of projective identification (Freud, 1920).

4. Chasseguet-Smirgel (1987) argues that unacknowledged and uncompensated guilt remains in unconscious collective memory across the generations, causing equally unconscious dread of retaliation and the acting out of propitiatory gestures within otherwise unrelated cultural and political movements – a kind of collective talionic law. She focuses upon the fear of mass environmental pollution and of the dangerousness of the polluted environment that underlie the large-scale support for the Green Movement in post-war Germany. Her analysis of Fascist mass murder, which could apply to other historical situations as well, requires us to make a moral distinction between kinds of violence. One way to put it might be to say that moral judgement permits a distinction between blood spilled within a structure of primitive phantasies and blood spilled in other ways: only the former calls out for revenge. Of which sort are the phantasies surrounding the arming for mass killing – even the apparently humane restraint in releasing such weapons in an ambience of readiness to use them?

5. Bakan sees the drawing back from child sacrifice (in particular, sacrifice of the first-born around the seventh century BC) both in terms of omnipotence and in terms of the advent of patrilocal and patrilineal marriage. The sacrifice of the first-born was a sacrifice to matrilineal deities. The father

as protector was associated with stopping it, and with substituting symbolic sacrifice, in the form of animals, for the literal sacrifice of children (Bakan, 1979, pp. 148–9). Thus an advance towards the symbolic was also an attack on matriarchy. I raise it here to highlight the complexity of unconscious conflictual phantasies that can be activated when actions touch upon omnipotent phantasies.

REFERENCES

Bakan, D. (1968) *Disease, Pain and Sacrifice: Toward a Psychology of Suffering.* Chicago: University of Chicago Press.

——— (1979) *And They Took Themselves Wives: The Emergence of Patriarchy in Western Civilization.* San Francisco/London: Harper & Row.

Bovensiepen, G. (forthcoming) 'Thoughts on the mythical structure of consciousness of the West German power élite', *Free Assns.*

Chasseguet-Smirgel, J. (1987) ' "The Green Theatre": an attempt at interpretation of group manifestations of unconscious guilt', in *Sexuality and Mind.* New York: Columbia University Press, pp. 109–27.

Cooter, R. (1982) 'Anticontagionism and history's medical record', in P. Wright and A. Treacher, eds *The Problem of Medical Knowledge: Explaining the Social Construction of Medicine.* Edinburgh: University of Edinburgh Press, pp. 87–108.

Durkheim, E. (1895) *The Rules of Sociological Method.* The Free Press (Collier-Macmillan), 1938/1964.

Easlea, B. (1981) *Science and Sexual Oppression: Patriarchy's Confrontation with Woman and Nature.* Weidenfeld.

Figlio, K. (1978) 'Chlorosis and chronic disease in 19th-century Britain: the social construction of somatic illness in a capitalist society', *International Journal of Health Services* 8(4): 589–617.

——— (1985) 'What is an accident?', in P. Weindling, ed. *The Social History of Occupational Health.* Croom Helm, pp. 180–206.

Freud, S. (1914) 'On narcissism: an introduction'. *S.E.* 14, pp. 67–102.

——— (1918) 'The taboo of virginity'. *S.E.* 11, pp. 191–208.

——— (1920) *Beyond the Pleasure Principle. S.E.* 18, pp. 1–64.

——— (1939) *Moses and Monotheism: Three Essays. S.E.* 23, pp. 1–137.

Ledermann, R. (1981) 'The robot personality in narcissistic disorder', *J. Anal. Psychol.* 26: 329–44.

Levidow, L. and Young, R.M., eds (1981, 1985) *Science, Technology and the Labour Process: Marxist Studies.* CSE/Free Association Books, vols. 1 and 2.

Parsons, T. (1951) *The Social System.* Routledge & Kegan Paul.

——— (1958) 'Definitions of health and illness in the light of American values and social structure', in *Social Structure and Personality.* Collier-Macmillan, 1964, pp. 257–91.

Searles, H.F. (1960) *The Nonhuman Environment in Normal Development and in Schizophrenia.* New York: International Universities Press.

Segal, H. (1987) 'Silence is the real crime', *Int. Rev. Psycho-Anal.* 14: 3–12.

Teich, M. and Young, R.M., eds (1973) *Changing Perspectives in the History of Science: Essays in Honour of Joseph Needham.* Heinemann.

Webster, C. (1975) *The Great Instauration: Science, Medicine and Reform 1626–1660.* Duckworth.

Wilke, G. (1984) 'The importance of the perception of health and illness for social order and conflict: aspects of class and cosmology in a German village', paper presented to the workshop, 'Perception in History and Anthropology: The Problem of "Otherness" ' organized by the German Historical Institute, London.

Williams, R. (1984) *Keywords: A Vocabulary of Culture and Society.* Fontana.

7 GENDER AND THE PHANTASY OF OMNIPOTENCE
Case Study of an Organization

Sheila Ernst

THE CONTEXT

IN GROUP ANALYTIC THEORY it is necessary to understand the meaning of what happens in the group within the broader matrix of the context within which that group exists. I think this principle can be applied more generally and that what I have to say about omnipotence and gender has become more significant to me and I hope will be to you too because of the particular political context.

The fear of chaos and the question of who can offer control form an important sub-text to political struggle in Britain in the 1980s. In two general elections Conservative publicity material suggested that a Labour victory might lead to disruption and chaos; through images of the 'Winter of Discontent' and hints of Labour's plans to effect a complete military surrender, combined with the prospect of disruption in schools and family life, a scenario was portrayed of a Labour Britain, dominated by industrial strife, unable to protect herself from external enemies and with 'innocent' children unprotected by the police (who had recently been refused entry to some schools) and wide open to exposure to all kinds of sexual depravity (being allowed to read books which portrayed lesbians and homosexuals).

Both Labour and Conservative leaders have attempted to portray themselves as the party who can take control. A small but telling illustration was Mrs Thatcher's determination to hold her party's conference in Brighton, where it had previously been bombed by the IRA, to show them that they cannot terrorize her. This masterful public gesture was worth her spending several million pounds of taxpayers' money on the necessary security measures. Meanwhile Neil Kinnock, the Labour Party leader, has been edging his party from an affirmation of the value of strong military defence (albeit non-nuclear) to dropping Labour's unilateralist nuclear policy as a way of denying the Conservative allegations.

I am preoccupied with trying to understand the success of Thatcherism and the difficulties that the Left is having in Britain in regrouping in any kind of effective way. The Left is either, as we have seen, competing on Thatcher territory in trying to project an image of control, or seems to be splitting into tiny groups removing themselves from the map altogether in their efforts to cling on to a 'correct line' (which is after all another more symbolic form of trying to gain control).

I have been thinking in particular about one of the potentially uncontrollable aspects of our lives and how it is dealt with by the Right and the Left. This is the politics of sexuality and the family. For the Right, the heterosexual family is to be upheld and sexuality is to be contained within the clearly defined structures of patriarchy. Thus, we may not have books in schools which portray the family life of homosexuals but it is acceptable to have a member of the British Government who is publicly known to be married, to have fathered his secretary's child, to have left her to manage on her own and to have been taken back into the bosom of his family (and incidentally to the cabinet too).

There is a growing, if minority viewpoint, literature suggesting that what the Left has to do is to take the *politics* of sexuality and the family into the heart of its politics as effectively as the Right has done. Yet the Left seems to find this very difficult to do. Cynthia Cockburn, in an interesting article on 'Masculinity, the Left and feminism' (Cockburn, 1988, pp. 303), describes her disappointment in going to the Chesterfield conference to participate in the reforming of the new Left and discovering that it was all to be done under the old white male Left slogans and preoccupations. There appeared to be no attempt to address people at the level at which Tory politics can touch them when they speak about the sanctity of family life. Thatcherism speaks to people's anxieties about losing their fantasized power in the world. Its politics allows people to avoid facing a reality in which Britain is a multi-racial society bristling with contradictions. (The need to struggle with the ineffectiveness of our welfare state, our economic system, our education system, would involve a level of admitting to doubt, failure and anxiety which both Left and Right might find unbearable.) What the

102

Right does is to capitalize on this anxiety by reasserting the interest of the dominant culture and it gets support because what it says appears to offer the re-establishment of a familiar and controllable world.

Cynthia Cockburn points to the contradictory position of the Left; its politics are dominated by those same fears of change yet it cannot, almost by definition, manipulate people's fears in the way that the Right does since in theory it represents change. She suggests that it is up to feminists to confront this issue by setting terms for working within the Left which include facing such issues.

Yet I think she underestimates the levels of anxiety and unconscious conflict which are involved. Those people who support the Conservative government even when superficially it might not appear to be in their interests perhaps do so because it allows them to maintain an illusion of a world in which things are under control; someone is protecting them from danger. People on the Left are also prey to those same anxieties. They have principles, theories and beliefs which can offer them a way of ordering the world. This can lead to an illusion of control or what I shall later refer to as a phantasized omnipotence. For the Left (and I include feminists here) it can feel safer to stay with these phantasies than to step out into an arena where risks must be taken and political power may be won or lost.

In this paper I suggest that some light may be shed on these political questions by the study of the different development of boys and girls and the implications of this difference for our understanding of an aspect of how large organizations work.

MASCULINE AND FEMININE PHANTASIES OF OMNIPOTENCE

Large organizations are often frightening and unwieldy places which generate some of the fears and phantasies which have been explored in the setting of specially created large groups. As Lionel Kreeger points out in his introduction to a collection of papers on the large group, 'the powerful forces of the large group must be acknowledged and respected, because of their potential use for either good or evil' (Kreeger, 1975, p. 25). The large group is usually defined as having more than forty members and is recognized to evoke the more psychotic mechanisms which are 'released . . . in a way which parallels the infant's primitive perception of external reality' (p. 24). While the large group is set up to explore such phantasies for therapy or training purposes, the large organization has to find other ways of dealing with them since there is an expectation that people in these organizations act as 'adults' and deliver the goods and/or services. A way of handling what is experienced as intolerable anxiety within the organization may be to resort to a state of phantasized omnipotence, thus maintaining the belief that everything is 'under control' at the expense of acknowledging what is really to be faced within the organization. Having observed elsewhere that phantasies of omnipotence are somewhat differently expressed by males and females, I want to see whether gender played a part in this process within organizations. I suggest that in the splitting and regression involved it is useful to look for a splitting of the omnipotence phantasy into a predominantly male or female mode which acts defensively by excluding the other gender. Phantasies of a predominantly 'masculine form' of omnipotence connected to mastery of the environment may predominate or phantasies of a more feminine nature may hold sway as in the all-powerful nurturing mother.

As with all splitting, both phantasies may coexist as long as there is no space for the contradictions between them to be worked through. The roots of this phantasized omnipotence lie in early infancy. As Winnicott has described it, the baby, emerging from an undifferentiated state, would be overwhelmed if he was suddenly to become aware of the degree of his total dependency and vulnerability. In his phantasy the world revolves around him, an illusion that his caretaker will try to preserve for a period until the baby appears to be ready physically and psychologically to be gently led into an awareness that he is not entirely in control. However, at the same time as sustaining this loss, he can begin to compensate for it by the growing discovery of his pleasurable capacity to 'master' aspects of his environment. This is not simply a linear developmental process; any of us, when we reach a certain anxiety level, may regress to omnipotent phantasies or activities. Personally, I resort to compulsive housework (a domain where complete control can be more easily imagined) when a really challenging piece of intellectual work needs to be done or a particularly difficult phone call has to be made.

You will have noticed that I referred to the infant/baby as 'he'. This was deliberate. Winnicott assumed that the early development of the boy and the girl were similar and used 'he' to write about both. I suggest that, though it is useful to see the girl infant as moving through similar developmental processes, she has her own particular version. (I will not go into this at length here – see Ernst, 1987.) From the earliest days, the mother's feelings about the girl infant who is the same gender as herself will be different. When the girl baby looks into her mother's eyes to see herself mirrored there what she sees will be affected by her mother's perception of her as female, as the same.

The mother conveys her own perception of the social and psychological position she has as a woman to her daughter. She sets both the arena within which her daughter will phantasize (body, home, children, others in need) and the basic psychological parameters of her development. The daughter may evoke in her mother her own repressed desires and her unresolved conflicts about how to deal with her longings, her envy, her competitiveness and her anger. The mother's identification with her daughter as a girl may be so painful that in her daughter's early infancy she may experience particular difficulty in holding or containing her daughter.

The mother communicates to the daughter the message that she must contain her own feelings, perhaps partly in preparation for her role as container of the feelings of others. Already the connections between mother and daughter are different from those between mother and son. They will affect the mother's creation of the illusion that the world centres around her daughter, and the way in which the daughter phantasizes herself to be in control. It is from these roots that a woman creates a closed system within which, in her phantasy, she is omnipotent. This may only involve herself – as in the anorexic's phantasy that she has total control of her bodily needs and the world reduces to her body or the agoraphobic's phantasy that by shutting herself into her house she shuts *out* that which she cannot control and is therefore omnipotent.

The system may also involve others. A woman may deny her needs by providing for others; through projective identification with the object of her care, in phantasy, she meets her own needs and is thus omnipotent. Or, she may hold herself responsible for all that happens, especially all that goes wrong. In this way she denies that others may affect her and in phantasy she is again all powerful (even if guilty).

Let us now look at how this is illustrated in a session of an analytic therapy group for women. The atmosphere is constricting. Though it is not obvious at first sight, the group is dominated and restricted by its collective phantasy of omnipotence. None of the five women in the group imagine that they have mastered the outside world. Far from it: Shirley, Tracy and Mary are visibly failing to do so. Tracy and Mary have difficulty in going out, and Shirley talks in the group about her inability to work for an exam which would enable her to

105

begin a career which she both longs for and is terrified of. All three women unconsciously restrict themselves; they keep themselves at home ('not living' as Shirley puts it) lest they panic when they are out in the world. Rachel and Marguerite have been able to function in the world but in this session the defences they use to do so become conscious as group themes emerge. The group is struggling (at a primitive level) with whether or not they can risk the uncontrollability of being alive and the implication of recognizing life, which is facing the ultimate possibility of death. As they present themselves in the group each woman shows how, in phantasy, she has control over her world: how she is, in phantasy, omnipotent, precisely through the ways she restricts herself or holds herself back from life, intimacy and power. Mary expresses this most clearly when she talks about being terrified of dying, but feeling that she is forty and has never been alive.

I have spent some time on the ways in which *women* phantasize themselves to be omnipotent, because, although all the experiences and symptoms will be familiar from our own lives and work, we do not usually see them as being the same as the more obvious forms of phantasies of 'mastery'.

Let us now turn to the study of an organization and see how both masculine and feminine phantasies of omnipotence may be used.

AN ORGANIZATIONAL EXAMPLE

A local government department is called upon to provide services to people who are increasingly needy within a framework of central government policy which is not recognizing many of those needs as valid and which is trying to curb local government power. The elected members, who are the local authority's employers, have an ideology which may be at variance with government views, and the employees have their own view of themselves as providing a certain kind of professional service to the public which they feel they have been trained for. The professionals are convenient whipping boys for the 'public' who don't want to believe in or recognize the level of cruelty, abuse and deprivation which exists and would rather blame the professionals for not doing their job properly. The clients also often blame the professionals for not helping them enough. You can probably recognize that this is a description of a social services department. This is the kind of conflict-ridden situation which social services managers are trying to 'manage'.

Imagine yourself to be a director of social services. You are trying to cope with government demands for compulsory competitive tendering for services, alongside the members' demands that you implement an equal opportunities policy. Your social workers officially supervised but often undersupervised from a psychodynamic perspective, reflect and even act out their clients' extreme distress. You might well find yourself wanting to impose some 'order' on to this chaos.

One kind of order which can be very appealing under such circumstances is the notion that if everything is well planned, researched, documented and systematized then it will be possible to have some control over the situation. The unconscious phantasy of omnipotence that the director has control over the service, through taking a scientific, rational approach and maintaining a strict hierarchy and adherence to bureaucratic procedures, is an apparently powerful way of dealing with chaos and with the unbearable contradictions which face local government.

This kind of masculine phantasy is of course not restricted by any means to men. Women in similar positions may often be found with impressive-looking flow charts pinned all over their office walls, shutting out certain painful areas of uncontrollability.

What evidence do I have for proposing that such a manager is operating on the level of phantasy and in a defensive mode, when on the face of it he is being entirely rational and (in my view) often establishing very useful management systems? A first indicator is a situation which should cause anxiety where no *overt* anxiety is being expressed. In relation to the present example a recent article in the *Guardian* (Clode, 1988) revealed that a quarter of all directors of social services in Britain have vacated their jobs in the past year. This should give rise to some anxiety among senior management. Yet in this example that I shall give senior management expressed no explicit anxieties. When something goes wrong that cannot be incorporated into the senior management's model of functioning, then the response reveals how much the mode of working has been based on phantasy.

Before looking more closely at a particular local example I want to emphasize that I do not see this department as being in any way more pathological than other social services departments or other local government departments or even private companies. I think such processes happen in most large organizations under pressure. Once identified and acknowledged, it is possible to work out a way of holding the anxieties which allows them to be confronted and worked through.

In a social services department the handling of a member of staff working with a case of child sexual abuse indicated to me that perhaps the department was unconsciously caught up in some omnipotent phantasies which in turn made sense of other things I had become aware of in the department's functioning.

A social worker, working on a child sexual abuse case, was sufficiently self-aware to realize that she was not able to function properly with the family and told her senior. The social worker requested some serious psychodynamic supervision from a consultant or possibly a family therapist experienced in such work, to help her to disentangle herself emotionally. This might appear to those working in the field of psychotherapy or psychoanalysis to be a very sensible response. However, since this social worker was already having difficulties with her work, it was seen within the department as a sign of inadequacy and incompetence. The senior social worker took the problem to his line manager. The social worker was severely questioned on her handling of the case and furthermore on her handling of other cases. Was her work schedule satisfactory? Her diary would have to be handed in to management for inspection. At the time I was offering a training course on child sexual abuse. Not surprisingly the social worker turned to me for advice. However, interestingly enough, management did not ask my advice even though the social services department employed me for precisely such purposes (i.e., as a staff consultant). I decided to take the extreme course of offering my advice, which is not my normal practice. It was politely turned down. This was a matter for line management and for disciplinary action if necessary. In the event the social worker was gently helped to resign.

Why had events taken this turn? Why was I not allowed to be involved? My analysis is that the social worker's confession, that she was losing her capacity to draw boundaries in her work with this family, was deeply threatening to management. It not only suggested that the procedures for working with child sexual abuse were inadequate but it also posed the possibility that drawing up 'better' procedures would not in itself be a solution and that the problem involved the uncontrollable unconscious (of which, of course, incest is a most potent example). To recognize the problem as psychodynamic as well as procedural would be to admit that the best planned, ordered and researched department could potentially fall apart. This would of course be a serious threat to the predominant phantasy.

This, in turn, illuminated for me why it was that other apparently well-thought-out plans and policies foundered in the actual implementation because there was no real room to deal with the human factor or with the contradictions involved.

The question of why was I not allowed to be involved leads directly into the other powerful alternative to the masculine phantasy I have just described. I think it is equally often to be found in an organization which is under the kinds of stress and anxiety we have noted. This phantasy takes a more feminine form in that a figure or section within the organization is endowed with maternal powers. Like a mother, this person/group is seen as being all powerful in her capacity to nurture and heal others. The others are, in phantasy, totally dependent on her. They are tied to her in a love/hate relationship. She lives out her phantasy that she can control difficult, painful and intractable feelings and circumstances. She 'suggests' that mother will make it all right and that we don't really have to take all those nasty procedures, council members and budgets into account. She suggests that through her personal magnetism she can help people to be human in the organization. What neither she nor her followers are able to acknowledge is that she has no *real* power in the organization. She has no power to hire or fire, to change policies or initiate new projects.

Such a phantasy may easily be maintained, often in conjunction with the masculine phantasy. My post within the organization was certainly seen in this way. When I arrived I was continually told how significant and important my predecessor had been – how much influence she had had and how powerful she was (this meant anything from the way she swept into the office to the fact that she knew lots of intimate things about people). It was clear that people were eager to imbue me with the same powers and it was tempting to see if I did in fact have them. Could I maintain the illusion of a kind of omnipotence, to be a wise sage and to maintain my distance?

It was incidents like the child sexual abuse case which revealed a different situation. My omnipotent phantasy – that being able to *understand* the organization gave me power – was revealed as a phantasy. I had no power. At the same time the projection on to me that I had 'special powers' was part of the reason for which I was excluded from the process. For, like a mother, I was seen as potentially very dangerous to the masculine form of omnipotent phantasy.

As Dorothy Dinnerstein points out in *The Rocking of the Cradle* (1988) it is possible, if costly and painful, for the masculine and feminine forms of these phantasies to be relinquished. She suggests

CRISES OF THE SELF

that both men and women need to mourn the loss of their archaic unity with mother and through this will come a more real appraisal of life and death. As I have tried to show, I do not see the issue as being of 'men' and 'women' but rather of the gender stereotypic traits which we manifest; and that in the organizational example I have given, the director and senior management need to give up their phantasy of omnipotence and recognize areas of human uncontrollability while I (and others in my sort of role) need to give up our illusory omnipotence and struggle for some real power, painful though both of these positions will be.

In the organization I have written about, some work has been done which has led to a reduction in the polarization of the two phantasies. As structures for working with child sexual abuse and other difficult areas are improved, space opens up for discussion and for including a psychotherapeutic approach. Of course this has to be pursued and struggled for. The recognition of my own lack of real power led me to work hard at finding ways in which the thinking time and understanding that I and others in my role could offer could be integrated into the regular work of the department and be publicly recognized and acknowledged. This has not always been the most clinically or theoretically satisfying aspect of the job but I believe that it can pay off. More recently, when a crisis blew up in the department which could prove traumatizing for social workers, although the staff consultant was not *invited* in to help, an offer of help was welcomed. Perhaps the phantasy of the all-powerful mother has diminished a little.

Perhaps we can now return to the political issues with which I began. Can this way of looking at an organization be applied to the current political situation? What are the phantasies of omnipotence purveyed by the two major political parties? Could an understanding of how phantasies of omnipotent control are influencing current political thinking be helpful in negotiating a new approach, as it was in the social services department? I don't claim to have the answers to these questions, but I hope to have said enough to stimulate some speculation and hypotheses.

ACKNOWLEDGEMENTS

I would like to thank the following people for their contributions to this paper: Les Levidow, Marie Maguire, Norma Anderson Maple and the psychotherapists' group at the Women's Therapy Centre.

REFERENCES

Clode, D. (1988) 'Disappearing directors', *Guardian*, 19.10.88.

Cockburn, C. (1988) 'Masculinity, the Left and feminism', in R. Chapman and J. Rutherford, eds *Male Order*. Lawrence & Wishart, pp. 303–30.

Dinnerstein, D. (1988) *The Rocking of the Cradle and the Ruling of the World*. Women's Press.

Ernst, S. (1987) 'Can a daughter be a woman?' in S. Ernst and M. Maguire, eds *Living with the Sphinx*. Women's Press, pp. 68–116.

Kreeger, L. (1975) *The Large Group: Dynamics and Therapy*. Maresfield Reprints.

8 PORNOGRAPHY AND BULIMIA

Gender and the Denial of
Psychic Reality

Marie Maguire

I N THIS PAPER, I explore some symptoms found predominantly in one sex, to see whether they might be gender-mediated attempts to solve similar underlying problems. Although perverse fantasies (where the inflicting of pain is central to the excitement) are widespread in both sexes, certain organized perversions, such as fetishism and exhibitionism, are almost exclusively found in men. Serious eating disorders are, on the other hand, much more commonly found among women. I focus on a bulimic woman, who binges and then makes herself vomit, and a man obsessed with pornography depicting explicit heterosexual anal and genital intercourse. I look at the childhood origins of these symptoms and the way they are manifested in the transference relationship. Finally, I explore possible ways they might resonate with or reinforce existing social attitudes and institutions.

It is notoriously difficult to define what pornography actually is, and to distinguish it from erotica, especially given that notions of social acceptability shift constantly. I therefore begin by highlighting some psychoanalytic ideas about pornography, which I link to the bulimic experience, thus introducing some of the themes that emerge from the case histories that follow.

According to Stoller (1975), in *Perversion*, at the heart of pornography is a fantasized act of hostile revenge. 'There is always a victim, no matter how disguised.' The pornographic fantasy used will encapsulate the viewer's sexual life history, which usually includes a passively experienced childhood trauma connected with sexuality or gender. Yet Stoller also stresses that pornographic literature and perverse sexuality are not distinct categories, that they form

113

part of a spectrum of human emotional life, since there can be no powerful sexual excitement without aggressive feelings or fantasies. Within pornography itself, there is a range, with the videos my patient uses occupying an intermediate category, between soft-core 'girlie' magazines and the most overtly sadistic hard-core material. Discussing the same theme, Meltzer (1973) refers to the 'knife-edge balance', where the depiction of passion in art hovers on the edge of pornographic destructiveness. This razor-edge can be the source of the greatest creative genius yet can easily tip over into caricature. He describes pornography as an attack on the viewer's inner world, on the capacity for love, creativity and reparation of damage to the self and others. What is attacked in pornography is the original source of life itself, the mother and her sexual relationship with the father. The infant's pain about exclusion having proved intolerable, that relationship itself is now debased and ridiculed in a parody of idealized romantic love.

In *Creativity and Perversion* (1984), Janine Chasseguet-Smirgel describes how, in some famous pornographic literature, the human body is used in brutally grotesque and fantastical ways. She describes the perverse impulse as the desire within all of us to extend the limits of what is possible, in the interests of avoiding psychic pain intrinsic to the human condition. These intolerable psychological realities include the loss of the infantile sense of fusion with the mother and the awareness of the inevitability of death. In order to avoid the recognition of loss, frustration and absence, all differences and distinctions are denied or obliterated, especially those between the generations and the sexes. The perverse state of mind has strong links with that of the toddler who struggles for independence and control over its own body at the same time as it fights to hold on to its powerful infantile sense of being at one with the mother. Conflicts about domination and control originating in this period are reflected in my male patient's preoccupation with fragmented images of anal and genital sexuality. Just as parts of the body are disconnected from the whole, human needs are divorced from any relational context. Pornographic sex is dissociated from love and never results in procreation.

There are also echoes of toddler power battles in the bulimic woman's attempts to subvert the digestive process and break the link between feeding and nourishment. In *Women's Secret Disorder* (1988), Mira Dana and Marilyn Lawrence describe bulimia as a perversion of the natural function of eating. The bulimic woman, overcome by unbridled appetite, abandons the most basic proprieties and conventions about the consumption of food. Bulimia also represents a caricature, this time of the process of nourishment. The hostility intrinsic to this parody is turned inwards toward the bulimic's own body which, like the pornographic image, is objectified and debased.

There are striking similarities in the family relationships of the man and woman I am going to describe. They were each born into families struggling to cope with extremely tragic wartime histories. Mr B's father, a skilled manual worker, never came to terms with traumas experienced as a Japanese prisoner of war. The family's difficulties were further compounded by financial hardship and the physical illnesses of Mr B's mother. Mrs K's German Jewish father became seriously depressed after losing his entire extended family in concentration camps. In Mrs K's early years the family suffered another series of major losses. Bereft of their husband's emotional support, each mother became overinvolved with these particular children. Both Mr B and Mrs K experienced their mothers as possessive and controlling, yet absent or preoccupied with their own problems at crucial moments. Both describe their mothers as having, unwittingly, aroused them sexually, so that the mother–child relationship became eroticized. Since neither mother could tolerate or negotiate such extreme emotional pain or conflict themselves, they could not help their children to develop the capacities to do so either. As a result, both Mrs K and Mr B were, like their mothers, prone to using addictive, escapist ways of avoiding the truth of their own emotional experience. Mr B could clearly see the connection between his mother's use of mass-market fiction as a defence against depression and his own addiction to pornography. Mrs K's mother, on the other hand, avoided the emotional realities of her own tragic life by immersing herself in fundamentalist religion, and expecting her daughter to find a similar solution to the traumas of her early childhood.

Mr B's and Mrs K's difficulties with their mothers were compounded by the lack of a father or other involved adult who could set benign limits, so helping them develop a sense of their own psychological boundaries. This contributed to their difficulties in developing an internal regulatory capacity of their own which might have enabled them to set limits on their physical and emotional appetites. Instead, they each remained preoccupied with struggles against a dominating internalized mother, who laid down the law, against which they rebelled. The conflicts about power and control which obsessed each of them were played out through Mr B's pornography and Mrs K's bulimia.

Mrs K's infancy seems to have been relatively contented. When she was eighteen months, however, her father, with whom she seems to have had a loving relationship, died. During her fourth year, her little brother was killed on the road when they were playing alone together. Unable to understand this accident, she held herself responsible. Mrs K remained constantly preoccupied with this second death. Her tendency towards binge-eating and compulsive sexual experimentation with children, and then adults of both sexes, began as an attempt to escape from this utterly unassimilable inner reality. Through her bulimia, which began at twenty, Mrs K attempted to vomit up a dead internal object which, because of her guilt, she had been unable to mourn. Sexual experimentation with both sexes, which at times became quite compulsive, had also been from childhood an attempt to escape from this utterly unassimilable inner reality. Her adult sexual relationships had a sado-masochistic quality. She and her husband had for a brief period shared the use of pornography. However, despite these rebellions against it, Mrs K had in fact internalized a strong religious prohibition against the free expression of sexuality, especially for women. This meant that her emotionally escapist activities focused predominantly around food, which she had been brought up to see as 'the only legitimate female pleasure'.

Mrs K's mother's own feelings of guilt and abandonment seem to have compounded her difficulties in helping her daughter come to terms with her brother's death. As a result, whatever capacities the little girl had developed to tolerate and digest emotional experience seem to have disintegrated. This was clearly evident in her early therapy sessions. She would rush in, flood me with desperate, disorganized emotion, gulp greedily at my interpretations like a starving infant, and rush off again to binge sweet milky food and vomit up the whole experience in secret.

Mr B's difficulties originated in the first year of his life, at the stage when feeding, sensuality and emotional experience are inextricably linked. Women, Mr B told me, abandoned him after six months. After this period of time, he began to find the therapeutic relationship excruciatingly difficult. Gradually, evidence seemed to emerge that he had experienced weaning from the breast at six months as the first in a series of humiliating, bitterly resented losses. Like his elder brother, he had slept in the parental bedroom until he was three. It

116

seems likely that he experienced this constant exposure to his parents' sexual relationship as a traumatic violation which he was forced to tolerate alone. The awareness that his father retained possession of his mother's body continually reinforced his pain and jealousy. He defended himself against desperate feelings of loneliness and exclusion by turning away from his parents to his own penis, reassuring himself constantly about his ability to satisfy his own needs. However, beneath this essentially oedipal pain and rivalry there seemed to be overwhelming infantile anxieties about losing his mother and going to pieces himself. His masturbation represented a defence against these very early fears of falling apart or ceasing to exist. It was also a rebellion against his mother, who later prohibited masturbation.

Mr B's uncertainties about what it means to be a man reflect these early anxieties. There was also an intense confusion between his parents about gender roles. He was seen as his mother's child, while his brother formed a closer bond with their father. Sensing that his mother expected him to be 'more than a son', Mr B came to experience himself as her life companion. His confusion was intensified by his strong identification with his mother and by his view of her as 'wearing the trousers' in the family. In his early sessions, Mr B consciously accepted his mother's opinion of his father as an almost pitiably passive character. In an early childhood dream however, his father emerged as a powerful, unassailable sexual rival, most compellingly as an evil knight who kidnapped a beautiful princess. It now seems likely that his childhood revulsion against touching his father masked a powerful sense of sexual fascination with a paternal body that, later on in his therapy, Mr B acknowledged as physically strong and handsome, 'a fine figure of a man'.

As the omnipotent voyeur of pornographic couplings Mr B unconsciously engages in a shifting kaleidoscope of painful and pleasurable identifications with each parent. Unsure whether the women he watches are crying out in anguish or delight Mr B satisfies his conflicting desires to keep the injured princess safe, while simultaneously punishing her for her unfaithfulness. He describes the pornography as being like a love-object which is always there when he needs it unlike a real partner whose wishes cannot be predicted or controlled. 'My dad stole mum away . . . she chose him over me. Perhaps when I see women being dominated, I feel I'm getting my own back.' Through his total power over the celluloid images in whose intercourse he can intervene at will, Mr B can reverse his helpless infantile exclusion, and revenge himself on both parents.

As infants become less physically helpless, control, especially over their own bodies and that of the mother, becomes a crucial issue. They have to come to terms with the painful reality that they are not the centre of their mother's universe, and that they cannot satisfy her in the same way as other adults can. For instance, they cannot in reality be her equal sexual partner.

The child needs to be helped by the adults around it to struggle with and to negotiate the inevitable frustrations and inequities of being small and helpless. It also needs to be helped to come to terms with the serious limitations of belonging to only one sex and the lack of the physical attributes of the other.

It is often suggested that there is a strong link between bulimia and some disturbance or lack in the relationship with the father. Mrs K's constant emotional oscillation between men and women seemed to reflect conflicting desires towards the parental couple, which remained unresolved because of her father's premature death. On the one hand, she wanted to come between them and have exclusive possession of each. She couldn't, she insisted, face the idea of her mother or myself being part of a sexual couple. 'It makes me feel ill.' On the other hand, after arriving an hour early for her session one morning, she acknowledged fantasies of bumping into the man in my life and luring him away. Nor, because of her own guilt about her brother's death, could she feel positive about herself or her parents creating new life. Yet on the other hand, she was aware of a desperate need to bring her parents together as a unit inside her, so that she could relinquish her obsession with them and build her own adult emotional life.

In her therapy, as in her life, she wants a woman when she is with a man, and a man when she is with a woman. This was illustrated graphically when, soon after a holiday break, feeling overwhelmed by a combination of rage and devouring need for me, Mrs K attempted to vomit up the therapy by visiting a series of male psychiatrists. One of them gave her a strict fatherly lecture when she finally refused his offer of treatment, having decided to remain in therapy with me. Yet, in reality her mother had acted as both parents and was, Mrs K told me, a 'sexually ambiguous figure whose behaviour was sometimes more male than female'. She associated the psychiatrist's apparent emphasis on adjusting surface behaviour with her mother's methods of control. Yet he also 'gave her licence', as she imagined her father might have done, to risk a period of depression if she gave up her bulimic symptom. Angry at the psychiatrist's confrontational style, she decided 'out of cussedness' that

118

she could now tolerate her feelings enough to give up bingeing and vomiting while remaining in therapy with me, 'rather than doing it with strangers'. In fact, she did give up vomiting, and although she still sometimes overeats, this has considerably lessened. Gradual signs of an increased ability to contain her emotions and avoid addictive activities especially during breaks in therapy indicate that she may now be beginning to internalize me as a bisexual object who can set limits and boundaries.

However, because in childhood there was, in reality, no other involved adult who could help her to separate psychologically, in the early stages of her therapy Mrs K remained preoccupied with an unusually intense physical identification with her mother's body. She experienced herself and her mother as identical, both simultaneously beautiful and repulsively fleshy. In her therapy sessions over a period of time, it was as if, in fantasy, she wrapped herself around me and became me. When this first happened, I had the sudden alarming feeling that, without understanding how or why, the ground had been cut from under my feet and I had lost all sense of who I was. When I expressed this feeling of intense disorientation, Mrs K then began to voice her fantasy of having stepped into my skin, sat in my chair and become the therapist rather than the patient. At this point, I began to regain my capacity to think and understand. During these sessions Mrs K arrived wearing clothes as similar to mine as possible. For the first time in her therapy, she became visibly enraged. Her anger focused around the fact that I wore an unpredictable colour, one she disliked too much to copy. If she could actually experience herself as being me or her mother, rather than a separate individual in her own right, then in fantasy she could control us. Imagining that she possessed all our attributes, she need not feel her usual sense of inequality and envy in relation to us.

Common factors in the histories of this man and woman include an overcontrolling mother, a lack of paternal intervention and the need to control and evacuate intolerable internal realities. Each used their bodies to cope with traumas connected to the solitary witnessing of family secrets. As a result of these events and family constellations, both developed uncertainties connected to gender identity or object choice.

There are also similarities in the actual symptoms. Most obviously, both are addictive, second-hand ways of dealing with and controlling emotional experience. Since other therapists have told me of

bulimic women patients who also have some experience of pornography as Mrs K does, I wondered whether there might also be a
more direct connection. Mr B and Mrs K both describe an overwhelming sense of self-sufficiency, an almost ecstatic feeling of pleasure and physical excitement which rapidly disappears, to be
followed, after the event, by intense sadness and shame. Each regrets
bitterly the need to rebel, through these secret self-abasing rituals,
against the veneer of total filial conformity or 'polished perfection'
demanded by their mothers.

In different ways, each symptom reveals a preoccupation with
sexual looking and with stereotyped notions about sexual attractive-
ness. There is a sense in which Mrs K sees her body as a pornographic object, which she tries to control. From infancy, Mrs K seems
to have experienced herself as a pretty, passive doll, to be displayed
enticingly and played with by others. It has, she says, taken her a
long time to realize that she can actively engage in, and feel herself a
part of, her own sexual life. This sense of objectification is reflected in
her concern with the physical functions of her body and its fluctua-
tions of weight. It also reveals itself in her anguished fascination
with attracting and repelling the advances of voyeuristic men. Mr B's
main preoccupation is with watching others. Yet, at the same time,
his own sense of himself as a passive object, awaiting the advances of
somewhat motherly princesses, may have been projected outside
himself on to pornographic female images.

The most significant differences between these symptoms are that
Mr B eroticizes his conflicts and projects them outside himself.
Through the use of food, Mrs K directs her own greed and destruct-
iveness inwards, towards her own body.

I am now going to look at the way in which these differences were
expressed in the transference relationship with me in the early stages
of psychotherapy. Mrs K's fear of damaging me was intense, since
she felt that her childhood rivalry had killed the little sandy-haired
brother who was now re-emerging in the transference relationship
with me. She expressed her needs for me in a more directly
emotional way, with overtones of sexuality. But, feeling internally
torn between men and women, she alternated between wanting to
possess me and experiencing me as a sexual rival. This bisexual
emotional state is common even among women who consciously see
themselves as heterosexual. It reflects the difficult transition girls are
expected to make between the mother with whom they identify and
the father who is supposed to be a sexual love object.

120

Initially, her intense need, rage and rivalry were evacuated secretly through bulimia and random, occasionally dangerous sexual exploits. During one of these encounters, she thinks she may have risked being murdered. As her brother's mysterious death was slowly reconstructed, from fragments of memory, family information and dream images, she communicated to me through actions and feeling-states her overwhelmingly powerful sense of guilt. I became worried by the strength of her urge to destroy herself or allow herself to be destroyed.

Mr B initially abandoned himself to the therapeutic relationship with the passive vulnerability of a very young infant. It was a long struggle, however, for him to begin to engage with me in a real two-way exchange. I often felt overwhelmed by his sense of despair about being genuinely close to another human being. He fought to maintain an illusion of being the centre of my emotional life, as he had imagined himself to be the focus of his mother's. After seeing a mechanic in the street mending a car he believed to be mine, Mr B embarked on one of a series of bitter and prolonged battles for control of my presence and the therapeutic environment. It began with him noticing a weakness in one of my chairs. 'Chairs that might break', he pointed out later, 'are like mothers who aren't there when you need them.' Soon, his attention shifted to the perimeters of my flat. He declared my neighbourhood dangerous and the door-locks flimsy. I might, he pointed out angrily, be intruded upon or attacked by violent men. Angry that I responded only with interpretations, he then stayed away for several sessions. During one of these he occupied himself with a pornographic book depicting a brutal sexual attack on a woman. He came back worried about having for the first time bought such overtly sadistic material. He did not want this to continue. But beneath this was a deeper anxiety, that the hostility he was becoming aware of within the maternal transference to me might become uncontainable.

Interestingly, given my focus on escapist psychological activities, I rapidly forgot the details of this attack. Presumably Mr B was projecting into me his intolerable anxieties about acting out his aggressive feelings, and I was reacting with an only partly conscious fear of male violence. This fantasized attack on my body, like Mrs K's attempt to take control of my physical presence, seemed to temporarily suspend my ability to think about the therapeutic material.

Feeling rage and need for me, Mrs K risks harming her own body, through bulimia, and being harmed by men through dangerous sexual encounters, while Mr B misses sessions and identifies with a

121

man's sadistic physical attack on a woman. These distinctly different transference reactions raise certain crucial questions about the inter-connections between internal experience, and the external world. I will begin by looking at the interaction between fantasy life and real actions as it emerged in the therapy of Mr B. Then I will look at these two therapeutic experiences in relation to patterns of male-female psychosexual development, bearing in mind that the reality of my own gender will have had a crucial effect on the transference.

Mr B gradually let me know that, when exploring any element of sexuality or aggression towards me, he became extremely anxious, as he had with his mother, lest the boundaries between fantasy and reality might become blurred. He experienced this with particular acuteness at the beginning and endings of the sessions, 'when the barriers go down and then come up again'. If we really looked at his inner feelings and fantasies, would we, he seemed to be wondering, be able to maintain the transference as an 'as-if' relationship? Would I be able to ensure that the professional boundaries remained intact, or could we be talking about a real love-affair, or an actual physical attack? In fact, Mr B's eroticized transference feelings were largely a defence against experiences of pain and loneliness and anxieties about disintegration during his first year of life, rather than an expression of adult sexuality. His fear of acting on those feelings was also connected to their origins in this earliest stage of development, when fantasy is inextricable from reality.

Just as pornography had provided an addictive means of escape from anxieties about enacting his fantasies within actual relation-ships, now Mr B became aware that he might be using the therapeu-tic relationship in the same way. Rather than tackling the hard work involved in genuine internal change, one part of Mr B simply wished to remain for ever enmeshed in a re-enactment of the eroticized relationship with his mother, where a facade of passive compliance belied a continual desire to rebel. To me he said, 'I was waiting for you to do all the work . . . become my girlfriend, take me out.' This part of Mr B wanted to modify but retain his dependence on porno-graphy. The ever-present danger for me was of underestimating the strength of his resistance to change. For instance, I might not detect the contemptuous rebellion beneath his pretence of emotional explo-ration, when his main preoccupation was a forthcoming weekend 'pornographic binge'. This replicated the way he had bided his time until his unsuspecting mother went shopping so that he could then raid his brother's hidden stock of pornographic magazines. Yet, a strong part of Mr B did not want simply to 'paper over the cracks',

122

and is determined to change. Despite continual setbacks, after four years of twice-weekly psychotherapy he has become gradually more able to think about and articulate his feelings, and to become a much more active participant in the therapeutic relationship. There are signs that as he becomes more aware of and able to verbalize his needs and his aggression, he may feel less need to retreat into pornographic fantasy for fear of harming others or being hurt himself. He is beginning to move towards finding some middle ground in himself between experiences of total passivity and anxieties about being overwhelmingly dominant in relation to women, and can now envisage the possibility of more equal forms of intimacy.

For social as well as psychological reasons, men seem more likely to experience their emotional needs as highly eroticized and directed almost entirely towards the opposite sex, as Mr B's were. The possibility of homosexual feelings then becomes extremely difficult to explore. Later in this paper, I suggest some developmental reasons for this reticence which characterized the early stages of Mr B's therapy. At first he rarely mentioned his father. This was partly an avoidance of his pain and jealousy about being dispossessed of his mother. However, it also reflected the strength of Mr B's fears about acknowledging sexual admiration or longing for his father.

I will now look at male psychosexual development. Boys are expected to make a quite sudden shift to identification with the father and to repudiate their infantile needs which become associated with the mother and femininity. The mother becomes an erotic love-object. Those infantile needs from which the boy has had to cut off so dramatically are covered over with a veneer of pseudo-adulthood. When these needs appear, they may, as in Mr B's case, be highly eroticized. This tendency is reinforced by the sense many men have that vulnerability is only acceptable within sexual relationships with women.

The fact that men's rivalry towards women is often far more intense and asocial than their competitiveness with their own sex reflects its origin in the earliest phase of life. Excessive aggression and contempt for women, and an overvaluation of the penis by men, can be seen as defensive against early infantile pain, humiliation and fears of retaliatory attack by the mother. The boy's feelings of envy and inadequacy in relation to his mother's procreative and nurturing capacities and her relationship to the father are all the stronger because he senses that, given his different gender, he will never in reality possess what she has.

123

In theory, the boy's identification with the father will link him up with external reality where as a male he has a privileged place. This will help him develop a sense of his own separateness from the mother and of his own value and creativity. The boy who, like Mr B, is unable fully to admire and identify with the father and enter into this male world, may retain an overwhelming sense of inadequacy and envy in relation to both sexes, but particularly towards women. He may feel, unconsciously, a strong desire to leave behind his early identification with his mother, combined with a terror of losing the possibility of that infantile intimacy, and a wish for revenge for being placed in this dilemma.

Men's tendency to project their aggression outwards may be related to their own physiological outerdirectedness and an identification with the father's psychological and social orientation towards the external world. It also reflects men's much clearer sense of the mother, the object of their earliest, most intense emotions of love and hate, as being quite distinct from them, separate and different. Feminist theorists often suggest that the male tendency towards 'mastery of the world' may also be a compensation for men's marginal role in procreating the species.

I am now going to look at some of the reasons why women might turn aggression inwards and express unresolved conflicts through their bodies. Little is actually known about the complex and vital interrelationship between women's experience of their bodies, their emotional lives and their role in society, although there have been some interesting psychoanalytic speculations about the connections between physiology and psychology. Erikson (1968) in research that initially suggests more biological determination than I would agree with, linked girls' tendency to conceptualize interior spaces, such as peaceful rooms, with the hidden containment of female wombs and genitals. Boys, on the other hand, drew fast-moving exterior scenes. Women's sexuality is much more subtle, complex and diffuse than men's, with pleasure-zones located all over the body. Although there is obviously an erotic element in physically located symptoms such as bulimia, it seems that women focus on their bodies as an entirety, whereas men's sexuality and emotional lives focus more specifically around their genitals.

Other reasons for women's tendency to internalize emotional life and express it through their bodies may connect more specifically with the mother-daughter relationship. The daughter, as I said earlier, must both identify with the mother and her female body, and separate from her psychologically. The boy may manage to cut off

124

more suddenly from his early female identification with the mother. As Dinora Pines (1987) points out, since women remain in constant contact with the rhythms and developmental changes of their bodies, their process of psychological separation from the mother is lifelong. It is also inextricably linked with each stage of the physiological life-cycle. Unresolved conflicts in relation to the mother will re-emerge, for instance, at puberty, pregnancy and the menopause. One conse-quence of this is that the woman's early feeling of envy and inade-quacy in relation to the mother's body remain more immediate and inescapable. Guilt connected with these feelings may be focused around the girl's own female organs and the inside of her body, where she may fear retaliation. While the boy can check that his penis is still intact, the girl's fears about damage to her reproductive and genital organs cannot be so easily allayed by reality. These fears may be reinforced in some girls by the onset of menstruation which may unconsciously be associated with harm to the interior of the body. As a result of these anxieties women may be more prone to an internal sense of rottenness, persecution or emptiness.

The effect of this is heightened because women's bodies and their ability to procreate and nurture are their traditional source of self-esteem. Yet the female body and motherhood are both simulta-neously idealized and denigrated. For instance, pornography follows the same visual conventions as more routinely available images of women's bodies. Women's sense of connectedness with infantile emotional and physical experience is all the stronger because unlike men they do not have easy access to an external arena where they can develop a sense of self-value.

These are some of the reasons for women's tendency to turn aggression inwards and to express their emotional lives through their bodies, for instance through eating disorders, psychosomatic symptoms and anxieties about their own physical appearance.

In this paper, I have attempted to locate certain underlying problems which this man and woman share. Mr B and Mrs K both lack a capacity to assimilate and contain painful and frustrating emotional experiences. Both are preoccupied with conflicts about control of an overpowering but unreliable internalized mother figure. This contributes to difficulties in making equal adult relation-ships. At the same time, neither of them has developed an internal capacity to regulate their own physical and emotional appetites. This seems to be connected with the lack of benign control from a father or other involved adult.

Each suffers from some form of confusion about gender identification or object-choice that leads to sexual compulsiveness or rigidity, rather than any ability to be flexible.

For both, internal conflicts are dramatized through the female body, the body of the mother, for whom each feels intense envy and a strong erotic attachment. In fantasy, each attempts to control, possess and attack the mother's body. But, while Mrs K uses food, the traditional symbol of female nurturing, and turns her aggression against herself, Mr B eroticizes and externalizes his unresolved conflicts. These quite distinct ways of dealing with conflicts about need, sexuality and rage connect both with differences in men's and women's psychosexual development and with the power differential between them in the external world.

Although in some respects extreme, the families I describe struggle with culturally typical dilemmas. It is problematic in itself that mothers who are often solely responsible for child development are also often isolated and unsupported in this role. The ill-effects of this marginalization of child-care are reinforced if, like these mothers, they lack both psychological capacities and cultural support for negotiating psychic pain and conflict. There is a widespread denial in our society that we must all experience loss and frustration, and there are few outlets for dealing with these inevitable emotional realities. This leads on an individual level to the increase of escapist, addictive activities such as the use of pornography or bulimia. At a social level, psychic pain is only visible when manifested in the most extreme ways, for instance in sexual abuse or violence against children.

Dorothy Dinnerstein, in *The Rocking of the Cradle and the Ruling of the World* (1976), argues that men and women collude in the carrying of different aspects of human experience because of our difficulties in facing up to fundamental realities of loss and death. For both sexes, images of women as castrated or deficient are, as Chasseguet-Smirgel (1964) points out, a denial of the power of the mother early in the infant's life. In our culture, the body of the mother is the scapegoat for all human ills. Through a denial of the procreative richness and strengths of the female body, women collude in their social powerlessness, whereas men cut off from the richness of their own emotional lives.

Feminists have focused on pornography as an extreme and concrete symbolization of male oppression of women. It is, in fact, a crucial point of intersection between the internal fantasy world and social institutions. The two cases I have described also raise important issues about the relationship of men and women to sado-

126

masochistic imagery. The increasing cultural emphasis on erotic imagery of submission and domination is, Jessica Benjamin suggests in her essay 'Master and slave' (1983), a reflection of a deep unsatisfied human need to transcend the boundaries of the self. She ascribes the popularity of sado-masochistic ritual to the fact that it allows this sense of personal transcendence without the loss of control. Because of our restrictive gender roles, she says, neither men nor women have the opportunity to simultaneously lose a sense of self while maintaining a feeling of control. Western society, organized around the devaluation of maternal nurturance and intimacy, is, according to Benjamin, becoming both dangerously destructive and also increasingly personally unsatisfying. She points out that traditional social outlets for the human need for transcendence are disappearing or declining. The experience of 'losing the self', of continuity, is, she suggests, increasingly difficult to obtain except in the erotic relationship, so that this relationship becomes seen as overwhelmingly important.

Any discussion of the interrelationship between women's physiological experience, gender-mediated behaviour and social power raises a series of fundamental questions. We need to know how open our early emotional life is to influence from the external world, and how our defences against early anxieties might later become institutionalized, for instance, in pornography or images that debase women. Similarly, the use of pornography raises questions about the relationship between what is enacted in sado-masochistic fantasy and individual acts of violence, on the one hand, and the pornographic industry, on the other. Clearly there is a relationship between gender-linked symptoms, early development and male-female power relations. Obviously, much more work needs to be done on these areas and, in particular, on the interconnection between biological realities, human needs and fantasies, and social forces.

ACKNOWLEDGEMENTS

My greatest thanks go to my patients for their generosity in allowing me to share their experiences, certain details of which I have altered in the interests of confidentiality. For giving me considerable help and advice at extremely short notice, I'd like to thank Tirril Harris, Anne Mhlongo, Marilyn Lawrence, Sheila Ernst, Joanna Ryan, Russell Southwood and my clinical supervisor, Dr Arthur Hyatt Williams.

REFERENCES

Benjamin, J. (1983) 'Master and slave: the fantasy of erotic domination', in A. Snitow, C. Stansell and S. Thompson, eds *Desire: The Politics of Sexuality*. Virago, 1984, pp. 292–311.
Chasseguet-Smirgel, J. (1964) *Female Sexuality*. Maresfield Reprints, 1985.
—— (1984) *Creativity and Perversion*. Free Association Books, 1985.
Dana, M. and Lawrence, M. (1988) *Women's Secret Disorder*. Grafton.
Dinnerstein, D. (1976) *The Rocking of the Cradle and the Ruling of the World*. Souvenir, 1978.
Erikson, E. (1968) 'Womanhood and the inner space', in J. Strouse, ed. *Women and Analysis*. Chicago: G.K. Hall, pp. 291–319.
Meltzer, D. (1973) 'The architectonics of pornography', in *Sexual States of Mind*. Strath Tay, Perthshire: Clunie Press.
Pines, D. (1987) 'Women's unconscious use of their bodies'. Lecture at the London Centre for Psychotherapy.
Stoller, R. (1975) *Perversion: The Erotic Form of Hatred*. Maresfield Reprints, 1986.

PART 3
CASE STUDIES
IN POPULAR CULTURE
AND POLITICS

9 BE YOUR OWN PERSON

Dependence/Independence, 1950–1985

Amal Treacher

> To reach a point where we can live alone and feel secure in our
> capacity to look after ourselves, without any hurtful sense of
> exclusion or inadequacy; or to live in the intimacy of a couple
> without feeling threatened or diminished in our sense of self,
> without drowning in symbiosis, would be to hold the fine balance
> of independence and dependence that seems so delicately
> necessary.
> LIZ HERON, *Changes of Heart.*

THIS QUOTE probably sums up some important aspirations and
hopes of many people living in present-day Western society,
that is, to be able to be an independent being knowing the
boundaries between self and others, and through that knowledge of
the self to be able to have a full and satisfying relationship with
another. Many of us seem to juggle with the particular complexities
of being independent, autonomous and self-reliant, of being our
own man or woman. A dominant interpretation is that to be one's
own man or woman is to be open, honest, able to explore and
overcome one's emotions, confidently sexual and of course orgasmic,
to know one's body and all its sensations, to be fluid and comfortable
whether in public or private. Many of these terms are inextricably
bound up with one another; for instance, to be fluid demands an
open, honest, freely expressed sexuality. The general imperative is to
be an independent individual sure in one's knowledge about oneself. But this imperative seems to be a contemporary phenomenon.

This paper will trace some changing definitions of the self from
1950 tó 1985. I will concentrate, in the main, on one aspect of contemporary subjectivity, that of independence. To do this I have read
closely the first issue of each month of *Woman* magazine, which is a
popular weekly magazine. Its features cover a range of female interests from cooking to clothes, home decorating to amusing anecdotes

about the family. Articles are published about the rich and famous who are represented simultaneously as both one of us and one of them. There is usually an article about a 'normal' member of the public who has overcome a tragic misfortune. The tone is warm, friendly advice with an emphasis on the belief that you (the reader) can achieve and be more than who you really are. This paper outlines some of the findings of the research, in particular about the problem page and some salient short stories; this approach is not intended to provide the definitive statement of what it means to be dependent or independent within this social period, but is offered as a way of tracing and exploring these changing definitions.

Woman magazine profoundly shared the consensus that the family was and is the central unit of society, and in the 1950s it both represented and perpetuated the belief that women's contributions to society were as loving, dutiful but not submissive, dignified, warm wives and mothers, equal but different to men. The ideal woman of the 1950s should have been 'feminine', 'demure', 'coy', and Helen Temple (the beauty and fashion editor) looked forward to 'the new appealing charm which will be ours during the coming decade' (*Woman*, January 1950). This new ideal ought to be achieved by all, and could therefore cut across class and economic status. Women could and should transcend their social and economic status by concentrating and developing their powerful femininity.

Much of the emphasis of the magazine was on the rules of good public behaviour. For example, an article published in January 1956, entitled 'Little things mean a lot', explored through different examples how women should behave and act towards others. The concentration was on putting others before the self, thinking of small gestures which will please other people and make them feel good about themselves. It was common in the 1950s for *Woman* magazine to publish articles on moral behaviour and attitudes, and the implicit theme of many of the columns was how to keep up good social standards. Many of the short stories were about rules of social conduct, and crude distinctions between good and bad abounded. Bad men were selfish, vain and lazy, but above all their badness manifested itself in their desire for sex before marriage. Good men on the other hand were quiet, gentle, successful and unassuming, and knew how to control their 'passionate tendencies'. Sex before marriage was dangerous and shameful, but after marriage it became sacred and beautiful. However, women were urged to think about how they might have encouraged men to want sex by the way they dressed, acted and gave the impression that their moral standards

132

were lower than they were. The responsibility for refusal was laid squarely on the female shoulder, and the consistent message was that it is often much harder for men to keep moral rules because of their nature, and therefore it was up to women to make self-control easier for them.

I will now outline a short story to illustrate some predominant themes of the 1950s. In 'Letter from Yesterday' by Kathleen Crawford (January 1950), a married man (John Martin) receives a letter from a past mistress, and the story opens with him trying to decide whether or not to go away for the weekend with her (Anne). The affair had happened during the war, when it was all so simple. Since the arrival of the letter John had been aware of a debate in his head trying to decide whether or not to go. 'He had even wondered if those insistent voices weren't audible to everyone else in the office.'

The narrative takes the reader from the tormented day-dreaming of John, to John the father playing with his son Peter, during which John rather carelessly loses the letter, panics, and is in a state of high anxiety. 'It was not by any means the kind of letter you wanted lying about for the world to read.' John begins to search for the letter, and looks in the chest of drawers, and while he doesn't find the letter he discovers that his wife Laura kept her things in one drawer so as to give him more space. John begins to realize the extent of his wife's selflessness. His wife walks in to find clothes scattered all over the floor and she mutters, 'What on earth? Oh, John, and with the Simpsons coming.' John still cannot find the letter, but the narrative makes quite clear his anxiety about what he would lose, and also his anxiety about what the world would think of him. During the course of the evening they have an altercation. John challenges Laura about her placidity, and asks if she never gets fed up. She remains calm and reminds John not to shout otherwise he will wake up Peter. He persists in challenging her to admit to her dissatisfaction, and she replies: 'That's a privilege I never indulge in . . . I can't afford to. I wouldn't want to jeopardize all the things I love for the pleasure of letting off steam when I'm tired and fed up and bored.' She repeats that she does get bored, 'but not often enough to play games with her happiness.' John now tenderly declares his love for her.

The narrative now shifts to his anger towards Anne. At the beginning of the story she was described as vital and exciting, but as John sees what he would lose she becomes represented as the wicked woman who could have broken up a marriage. John realizes that it is important never to think of another woman, and to think of his family. 'Let the past keep its memories – here was his life, here in this house. Here was his present and future too.'

The story clearly illustrates to women that if they are selfless, loving and patient, then their husbands will discover and appreciate their inherent goodness, will not leave and the marriage will not be at risk. It further reinforces the positioning of women as the lynchpin of the family. It is love, a woman's love, which will contain, and keep in order and harmony the family and the world. But much of what happens between Laura and John is as if it is a mother speaking or relating to her son. Many of the references in the story are to do with John's anxiety about what the world will think of him: not his family, nor his wife, but the world itself. Also, Laura's discomfort at finding clothes all over the floor is to do with people coming to dinner, and presumably what they would think, and not John's internal state nor why he is behaving so peculiarly.

The emphasis on love as a healing agent is vigorously underlined by Evelyn Home who was until 1974 the agony aunt of *Woman*. Evelyn Home portrayed women as being very powerful through their identities and roles as wives and mothers. It was through their love and inherent goodness that women could, and moreover should, hold the family together. The tone of the problem page is that of no-nonsense, straightforward talking and advice. The problems and answers are devoid of any emotionality. Evelyn Home in her replies discourages emotion, and the only feeling she ever expresses is that of pity or sympathy. One of her favourite expressions is 'If that is your emotion stamp on it hard'. The ethos is that of making the best of things, of not letting fantasy and day-dreaming get in the way of reality, and of insisting that if individuals utilize their common sense, and believe more in the goodness of the world, they will inevitably be able to overcome their difficulties.

The place of emotions, the importance granted to them and how they should be dealt with, reveals an important shift in the way identity was perceived and represented. During the 1950s the advice most oft-repeated was to control one's emotions and to let one's head rule the heart. The sin was to brood and dwell on one's self. For example, a correspondent writes in for whom at 25 her marriage is a failure and both her babies have died. She feels that there is no hope. She is advised by Home to stop feeling sorry for herself, that the past is over and she should now learn forgiveness (May 1951). To forget the past, not to open things up and to step forward is the advice given to women who were experiencing marital difficulties. The advice 'give your heart less to do and your head much more' was a

sentiment shot through many of Evelyn Home's replies. She acknowledged that everybody does wrong, but the best way forward was to
create a new life. To comfort another and to look after someone less
well off than yourself was a constant piece of advice to women. In
that way, it was represented, women would receive healing and a
cure through altruism and love of others. No attempts at psychological explanation or advice were given; the emphasis was on action
and doing good. The unforgivable was what was labelled in various
ways as 'self-indulgent', 'self-pity' and 'wallowing'.

Woman magazine in the 1960s becomes brighter, rather more
cheerful in its use of colour and its design, but it still retains its rather
warm and cosy tone of the close but distant friend. The most prominent shift is in the theme of sexuality. Affairs, relationships,
unwanted pregnancies were frequent problems on the problem page
in the 1950s, but a quiet voice of sexual discontent appears at the
beginning of the 1960s, and grows in strength towards the end of the
decade. This shift is most apparent on the problem page from the
middle of the decade on, where there now appear a number of
queries about sex, including how to take the sexual initiative with
husband, how to climax and questions about birth control. The
language previously used to describe problems related to sexual
practice is now more open. It moves from describing sex as intimacy
(which often left me in considerable doubt as to whether love or sex
was meant) to describing sex as sexual intercourse. Interlinked with
this supposed growing openness about issues of sexuality, there is a
growing emphasis on talking over problems and discovering one's
emotions. Evelyn Home shifts from recommending control of the
emotions to tentatively advocating the exploration of feelings. In
conjunction with these seemingly more open discussions about sex
and emotions there appear more short stories about women rejecting
their staid boyfriends and finding men who are freer and not tied
down by social conventions. Images of men diving into the sea,
cleanly flying like birds, and other metaphors for the independent
spirit begin to appear. Of course, the stories end in marriage, but it is
not necessarily the successful businessman who is portrayed as the
most eligible catch, but the man who is able to go his own way.
Advertisements too begin to use images of women freed by consumer durables, so women are often depicted as leaping in the air
released from domestic drudgery by the new washing machine.

My intention in stating these shifts and changes is not to argue
that there was a massive break between the 1950s and 1960s. There
was not, and indeed many of the changes that were beginning to

happen were still articulated within the framework of the family; further, many of the themes of the 1950s, such as love, understanding, control, doing good and being busy, strongly continued. A contradictory attitude in advice given to women on how to treat their husbands persisted. By contradictory I mean the fluctuation between seeing men as strong, domineering and unchangeable, and depicting them as rather weak and naughty boys of ten, exempt from much of the responsibility of what happens in relationships. The important question women had continually to ask themselves was whether they were an asset or a liability to their husbands. Evelyn Home now defines love, as opposed to her practice in the 1950s when she treats it as if it is a quality about which we all have innate knowledge. Love is the 'constant desire and intent to do and be good to the beloved'. Difficult phases come and go, she acknowledges, but 'they are almost always followed by a happy return of ardour and easy sympathy' (March 1962). However, an important change is now occurring, and that is around the issue of divorce. In the 1950s the general advice was, no matter how dreadful the marriage, stick it out. In the 1960s, while Evelyn Home does not openly encourage women to divorce their husbands, her general stance is that if the marriage has irretrievably broken down then divorce is the best solution. She treads a careful line, not advocating divorce and yet not dissuading women from that decision. She now begins to give general advice to women on how to go about the legal business of divorce.

Importantly, Evelyn Home begins to advise women to broaden their horizons. This is partly to make the marriage better, by stopping the woman being clingy and a burden on husband and family, and partly to better the woman's own life. A woman writes in saying that her husband has bettered himself, and that he is a wonderful man, but she is very anxious that he will have an affair. She wonders how he can be content with what she gives him. Evelyn Home replies that she could calm her fears 'By giving him more, more love and affection – freely without thought of return. Welcome him home with open arms, and not with questions, or a tight lipped expression. Make yourself independent. A part-time job would help, soon you'd be so busy living your own life you would not have time or desire to try and live every minute of your husband's' (June 1962). Women are now being actively encouraged to develop their own identities in their own right, and not just as wives and mothers. At the same time that Evelyn Home is recommending that women develop interests outside the home, mothers are writing in to complain that their daughters are not independent enough and daughters are writing in

136

to reproach their parents resentfully for not allowing them to be independent. Evelyn Home advises a young woman that what she needs is 'a strong dose of bravery and independence to break away from home and from your fiancé until you are absolutely sure of what you want to do with your future' (March 1961).

As stated earlier, there were more letters expressing concern and anxiety about sex. These were dealt with more openly, and the letters and answers printed out in full, and not just the tantilizing covert reply placed in the bottom right-hand corner. There were many queries about birth control, some expressions of doubt about whether or not parenthood was natural, and some anxiety expressed about whether or not individuals could necessarily cope with parenthood. Orgasm now appears in the public arena of the problem page. Evelyn Home's responses include 'Women need slow and careful initiation to more serious union and men need to learn to control themselves to help their wives', and 'Many women never experience the brief physical climax to lovemaking, but they love the unique closeness and tenderness of intimacy, the sense of being so dearly wanted and the family that has resulted from sexual union'. There is a tendency to blame women's lack of sexual responsiveness for their husbands having affairs, and they are told that they 'must realize how you have humiliated him by undervaluing him sexually'.

These shifts in the meaning of what it is to be a wife and mother become stronger in the 1970s, and more consolidated in the 1980s. *Woman* magazine as a whole package carries the messages 'be freer, more independent, juggle work with managing a family, be yourself'. The new messages and themes proclaim a new identity and roles for women as knowing consumers with power, knowledge and skill, as part-time working mothers, as cooks now able to produce more interesting and cosmopolitan food, as women who are more sexy and able to have a satisfying sexual time with their husbands, as individuals who know where they are going, what they feel and how to talk about it.

Anna Raeburn (the agony columnist from October 1974 till the late 1970s when Virginia Ironside took over) actively encourages the pouring out of emotions, so that the problem page becomes focused on understanding the self through the expression of emotions; words such as guilty, miserable, depressed, sad, angry and jealous were written on to the page with a vengeance. Anna Raeburn's emphasis was on women becoming independent, continually having honest dialogue with their spouses and family, and facing up to the responsibilities of their decisions and choices. Honesty becomes the new

137

moral virtue, and this, coupled with the emphasis on developing self-esteem and more confidence, gives the representation of women in *Woman* magazine a different flavour to that of the 1950s. Through its articles and visual imagery, the magazine advocates individuality, independence, freedom and talking things over with complete honesty.

The problem page is always reliant on the expression of emotionality and emotional difficulties for its existence. However, the recommended way of handling emotions does change over this period, from action and 'stamping on' being advocated as the correct way to deal with difficulties to expression becoming the mode of dealing with feelings. The advice encourages women to express and not repress, and women are told not to feel guilty but rather to deal with whatever it is they are feeling. The columnist begins to explain the role of emotions and defence systems and to argue that not to express emotion causes great strain. For example, a woman writes in to say that she is deeply depressed and is on anti-depressants. Her husband is fed up with her and locks up the phone in an attempt to get her to pull herself together. Ironside tells her that she doesn't need to pull herself together, but rather to let go and discover the reason for her depression. She remarks that depression is too deep-rooted for drugs. She suggests that the woman sees a psychiatrist in order to have therapy, and that she contacts MIND (February 1982).

The stress is on being honest, getting to know one's emotions and expressing them, and these imperative are interlinked. The demand is to be honest to oneself, to face up to the truth and to take responsibility for whatever happens and the choices one has made. Previously, Evelyn Home used to recommend that the reader forget and put the past behind her, but a shifting emphasis occurs and Anna Raeburn and Virginia Ironside recommend to the reader that they get to know their past in order to discover who they are. Simultaneously, women are encouraged to talk things over, speak about it. Speaking and talking things over is presented as the new cure-all, and, as Rosalind Coward remarks, 'Talking out your problems with your nearest and dearest is a primary solution offered by the advice columnists. And "Have you tried talking about it?" is one of the most common questions asked by the agony aunts' (Coward, 1984, p. 135).

Talking about it is represented as the royal route to self-discovery and also the path to a true relationship. Talking things over with one's partner is the commonest piece of advice to those in difficulty.

Be open, confide in each other, take the risk and tell him/her and all will be well, or at least if not better then at the very least you will discover more of who you really are. A clear example of this is the advice given by Irma Kurtz (the agony aunt on the monthly *Cosmopolitan*) to a man who writes in because his wife is leaving him and he does not know how to deal with this. It is worth quoting the reply in full. Kurtz advises him to:

> Talk to her. Talk to her for her sake and, above all, for your own. Talk to her so you will know, if the marriage must end, that you did everything you could to save it. Talk to her so your children know that their father is a man of feeling. Talk of her because you have loved her, maybe you do love her, and maybe she never knew. Talk to her because we cannot guess each other's feelings or take them for granted. Talk to her because she needs to hear but, even more, because you need to talk. If she seems not to be listening, talk to her anyway; and if she starts to talk, listen to her. Please, talk to her. (*Cosmopolitan*, February 1982)

This contemporary imperative to know and possess the self is clearly illustrated by a short story entitled 'Valentine', published on 14 February 1985. The tale opens with a woman looking at a card which apparently expresses and describes how she feels. She begins to reflect on her life and to reminisce. She remembers her marriage to Michael and how during her time with him she lived in a state of terror and gloom, in fear of what he could do and actually did to her. Michael is described as emotionally withholding; his 'power lay in distance; withdrawal'. When she displeased him, he did not make love, and she experienced him as paralysing and sapping her of her life. However, she has now divorced him, and while she is in a state of disbelief about how and why she tolerated her marriage, her relief that it is over is strong. To mark this change of events, and the fact that she is taking control of her life, of herself, Stella – the female protagonist – is changing her surname. When asked if she will be happy, she has no doubts – she is now positive, sure.

The narrative takes the reader through her relationship with her current and permanent love, John, and we discover that love and kindness had come as a revelation to her. Stella now knows through her new man that love is about talking, listening, exploring, and that relationships can be good and full of love. Further, that it is 'possible to embrace life' and to 'wake up longing for the day' and 'whispering a prayer of gratitude that life exists'.

We now reach the climax of the story. It is Valentine's Day, and Stella in a state of anxious excitement moves as though an 'unseen audience could appraise her'. She sets out on the table her post – her banker's card, cheque book – the stuff of life. In the middle of this she lays out the most important object – she relishes it, almost fetishizes it – and this is her passport. All of the necessities of contemporary living have now been changed to her maiden surname. She has reclaimed her self, found it and possessed it. She declares to John that she feels younger and lighter. She can be her own self. In what is represented as an almost inconsequential moment she hands John his Valentine's card; however, the reader is encouraged to revel in the central and most important moment, when Stella opens the card that she has purchased for herself, and the message inside reads – 'You're O.K.'.

Love in this 1980s tale is portrayed as a quality through which you can discover yourself. The relationship is about self-discovery and retaining the self, and not being drowned in another. Love is knowing who you are.

In all then, the main change of emphasis in representations of female identity is from women gaining security, respect and power from marriage and the family to women gaining security and understanding from the self and the family. The stress changes from doing your best for others and your family, from a way of being that emphasizes doing and especially doing good, to demands that women think about who and what they are, and assert that knowledge in order to face up to the responsibility of themselves and their choices. This is not to suggest that the importance of the family was eroded and undermined by *Woman* magazine, but that it represents the belief that women can gain separate identities simultaneously outside and within the family.

The notion of an independent individual is deeply embedded in our common-sense understanding of the social world that we exist in. The demands for independence are diverse, from Thatcherism's call that we stand on our own two feet to many feminist demands, and to much of the thinking and practice of the humanist psychology movement. The *Independent* newspaper's advertising makes much of the notion of individuality. Its message – 'It is . . . Are You?' – offers testimony to the almost fevered need to be independent, and its use of peas in the pod imagery plays on people's fears that they will be seen to be, or will actually be, the same as everyone else. The notion of the free individual abounds, and none of us are immune to its effects.

140

While maturity was the goal of the 1950s, it is now independence and individuality. From immaturity being the mark of the pathological person, dependency is now seen to be the sickness. As Barbara Ehrenreich argues in *The Hearts of Men* (1983), psychology, and I would add other subcultures and other theoretical frameworks, discarded maturity as the goal and embraced growth as the new ideal. Further, Ehrenreich argues that in the 1950s the code word for male discontent was conformity, which was and is the antithesis of Americanism. It was argued that conformity destroyed men's souls, in fact their very masculinity. Conformity was emasculation. Women were the villains in this scenario, for in their supposed wish for security they suppressed the male's desire for adventure. 'All women want is security. And she's perfectly willing to crush men's adventurous, freedom-loving spirit to get it', runs the heading of an article in *Playboy* in the late 1950s. But it is not just the likes of *Playboy* magazine which argue that female energy is likely to be destructive and oppressive. Betty Friedan in *The Feminine Mystique* wrote about the housewife that her 'misdirected energies were a toxin spreading outward through the family to the nation' (quoted in Ehrenreich, p. 101). The solution was, according to Friedan, that women should return to work otherwise 'their wasted energy will continue to be destructive to their husbands, to their children, and to themselves' (p. 102).

This argument is more than reminiscent of Evelyn Home who often advised women that men, because of their nature, needed more freedom and independence. Women, therefore, have to curb their innate need for domestic security in order that their husbands can fulfil themselves. The later representation of women as independent and autonomous, in their own right and yet within the family, was prefigured in the advice that women should develop a separate life from their men in order to let them develop their personal capacities. For example, in 1958 *Woman* published a short story entitled 'The Cool Green Trees'. In this story, a young couple meet, fall in love and marry. The male protagonist is represented as a creative artist deeply involved in his work but in a deep dilemma of love versus art. Love initially wins out. The woman is represented as someone who would do anything for her man. The story unfolds and it becomes obvious to the reader that the male protagonist is feeling constricted and unhappy. His wife, despite being pregnant, senses this and lets him go in order that he can become an artist. Two years later, when she has struggled through and is bringing up their child, she receives reviews of his art show in France. She rushes over to Paris, they are reunited, and are represented as now being able to be really together because he has discovered his inner potential.

From popular psychological texts to many political discourses, dependency is seen as the new evil, something which is toxic, poisonous, a tough weed, and the killer of people's spirit. It must be got rid of. This is most clearly articulated by the humanistic psychology movement, which argues that the purpose of growth is to allow people to discover their inherent free spirit and their innate individuality which society has conspired to squash. The belief is that it is only when individuals are able to look after and take care of themselves and know who they are that they will be able to enter a 'full-filled' relationship with another. However, even when one is within a relationship the demand is to put the self before the other, to allow oneself and others to grow and become liberated. This position is clearly expressed by the author of a popular psychology book: 'Dependency in physically healthy adults is pathological – it is sick, always a manifestation of a mental illness or defect' (Peck, 1985, p. 98). People who are dependent are parasitic, passive and, apparently, in a constant state of wishing to receive care. Their greatest sin is that they purchase security at 'the price of freedom', which means they are in relationships which serve 'to retard the growth of individual partners'. Worse, dependency 'seeks to receive rather than to give. It nourishes infantilism rather than growth. It works to trap and contrict rather than to liberate. Ultimately it destroys rather than builds relationships, and it destroys rather than builds people' (ibid.).

A fragile and perhaps paradoxical position is maintained in humanistic psychology. It is permissible to have dependency needs, and yet the individual cannot be dependent. People should gain knowledge of their dependency needs so that they can accept them, not so as to negotiate from them, but rather so that they can overcome them. Underpinning much of the thinking about dependency is the view that it is crucial to be independent and self-reliant, because if you rely on others they will inevitably let you down. Others can never come up to your expectations, your needs, your fantasies of them. This points towards a strong paradox within humanistic thinking. While people are theorized as being good, generous, and with having the ability to unfold into their unique and creative selves, they are also somehow bad, greedy and out for themselves. In this almost paranoid view of the world, people by necessity have to protect themselves from depending on others.

142

It does seem as if much of the reaction against dependency is based on disappointment. We can see this in terms of disappointment at the loss of that early and necessary symbiotic union and closeness with our mothers: profound disappointment that we all wanted more of our mothers than we could have, and the resulting frustration and rage about the inevitable loss incurred at that break from the symbiotic union so that we could enter the social and cultural world. This fundamental loss of that primary dependent relationship is, I suggest, what leads to this desperate reaction expressed in the language of autonomy and independence. This is an unconscious psychic defence that tries to ensure that the dependent relationship and the disappointment, pain and humiliation which it occasioned should never be repeated.

Christopher Lasch has provocatively argued that much of contemporary culture is predicted upon and actively encourages the narcissistic personality and narcissistic ways of being. Common psychoanalytic understanding of narcissism is that the individual is self-absorbed and self-adoring, and that these two interlinked traits arise from, and reinforce, a denial of the needs for others. The individual is unable to give and simultaneously to take from others. While within psychoanalytic theory the term narcissism has various usages, the prevalent understanding is that narcissism involves a positive libidinal feeling towards the self.

Freud initially theorized narcissism as a stage in sexual development, where the infant takes his own body as his love object. Narcissism within this formulation is a stage between auto-eroticism and the development of the capacity for object-love by the subject. However, in the essay 'On narcissism' (published in 1914) Freud developed the concept of narcissism which he now theorized as being interlinked with the development of the ego. The subject is now theorized as always in a process in which the ego is invested with his/her libido or the object is invested with his/her libidinal energy. The ego is now theorized as a reservoir of libidinal energy, held ready to be sent out or reabsorbed back into itself. Within this essay Freud put forward two main paths towards the choice of an object – the narcissistic path, whereby one loves according to the image of oneself, what one was, someone who was once part of oneself or how one would like to be. The other path – the anaclitic path – is one in which the subject loves the woman who once fed it, and the man who had protected it.

The current demands are that we get to know and idealize the self, so that we can overcome, either on our own, but if necessary with the

143

help of others, who we are. The contradiction in these demands is that we know who we are in order to overcome the self, but also in order to be able to satisfy and love oneself. These demands and conceptualizations of the self are prevalent aspects of narcissism. The self feels empty, alienated and isolated; what is required is not an other with whom one can have a full relationship, but one who can be a mirror reflecting back to the subject a sense of his/her importance, his/her self. The self fills his/her own body and ego up; it cannot take in the other, except as that which reflects.

In 'Valentine', Michael is portrayed as that which has to be given up, that Stella had to rid herself of, because his cruelty lay in sapping her of her life. She was not able to blossom, grow and develop; instead her demands for his approval required her to become what he wanted her to be. In this representation of a sado-masochistic relationship the female protagonist had to give herself up in order to be loved. However, the narrative constantly warns the reader of the dangers in this, and language is utilized to reinforce constantly that this state of affairs is unhealthy. There are a number of interpretations as to why that fictional relationship was pathological, but the representation was that the difficulty lay primarily in Stella losing herself: she did now know who she was. The narrative compels the reader to celebrate the moment when Stella finds herself, rediscovers and possesses her maiden surname. John, her lover, while crucial in that he has helped her to discover who she is, is really on the sidelines; he is unclear and hazy, except as a supportive mirror. He is very much the appendage to the narrative, her love for him utterly forgotten as she celebrates who she is.

This story supports Lasch's thesis that the emphasis and the mood of modern society is on living for the moment, that the values affirmed and encouraged are those that centre on the well-being and salvation of the self, for 'people today hunger not for personal salvation, let alone for the restoration of an earlier age, but for the feeling, the momentary illusion, of personal well-being, health and psychic security' (Lasch, 1978, p. 7). Lasch argues – problematically, for feminists and some social theorists – that this has occurred because of what he perceives as the breakdown of the family, and poor paternal and maternal authority.

Sennett sees the breakdown of the boundary between private and public as having been in progress since the eighteenth century. In *The Fall of Public Man* (1977) he persuasively argues that the public arena has been eroded since the eighteenth century, since when the emphasis on that which is interior and private has been increasing.

144

Sennett is critical of much of contemporary society, but in particular what he terms as the Tyranny of Intimacy. By this he means that we now feel and think that we are not being authentic, truthful and honest, and that we are not engaged in meaningful dialogue, unless we are exchanging inner feelings, or revealing some inner aspect of ourselves. In short, we are compelled to confess, and we are profoundly and inevitably engaged in this principal burden of knowing ourselves.

The drive to confess, to talk it over and to overcome is illustrated by the large increase of referrals on the problem page. During the 1950s Home occasionally recommends the correspondent to seek professional help; this was mainly in order to save the marriage and to put it on a better footing. Women were occasionally encouraged to see a priest or a psychiatrist. However, during the 1960s the increasing recommendation is that professional and expert help is sought. The marriage guidance counsellor, social worker, probation officer and psychiatrist replace the priest and the family as the founts of wisdom. Most letters receive a plea to get help in order really to explore the problem. In a study of problem pages in women's magazines Mary Louise Ho (1981) states that, in 1980, 97 out of 138 letters meet with the recommendation to seek professional help. The increase in referrals to professionals for help is interlinked with the belief that it is possible to talk things over and to overcome one's difficulties. Individuals are also urged to seek therapeutic help in order to better their own lives. 'A psychiatrist or group therapy would be better long-term solutions' is the constant advice given to those in psychic distress. Or: 'You need the help and advice of a real expert. Explain your fears to your doctor, and ask to see a specialist. And seeking a cure will be your first step towards real health.'

The increase in referrals is of no surprise for we believe that if we understand ourselves and discover our inner being, our sexuality, we will inevitably reach that which is distinctive, unique and individual about our being. We perform on ourselves a series of techniques to reach this internal truth. We are constantly performing on ourselves as we go about our daily social lives using, in Foucault's terms, a series of techniques and technologies. Foucault argued that these techniques 'permit individuals to affect, by their own means, a certain number of operations on their own bodies, their own souls, their own thoughts, their own conducts, and this in a manner so as to transform themselves, modify themselves and attain a certain state of perfection, happiness, purity, supernatural power' (Foucault, 1982, p. 10).

These technologies of the self, which we perform daily as we go about our personal and social lives, are not discourses and practices which conceal the true and unique individual self, but rather they constitute the centre of our being, subjectivity itself. We are all involved, and in an active relationship, with these technologies of the self in order that we can gain knowledge of the self and so achieve growth and development, make minimum demands, have few needs of others and, crucially, assert who we are. Perfection of the self, the goal of contemporary subjectivity, is, in part, equated with being independent and autonomous, knowing who we are and achieving our potential. To strive relentlessly for more is the current mode of being. The discourses that encourage independent, knowing subjectivity circulate across the political spectrum, in popular weekly magazines, and in the humanistic psychology movement. The technologies of the self and the discourse of interior subjectivity involve us in the search for independence and autonomy. The hymn is subjective experience, our preoccupation is the self, and the tyranny is that of intimate yet independent communication.

REFERENCES

Coward, R. (1984) *Female Desire*. Paladin.

Ehrenreich, B. (1983) *The Hearts of Men*. Pluto.

Foucault, M. with Sennett, R. (1982) 'Sexuality and solitude', in R. Dworkin, C. Miller and R. Sennett, eds *Humanities in Review*, volume 1. Cambridge: Cambridge University Press, 1982, pp. 3–21.

Friedan, B. (1963) *The Feminine Mystique*. Pelican 1983.

Freud, S. 'On narcissim: an introduction'. *S.E.* 14, pp. 67–102.

Heron, L. (1986) *Changes of Heart: Reflections on Women's Independence*. Pandora.

Ho, M.L. (1981) 'In the tradition of the wise woman', *Spare Rib*. February 1981: 31–4.

Lasch, C. (1978) *The Culture of Narcissism*. New York: Norton.

Peck, M.S. (1985) *The Road Less Traveled*. Rider.

Sennett, R. (1977) *The Fall of Public Man*. Cambridge: Cambridge University Press.

10 AMNESIA, ROMANCE AND THE MIND-DOCTOR FILM

Jed Sekoff

> *Probing the human mind can be a wee bit like opening Pandora's box . . .*
> *sometimes people have no wish for their unconscious lives to be revealed.*
> DR ANDERSON, PLAYED BY IAN HOLM IN *Return of the Soldier*

THE FILM THERAPIST has proved to be an enduring figure in British and American movie making. Since *Dr Dippy's Sanitarium* in 1906, the figure of psychoanalyst, psychiatrist or mental practitioner has surfaced in over 250 films. Whether the kindly and wise analyst typified by Ian Holm's character in *Return of the Soldier* or the psychopathic psychiatrist played by Michael Caine in *Dressed to Kill*, the figure of the mind-doctor, of the 'physician of the soul' has been a recurrent image across close to a century of movie making.

This essay is posed as a reflection upon this curious history. Why should we find such a persistent imagery regarding what after all is a practice encountered by only a minority of movie-goers? Why do film-makers return to a subject that has generated so many mediocre, often terribly bad movies, and only rarely films of sustaining humour, intelligence and interest?

On second thoughts, such questions may not be the most reliable opening to our subject. One problem is that questions about relevance and taste do not seem to have influenced the prevalence of other genres, the Western or the horror movie, for instance. Another difficulty is that exploring such questions starts us down the treacherous path of grappling with the complex problems of understanding 'cultural determination'.

Yet such complications are not easily skirted. As soon as we turn our curiosity to a cultural phenomenon, we are immediately caught in a morass of questions regarding the interrelation of culture, history, social forces and, for my purposes, of psyche, society and

147

cinema. As Dr Anderson/Ian Holm warns us, we might pause before opening ourselves up to such complexity.

I hope to avoid getting mired down by such questions by the expedient of stating at the outset some anchoring premises, questions and problems that will guide the essay. Even a beginning screen-writer knows the hazards of delaying the narrative just to set the scene. However, it soothes me a bit to note the general direction of my attention, if only as a way of acknowledging the paths inevitably missed.

I begin from the basic viewpoint that film must be understood as potentially embodying, disguising, challenging, containing, exploring, producing and so on the conditions of our cultural and personal lives, as well as the meanings we weave around them.

To help begin, some ideas of the critic Raymond Williams should prove helpful. Williams stressed that language and signification are 'indissoluble elements of the material social process itself, involved all the time both in production and reproduction' (1977, p. 99). That is, the meanings which constitute culture and consciousness must be understood as embedded in, not just reflective of, historical forces and processes. Williams charts the movement of cultural (and implicitly of personal) life through his description of what he terms 'structures of feeling'. This term designates a 'cultural hypothesis' which seeks to depict the elements of lived social experience, always in process, that make up a given historical period's substance, its 'feeling'.

Williams deliberately chose this subjective and ambiguous term to move beyond the formal constraints of concepts such as 'ideology' or 'world-view' in order to capture the interlocking nature of social and subjective experience.[1]

From a quite different perspective, another thinker who may prove helpful at the start of this interpretive effort is the philosopher Stanley Cavell. Cavell (1981) has written intriguing essays on film, starting from a simple, even deliberately naïve idea of film as 'conversation'. A film may be combed for meaning in various ways. Still, to take films as speaking to us, to understand the cinema as embodying conversations (discussions that for Cavell exist within a film and between films as well) is a useful starting point to build our reading.

The conversation that I wish to engage in around the mind-doctor films seeks a discussion of the following problematic. Namely, how does the genre of the mind-doctor film speak to the specific doubts, anxieties, questions and problems of various 'structures of feeling' in the modern era?

148

When we look at these films, I am interested to see if we can discern a history of a culture's feelings, thoughts, worries, experiments, answers, absences and so on – a history that somehow the figure of the mind-doctor is eminently suitable to portray. As we look more closely at this history, we shall find that mind-doctor films are 'conversing' about the threat of fragmentation posed to two forms of experience in the modern era, namely, our experiences of desire and of memory. However, this is getting way ahead of our discussion. It's time to roll our first movie.

NOTATION AND PUNCTUATION

'Hello, I'm Dr Fritz Lehman,'
'Oh well, that's all right. You can sit down, I don't mind.'
– Introduction of Fritz Feld (Dr Lehman) to Katharine
Hepburn (Susan Vale) in *Bringing up Baby* (1938)

In many, perhaps most, of the mind-doctor films the figure of the mental healer or the theme of psychology plays only a peripheral role. Yet we may think of the various film characterizations of analysts, psychologists and psychiatrists not as random appearances but as notations or punctuations which play a crucial role in establishing specific kinds of film 'conversation'.

Two examples of this idea of notation come to mind from the films *Bringing up Baby* and *My Favorite Wife*. These intriguing movies of the thirties may be related to a genre of film described by Stanley Cavell as 'comedies of remarriage', a series of seven or so films that explore human relationships within a plot structure wherein a man and woman fall in love – again.

Cavell views these comedies (which include *The Philadelphia Story*, *It Happened One Night* and *The Awful Truth*) as revolving around a series of questions involving love and commitment. For Cavell, these films provide an illuminating artistic inquiry into the American 'pursuit of happiness'.

Be that as it may, it is intriguing to find mind-doctors as characters in several of these films. In both Howard Hawks's *Bringing up Baby* (1938) and Garson Kanin's *My Favorite Wife* (1940) psychiatrists make brief appearances. In Hawks's film, Fritz Feld appears as Dr Lehman with a monocle as well as a central casting foreign accent. *My Favorite Wife*'s Dr Kolmar is missing only a pipe or cigar to complete his regalia of goatee, glasses and Germanic pronunciation.

149

Such comic turns are all too familiar. Perhaps the French or Swedes have their equivalents, but Anglo-American films are noticeably peopled by caricatured foreigners, whom one assumes provide comic reassurance that strangeness lies in others, not at home or within. The psychiatrist as 'funny foreigner' may be read as a notation that marks the boundaries of other-ness, specifically, that otherness lies out there – in someone as well as some-place else.

With the mind-doctor, foreignness is only part of the figuration of other-ness. These poor creatures fill the screen with odd grimaces, tics and stutters, and all manner of bizarre walks, gestures and behaviours. Feld (who later found a peculiar niche as an actor playing a waiter who made a popping noise when his hand was briskly cupped over his mouth) signals his strangeness with just such a grimace in his first scene in *Bringing up Baby*.

Let's turn to that opening scene. We meet Dr Lehman in the middle of a rather frantic encounter between Cary Grant and Katharine Hepburn. Grant plays a rather staid palaeontologist, one day away from his wedding to an even more staid assistant. Hepburn is the flaky young heiress, Susan Vale, who wreaks havoc on the poor doctor. By the second scene of their meeting, Hepburn has managed to damage and steal Grant's car, trip him and crush his top hat, have him accused of purse snatching and apparently upset his chances of receiving a million-dollar donation. This brief resumé of disaster hardly does justice to the manic overturning of language and social rules that accompanies the meeting of our destined lovers.

In the midst of their initial meeting, we find Feld/Dr Lehman at a dinner club where we join him as witness to the apparent craziness of our protagonists. Feld marks his witness through his authority as a psychiatrist (Feld: 'I lecture on nervous disorder, I am a psychiatrist'; Hepburn: 'Oh, crazy people'), his foreignness and grimace, and the following interpretation: 'The love impulse in man frequently reveals itself in conflict.'

As the disorder of the film escalates, Grant loses himself in the wilds of Connecticut seeking a lost fossil ('My intercostal clavicle. My bone. It's rare, it's precious') and a lost leopard, named Baby (calmed by the song, 'I can't give you anything but love, baby'). Dr Lehman pops up several times, his role escalating from the comic to the authoritarian. When Susan/Hepburn is found singing outside Lehman's house to the leopard on the roof, Lehman at first cajoles and then binds and gags her. By the film's denouement, the psychiatrist is participating in the interrogation of Grant and Hepburn at the local jail. Indeed, the film's mind-doctor virtually merges with another character who pops up along the way, the town sheriff (portrayed as a country bumpkin).

Authority, social convention, indeed rationality itself appear to be buried – along with Grant's brontosaurus bone – by the pleasure, spontaneity and urgency of 'true love'. Love is presented as craziness, yet we the viewer are let in on the secret, namely that passion demands such craziness. The mind-doctor surfaces as witness to a 'madness' that challenges the regime of order and routine.

The mind-doctor is ideally suited to punctuate a conversation about the relative merits of order versus disorder, of rationality versus the forces that press against logic or restriction. Who else is the familiar of irrationality and of madness? The artist or writer, perhaps even the madman – yet, who else claims the right to mark the boundaries of mental order, a claim reinforced with legal and social backing? This dual role, as familiar of the unknown and at the same time as arbiter of the psyche's order, locates the figure of the mind-doctor on a fulcrum between order and disorder. Here, we find one source of the mind-doctor's symbolic power.

The artist is a figure who also is given symbolic value as familiar of the unknown. Yet this usually takes the form of a romantic portrait of their suffering for such knowledge without any authority attached. Physicians also deal with the unknown, with the mystery of the body. They figure in movies as 'familiar of death' generating 'conversations' about life and death, youth and age, accident and fate, indeed all manner of morbid preoccupations with the body's eventual demise, often signified as the snatching of life from death's door.[2]

In *My Favorite Wife*, Cary Grant stars opposite Irene Dunne in another improbable romance. The story involves a wife stranded on a desert island for seven years who returns to civilization (and its discontents) on the wedding day of her husband, the latter having presumed her dead, lost at sea. A series of complications follows, including Grant's difficulty in informing his new bride of his wife's return and the revelation that Irene Dunne's seven-year island sojourn was spent with the handsome Randolph Scott.

The hapless bride Bianca/Gail Patrick consults a psychiatrist about her husband's reluctance to consummate their marriage. Dr Kolmar comes upon Nick/Cary Grant as he nervously picks up some clothes for his first wife. Preoccupied with the question of Dunne's fidelity, Grant sorts through her wardrobe. He holds up various outfits as if

151

imagining them on himself, all the while under the doctor's watchful eye.

Here, the mind-doctor's gaze is brought to another form of love's disorder, the upheaval of sexuality. *My Favorite Wife* is filled with anxiety about fidelity, about the strength of sexual desire versus the loyalty of love. Even sexual identity may playfully topple under the dizzying demands of passion. Again, the protagonists' craziness is but a foil that stabs at the madness of placing order above love. Again, the psychiatrist (like the hotel manager watching Grant run between the rooms of his two wives) is figured as a hapless authority, a representative of sense and order whose expertise is shown as sense-less.

In our two examples, we come upon a genre of film that appears to argue for the curative power of disordered passion. Or is it the saving grace of true love? Or perhaps, the threat that women's sexuality poses to masculine power, a threat best tamed by the remarriage of man with woman? Many such readings might be taken and many questions remain unanswered as our Pandora's box rapidly expands.

For the moment, I wish to note only that the position of mind-doctor as symbolic notation does not depend upon the particular argument taken or question posed. In another film, the mind-doctor's authority might have been valued rather than ridiculed (let's say in *The Three Faces of Eve*). Or in yet another movie, the subversion of stifling convention is possible only with the help of the mind-doctor, rather than against him (as in *Now Voyager* and *Ordinary People*).

Viewed as comic or serious, good or evil, esteemed or dismissed, the symbolic power of the mind-doctor lies not in a specific valuation, but rather in its usefulness as a currency to 'exchange' ideas on the edge of the unknown, on the border of madness, and on a terrain of passion and the mind's strange wanderings.

There is another aspect of punctuation easily missed, precisely because this form of notation directs attention away from rather than towards a theme. Punctuation may also serve as distraction, as disguise, as sleight of hand. We are directed towards one location, thus effacing another. The mind-doctor's arrival on the scene invariably heralds the appearance of the personal, of the intimate, of the psychological. Public life and social discourse recede from our view. What might otherwise be seen as social or political terrain is marked as private territory.

152

Later, I will expand upon the ways the construction of films acts as 'modes of containment' – a term I will use to describe avenues for the containment of various conflicts and conditions. The displacement of social contradictions on to a theatre of emotional conflict is one expression of such 'containment'.

To take up our initial film sampling, these two depression era films are curiously devoid of reference to the conditions of the day. In *Bringing up Baby*, Hepburn/Susan Vale treats all objects of the external world – including a million dollars – as trifles, mere playthings devoid of substance or interest. The terrain of *My Favorite Wife* is a land of flights to Yosemite, chartered planes, year-long cruises, private clubs, second homes and resplendent pools. The protagonists of both our films inhabit worlds in which the problems of sustaining oneself in a time of unemployment, uncertainty and unrest simply do not exist.

Yet, are things so simple? Manifestly, we find a world pieced together with a kind of lightness of being – at least of material being. On gossamer wings our Grants, Hepburns and Dunnes float above the material world. Their images are troubled only by weight of personal conflict, no other heaviness binds them. Indeed, their images live on beyond the constraints of even physical being. The presence of the mind-doctor is one punctuation among many which emphasize that the interior life of our 'movie stars' floats above the world's external constraints.

On the one hand, the social world beyond the frame of the screen is darkened. We may read the effacement of social life in the elevation of interior drama, an elevation partially signalled by the mind-doctor. Yet paradoxically, this very effacement seems to speak to the world beyond the screen. The reversal of the physical world's longing, deprivation, material struggle, as well as the overturning of external time, of death, of materiality, highlights – as does all repression – precisely that which such punctuation negates.

The punctuation that draws attention away from the social sphere may be understood *both* as a sleight of hand that disguises the world and as a poignant attempt to challenge and overturn the world's impingements. And so a simple reading of 'containment' is not possible. We note the turning away from social contradictions. Yet, perhaps the power of these films is precisely the ability to give notice to the life of the interior (at least a certain version of this life) as counterpoint to external oppression. Such contradictions will come to our attention again.

Before moving on, there is one other theme taken up in our 'remarriage' films that will prove central to the mind-doctor movie proper. Solely as punctuation mark, the figure of the mind-doctor does not appear capable of carrying the weight of this thematic and so it is symbolized by other characters, other action. The theme is time, more accurately, our ability to bring meaning to the passage of time. This is memory, the challenge of marking time with our remembrance.

Susan Vale/Katharine Hepburn has one day to intervene before Cary Grant/Dr David Huxley is married. Irene Dunne/Ellen returns with only hours to prevent the consummation of her husband's wedding. Time is compressed, but time is also elastic. Hepburn and Grant lose track of time as they wander in search of leopards and 400-million-year-old bones. Dunne spent seven years on a desert island and time bounces to and fro upon her return – minutes to disrupt a honeymoon, hazy weeks to re-establish a marriage, and the calendar turned topsy-turvy when Grant dons a Santa Claus costume at the wrong time of year finally to win back Dunne's heart.

As the boundaries of time are questioned, so too are questions raised about the nature of history and remembrance. How strong are the ties of remembrance? What hold does the past have on the present? Does our future lie in opposition to or in alignment with our past? Such conversations may be discerned in the representation of memory throughout these films. There are simple notations, like the marvellous gesture of Cary Grant's double-take in *My Favorite Wife* as elevator doors close over his first glimpse at Irene Dunne. And there are complex problematics: the two pasts that must be faced, the two wives who must be jettisoned, and the hold of memory on a couple who have never forgotten their love or on children who can no longer remember their mother.

Irene Dunne, disguised as their mother's friend, talks to her children about their remembrance. She asks them about her possible return. What if she weren't really dead, what if she were only sleeping? As if to say, what if the past wasn't what it seemed, what if we could remake it? Her son replies, 'No, our mother wouldn't play a dirty trick like that on us.'

As we turn to the mind-doctor films proper I hope to show that such symbolizations involving memory and history (personal and social) are central to the genre. Indeed, that which propels the mind-doctor to the centre of her/his own genre is precisely the need for 'conversation' about these vital problematics.

SPELLBOUND: AMNESIA, LOVE AND THE ROMANTIC CURE

'I'm here as your doctor. It has nothing to do with love . . . nothing at all . . . nothing at all . . .'
– Words spoken by Ingrid Bergman/Dr Constance Peterson as she kisses an amnesia-stricken Gregory Peck in *Spellbound*.

The peace of Green Briar Manor, psychoanalytic sanitorium, is unsettled with the arrival of a new director – Dr Anthony Edwardes, renowned author of *The Labyrinth of the Guilt Complex*. Gregory Peck plays Dr Edwardes and his first meeting with his new staff draws him instantly to Dr Constance Peterson, the beautiful, brilliant and emotionally repressed psychoanalyst portrayed by Ingrid Bergman.

A love affair blooms, but trouble is on the horizon. For Dr Edwardes begins to display some peculiar behaviour. Lines impressed in a table cloth set him off in anger. He seems hesitant in discussing his work. The pattern in a robe leaves him dizzy. Finally, he collapses in the clinic's operating room.

Headache, dizziness, bursts of temper, these symptoms are indicators to well-versed film diagnosticians of a particular movie disorder, namely, the melodramatic distress known as 'amnesia'. The amnesiac of Anglo-American film may often be identified by this triad of symptoms, in addition to a certain glaze in the eyes, an uncertainty of speech or a tendency to sudden collapse.

Peck is soon revealed as an impostor, an 'amnesiac' who has taken the murdered Dr Edwardes's persona and place. With only the initials J.B. engraved on a lighter as clue to his real identity, Bergman takes psychoanalytic charge of the case (a treatment no doubt complicated by her analysand's flight from pursuing detectives and police).

We will return to the case/chase in a moment; however, we first need to be clear about our patient. As Harold Searles notes in his classic article, 'The patient as therapist to his analyst', the question of who needs cure is not always clear in an analytic treatment. So too in the mind-doctor films, for the analyst is often pictured at the centre of the need for cure, as joint seeker of transformation.

In *Spellbound*, we are signalled the plights of our protagonists by the only two patients we meet at Green Briar. Suffering from a 'guilt complex', Mr Garmes (played by Norman Lloyd – known to television viewers as Dr Aushlander of *St Elsewhere*) is convinced he has killed his father. Bergman offers him the following interpretation:

People often feel guilty over something they never did. It usually goes back to their childhood. The child often wishes something terrible would happen to someone, and if something does happen to that person, the child believes he has caused it. And he grows up with a *guilt complex* over a sin that was only a child's bad dream.

This is actually not a bad interpretation. Indeed, it reflects a level of complexity regarding the psychic determination of symptoms that dissipates as the film turns to external, traumatic explanations.

Mr Garmes's problem mirrors Gregory Peck's dilemma. Peck/J.B. comes to believe that he has killed Dr Edwardes and we are left in tension as to the 'facts' of the mystery. Could Gregory Peck be the murderer? Or, putting aside our familiarity with the usual fate of movie stars in pictures, does an amnesiac, a person lost to memory/history, represent a threat? Garmes again poses the problem when he runs amok and slashes his throat.

Our other Green Briar patient is Miss Carmichael. Brief appearances at the beginning of the film make little sense until one understands her role as punctuation for Ingrid Bergman's dilemma and for Dr Peterson's patienthood. For Miss Carmichael is the 'lady in red' – a sultry, sexy nymphet, whose sexuality oozes with threat. She scratches a male analyst and throws something at poor Ingrid, whom she calls 'Miss Frozen Puss'.

The contrast is clearly, indeed brazenly made, as we look across the desk at Dr Peterson with her hair in bun, glasses and a visage that clearly carries no thoughts of romance or sex. Cajoled into an afternoon walk with the new director, Bergman informs him of her belief that:

> the greatest harm done to the human race has been done by poets
> . . . They keep filling people with illusions about love, writing
> about it as if it were a symphony orchestra, the flight of angels . . .
> people fall in love – as they put it – because they respond to certain
> haircuts or vocal tones or mannerisms that remind them of their
> parents . . .

She believes love is stuff for silly schoolgirls; a scientific attitude brooks no such nonsense.

Here we have Dr Peterson's disorder: she suffers from a love-sickness. The film describes her illness in several ways. She holds an unhealthy attachment to science – that is to say, unhealthy for a woman. Indeed, the inhibition of 'femininity' and the false adoption of 'masculine attributes' is an important diagnostic strand in many mind-doctor films (though not without contradictions that I will return to shortly).

Bergman/Peterson is shown as emotionally repressed, preferring intellectual work and a solitary life to the vagaries of emotions. This emotional suppression also implies a sexual frigidity. It does not take a Freudian perspective to read the double meaning in the label of 'Miss Frozen Puss' or the symbolism of four doors opening down a long hallway when Peck first kisses Bergman. Peck's diagnosis of Bergman's troubles is more succinct, 'Professor, you are suffering from moko on the goko'.

So, with our two pairs of patients we meet our two problematics once more, namely Desire and Memory – this time intertwined through the figuration of amnesia. Bergman suffers a disorder of desire which involves an amnesia. She 'forgets' the rules of the analytic process. She no longer remembers her previous path of existence. Peck suffers a disorder of memory which involves a peculiar amnesia of desire – he has not forgotten how to love, quite the contrary, instead he has 'forgotten' past associations which might encumber his desire.

'Suffering' and 'disorder' have now taken on additional meanings. For if our protagonists suffer from disorder, they are also in need of this suffering – it offers release and relief. The psychoanalytic reading of symptoms as compromise formations reminds us to account not only for the pain of symptoms, but also for the defensive function of symptomatic construction (what greater imagined pain is being avoided), as well as the gratification offered by the symptom in compromised form.

Peck and Bergman are pained by their problems. We may join the speculations as to the necessity of their symptom construction – Bergman's diagnosis of Peck's traumatic guilt or Peck's interesting assertion of Bergman's moko on the goko (translated in the film's plot as the latter's fear of emotionality or femininity). We must also appreciate the gratification offered in their symptoms. In their amnesias each is released from the ties that bind. Each is untethered from past responsibilities, roles, paths and identities. A statement of Peck's to Bergman sums up this release. To a worried look he responds, 'No darling, I can't remember a wife'.

Perhaps this offer of release is the pleasure principle which guides our watching of this film. The amnesiac plot offers a site in which we may join in the gratifications of our protagonists, while sharing their suffering with them. In a libidinal language, we might be seen as enjoying the play of tension around suffering and release, conflict and resolution – a tension whose burden is bearable in successful films. What Freud termed the 'adhesiveness of the libido' is thrown into question. A tendency for desire to 'stick' to prior satisfactions is overcome, the pleasure principle unleashed to find new objects of desire.

We have other psychoanalytic languages besides a libidinal dialect to interpret the disorders traced in *Spellbound*. Whatever interpretive lens we choose, symptoms may be understood not only as the by-product of energic vicissitudes, but *read* as texts, that is to say as signifying constructions. The principal word in our film text is 'amnesia', which is from the Greek, *amnestie*, translated as 'oblivion'.

The fall into oblivion – or more precisely the struggle with such a fall – crystallized in the symptom of amnesia is the generative foundation for the film conversation of *Spellbound*. As it happens, *Spellbound* marks only an early example of such conversations. For the 'amnesia film' represents an intriguing subset of mind-doctor films. In addition to *Spellbound*, we have the prominent examples of *Random Harvest* and *Return of the Soldier*.[3]

At the simplest level, the amnesiac plot no doubt persists because of its implicit dramatic qualities. From the start we have tension, mystery, conflict, with the potential for release and resolution. Yet, a more persistent reading may be rewarded with a more interesting conversation about these amnesiac film structures than a simple call to their quality as vehicles for melodramatic entertainment. Therefore, let's return to our movie with popcorn in hand.

The plot of *Spellbound* unfolds roughly as follows: revealed as an amnesiac, Peck takes flight, pursued as a suspected murderer. Against all advice, Bergman follows after him as they pursue the solution to his amnesia. A visit to Bergman's old training analyst provides valuable help. Dr Alex Bruloff is our funny foreigner psychiatrist, but as played by Michael Chekhov (nephew of Anton) he exudes wisdom, warmth and charm. He also provides some memorable lines.

For example, when told that Peck and Bergman are a honeymoon couple, Bruloff advises them to get to bed, 'and when you wake up in the morning we will have breakfast and analyse your dreams'. The wily analyst is not fooled by the marriage disguise, and offers both help and warning. When Bergman protests that he knows science but she knows Peck's heart: 'the heart can see deeper . . . I couldn't feel this pain for someone who is evil', Bruloff responds, 'This is Baby Talk'. To Peck, who resists dream analysis because he doesn't believe in dreams, Bruloff retorts, 'He doesn't believe in dreams. Freud is hooey. You are a fine one to talk, you got amnesia, you got guilt complex, you don't know if you are coming or going. But Freud is hooey, *this* you know.'

Bruloff also speaks decidedly unendearing lines about the faults of women: 'Women make the best analysts, until they fall in love, then they make the best patients.'

Yet, the portrayal of Dr Peterson runs counter to this claim, for in a sense she does make the best analyst. She will solve the mystery after all. In addition, she makes the best analyst because of her detective skills and because she is able to bridge the gap between intellect and emotion. The detective with a heart – a favourite genre of American cinema – is one theme making itself felt in *Spellbound*.[4] Perhaps more important, the film offers a portrayal of woman as redeemer. It is Dr Peterson's access to her 'femininity' that acts as a fulcrum across which transformation may occur. And so we have a contradictory portrayal: a strong, brave, effective woman – yet a woman whose power is allowed to blossom only within the boundaries of a particular version of the feminine, and a particular version of love for a man.

With her mentor's help, Peterson begins to decipher the famous dream sequence of *Spellbound*. Salvador Dali designed the sequence, originally lasting some twenty minutes of which about two minutes survive in the film. Alfred Hitchcock and script-writer Ben Hecht dosed the denouement to their 'amnesia film' in two portions. Peck regains his identity in a dramatic scene at the edge of a mountain cliff. With Bergman at his side, he skis to the precipice, the final trigger that recovers a memory of a repressed childhood trauma. At play one day as a boy, he slid off the edge of a porch banister, accidentally pushing his brother on to a spiked fence. According to Bergman/Dr Peterson's interpretation, the guilt from his brother's death underlay the present amnesia. Peck had witnessed Dr Edwardes's death on a ski slope and then linked the two events together, the amnesia a psychic cover for repressed guilt.

Alas, the hard-won interpretation proved incomplete, for a bullet was found in Dr Edwardes's body. Peck is sent to prison for the crime. However, the dream proves to be the royal road – at least the road to the murder mystery. The dream elements point to Dr Murchison/Leo Carroll, the director of Green Briar Manor whom Dr Edwardes was slated to replace. John Ballantine is restored to himself, while Dr Constance Peterson has found the fire of love burning beneath her psychoanalytic mask.

Hitchcock later termed *Spellbound* 'just another manhunt story wrapped up in pseudo-psychoanalysis' (Truffaut, 1967, p. 118). The characterization of the film's analytic content appears fair, but the film is far from 'just a manhunt'. Rather, *Spellbound* sets in motion a 'quest', a heroic journey of rescue and restoration. Powered by the force of love, aided and abetted by Freud's 'science', our protagonists are sent forth as travellers along a road darkened by a number of threats, as they search for truth, love and transformation.

Thus in the structure of *Spellbound*, we note a journey, or more explicitly a hunt, a quest. Our protagonists are hunters in search of memory and desire, of restoration through love and remembrance. Our protagonists are the hunted. They encounter opposed forces of misunderstanding, deceit and hate along their winding path. Out of this journey, with its tests and struggle, comes a transformation, a restoration of the world's order, a repair of the discord, and a resolution of our protagonists' problems of passion and identity.

The critic Northrop Frye has described similar narrative structures in his writing on the 'romance'. For Frye (1957, p. 193), romance displays the 'search of the libido or desiring self for a fulfilment that will deliver the subject from the anxieties of reality'. Yet romance is not simply wish, but rather the creation of a stage upon which an ethical struggle may ensue, a struggle between the forces of good and evil, and between the ascendancy of the ordinary or the extraordinary in the world.

In looking at *Spellbound* as a 'romantic quest', we are viewing its structure as a narrative of desire, as a signification of the wish that life may be transformed. This desired transformation is powered by the release of the extraordinary into the world, but finds its resolution in the triumph of love over hate, of passion over the mundane. In other words, hopes for a cure to what Nietzsche termed 'the disease called man' are based on the faith that love can conquer all.

Let's skip to the last scene of *Random Harvest* (1942), directed by Mervyn Leroy. In the final sequence, Ronald Coleman is led by Greer Garson down a garden path that leads to a small cottage. The gate, the path, the trellis and door, all seem oddly familiar. Yes, for they had walked here before, years past. This was the hideaway where Garson/Paula Ridgeway and Coleman/Major Smith had spent an idyllic interlude as she nursed him back from the 'shell shock' he suffered at the front in the Great War. This too was their home when they married and had a son.

Only Ronald Coleman has no such recognition. Up until these moments on the path he remembers nothing of those years together.

160

For life's 'random harvest' had served Coleman a peculiar fate. He had lost his identity twice. Firstly, British officer Coleman was found in a foxhole bereft of memory or identifying papers. 'Major Smith' was consigned to the 'Melbridge County Asylum' until Greer Garson's radiant Paula Ridgeway offered Coleman/'Smithee' the renewal that only love not medicine could bring. However, tragedy (or rather melodrama) intervened a second time. A blow to the head retrieved Coleman's memory of his previous life, yet stripped him of any recollection of his life with Garson, of their marriage or of their newborn son.

Tearful audiences have suffered with Garson the long journey that brings her for the second time to that cottage threshold, a journey involving a lost husband, a dead son and, in another twist of fate, years of quiet service as secretary to the lonely Coleman, returned to his life as the wealthy J. Railsberg. We fear disappointment as once again our fated couple stand on the garden path. But we receive the sign that love does win out after all. The light of recognition shines on Coleman's face. The dark veil of amnesia lifts at last, as a familiar key in the door and a kiss on the threshold finally unlock memory's secrets.

In *Random Harvest*, we come across a variation of the figuration of the mind-doctor in the amnesia film. Actual psychiatrists remain at the borders of the movie. It is the figure of Greer Garson who is the pivot of the romance and of the cure. Yet, it is intriguing that Garson is very much portrayed as a therapist, not simply as a lover. When she first meets Coleman, he is barely functional – memory lost, speech impaired, wandering aimlessly through the streets. Our substitute doctor takes charge, partially with a maternal air, but centrally with a therapeutic ethos. This is much as in Hitchcock's *Marnie* where it is the husband, Sean Connery, who substitutes as analyst – he even reads *The Sexual Instinct* on their honeymoon cruise – for the traumatically repressed Tippi Hedren.

Visually, Garson's role as therapist is marvellously played out in a scene in her dressing room, not long after their initial meeting. Garson's Paula, a plucky music hall performer, sits the Major down, then finds her own chair which she straddles in a gesture both confident and sensuous. She then conducts what appears to be nothing other than a therapeutic session. Garson: 'Well, now. Talk with me, tell me all about yourself'. Coleman: 'I'm all right . . . really . . . it's just my speech . . . it's just my nerves'.

The figure of the mind-doctor is not absent from the film, rather the figuration is established by an interesting split. Greer Garson *becomes* the mind-doctor nurturing Coleman back to health. Coleman's psychiatrists are figured as impediments to the cure and so the film cedes their healing function to the true carrier of transformation.

We now have sketches of two films whose elements may be used to describe a particular genre of film, what I will term the *romantic cure* scenario of the mind-doctor film. The amnesia film sets forth the essential structure of the genre of the romantic cure. The structure is born with an initial disruption signified by amnesia, carried by a journey of discovery, and terminated with a cure of remembrance and love.

As we look back at *Spellbound* and *Random Harvest*, I believe we can discern a cinematic narrative that establishes a conversation around a variety of questions about passion and identity, desire and memory. Can passion transform the world, change our being? How does love relate to feeling alive? What disruptions follow in love's wake? What dangers does desire unleash? What makes up our sense of who we are? Are our pasts surmountable? What burden, what price do our histories impose upon us? Paraphrasing Samuel Beckett (1957, p. 22), is memory a 'clinical laboratory stocked with poison (or) remedy, stimulant (or) sedative', or, as Beckett mused, all of these? How do we locate ourselves in the present or point ourselves toward the future in relation to what has come before?

Yet while many questions are possible, there must be limits to the terrain sketched out by a particular film or genre of film. Indeed, upon reflection perhaps it is precisely the mapping of limits, the ordering of questions, and the marking of boundaries to our conversation that these films accomplish. If questions are posed, do not answers follow?

The romantic journeys we witness in our two specimen films may be read as nothing less than a moulding of answers to the myriad of disturbing questions they raise. 'Answers' are moulded as the romantic quest leads us along on its path toward cure. Certain paths are offered, others refused or absent.

The path most clearly illuminated highlights the transformative power of particular versions of desire. 'True love', the heart over the mind, marriage that places the couple beyond the reach of a misunderstanding world (the heart in a heartless world), the healing power of 'feminine' care, all are offered as answers to the problems of our protagonists.

The romantic cure is also read through a particular version of memory, a version – as we shall trace in more detail shortly – that reduces history to traumatic events. We are offered a past that can be

162

retrieved, rather than one that must be struggled with and continually re-established.

Such offering of answers represents a narrowing of imagination, a reduction of possible visions. In a previous work I have termed similar effects in psychological life *modes of containment* – the term attempts to describe unconscious strategies that deflect, stall, channel, efface and/or contain contradictions deemed unbearable (see my discussion of Jameson's notion of 'strategies of containment', Seckoff, 1982).

In cultural life, such modes of containment work to 'repress' inherent contradictions, whether the latter are social or personal. Genres such as the romantic cure scenario may be viewed as offering conventions that channel various problems and questions along more or less fixed lines. Whatever surprises a particular filmic quest holds, we come to depend on certain predictable encounters, fixed guideposts and stereotypical solutions.

The romantic cure scenario is in essence only a variation of a broader form of containment offered by mainstream Anglo-American film (what is often generically dubbed the Hollywood movie). Roland Barthes (1974; 1975) writes of a classic narrative structure that tells a story organized around enigma and resolution. A disruption of a given order takes place and the task of the narrative is to resolve that disruption and set up a new equilibrium. Numerous film theorists have written about such a narrative structure.[5]

For example, Colin McCabe (1974) offered the concept of a 'classic realist text' which cannot deal with the real as contradictory. Whatever apparent contradictions appear in a 'realist' film, a 'dominant discourse' is coded as taking precedence. Stephen Neale (1980, p. 26), however, described the delicate balancing act required to sustain the equilibrium of the classic realist text as the playing out of a tension between 'process (with its threat of incoherence, of loss of mastery) and position (with its threat of stasis, fixity, or of compulsive repetition (which is the same thing in another form)'. Stasis or stability would soon lead to impatience or boredom. What is needed to sustain an audience's interest is an oscillation between 'delicious instants of risk and repeated temporary returns to equilibrium' (Johnson, 1976). I have described a similar process in the psychotherapeutic clinical situation (1982). All the above are quite reminiscent of Freud's theory of the joke (1905).

Stephen Heath (1977), among others, has drawn on Lacanian psychoanalysis for a theory of 'suture', an idea which parallels my notion of 'modes of containment'. Bypassing an interrogation of the Lacanian *'écriture'*, we might quickly situate the notion of 'suture' by reference to Lacan's focus on 'alienation'. Lacan describes a subjectivity born in alienation and thus destined to a perpetual striving of the 'I' ('ego') to fill in the gaps between desire and fulfilment. The 'suture' in one sense is the striving of the 'I' to close the gaps faced by desire, a striving forever frustrated, yet forever attempted.

The idea of 'suture' has been used to explore the formal aspects of what Christian Metz (1982) termed the 'cinematic apparatus'. For example, at a very basic level the film spectator must 'suture' the discontinuities of the formal properties of the film – the multiple frames and images that are threaded through our 'perceptual apparatus' into continuous motion. At another level, the realist style of camera placement, shot structure and continuity editing presses the spectators' identification with the film's characters in such a way as to allow a bridging of gaps of time, distance and the gulf between image and actuality.

'Suture' may also be used to describe the moulding of cinematic narrative in ways that work to contain conflicts and contradictions. Several writers with a feminist perspective – notably Laura Mulvey (1975), Griselda Pollock (1977), Christian Viviani (1980) – have turned particular attention to the role of women in classic realist texts as the site of 'suture'. We have touched on this 'containing' and 'suturing' process in *Spellbound* and *Random Harvest*.

In both these films, gender divides the protagonists. While both male and female roles suffer disruptions, the healing power of love is carried through the presence of the women. Bergman and Garson 'suture' the gaps into which Peck and Coleman have fallen. In both films, the woman's body is used as gesture, as object. A desire for this object binds viewer and male protagonist in the journey towards restoration and resolution.

While both films display a 'fetishized' appropriation of their women stars, as well as generating a 'suturing' of desire within the ties of marriage, there are countervailing currents to this mode of containment. As noted earlier, both women are clearly shown as powerful and effective. Each displays the virtues of intelligence, courage, conviction and commitment. Stanley Cavell (1988) in his discussion of 'remarriage comedies' notes the emergence of a cohort of women (actresses and women's roles) whom these films signify as important, vital and carrying the capacity to transform the world.[6]

164

Perhaps the romantic cure genre reflects a parallel cohort, a similar 'structure of feelings that coalesced in the 1930s with the disruption of former modes of social cohesion. With this disruption there also arose a hope for new direction staked on the sensibility and sensitivity of a 'new woman', of an imagined, yet still 'unknown' woman that these films struggle to chart. (Cavell [1988] has recently written about a series of films he calls 'the melodrama of the unknown woman'.)

If this hypothesis has value, we might read our films as engaged in 'conversing' about the value, power, limits, threat and so on of this emergent 'feeling' around woman and desire. Despite its limits this 'conversation' afforded a wider range of possibilities regarding gender than many other film genres could generate or tolerate.

For example, in the 1950s a genre of mind-doctor films emerged that might be called the 'domestication scenario'. In films such as *Lady in the Dark* and *The Lady Says No*, we find a heavy-handed use of the figure of the mind-doctor to contain, or more accurately, to crush any strivings of women to emerge from existing sexual roles.

In *Lady in the Dark*, fashion magazine publisher Ginger Rogers consults psychoanalyst Barry Sullivan regarding emotional and physical distress. Provided with dream material which points to Rogers's wish for marriage (and her producer's wish for a dance sequence), Sullivan interprets her dilemma. Her problem, he divines, is that she 'wishes to dominate men when she needs to be dominated by them'. Such domination is provided by the gruff Ray Milland, who in a horrific final scene is handed Rogers' heart, job and chair – as she plops to the ground before him, grateful to be a woman again.

The Lady Says No starring David Niven is another attack on 'ladies' (in this case a woman psychologist) who are afflicted with the delusion that they may enter male domains, or worse can envision life without a reliance on men.

At the outset, I marked two thematics that I thought would prove central to the mind-doctor film. Thus far, 'conversations' about desire have occupied this reflection. The mind-doctor film may be interpreted as occupied with questions concerning 'desire', that is, with the vicissitudes of love, hate, sex, aggression, wish and phantasy. On this view, the 'structure of feeling' evident in one genre of mind-doctor film, namely, those films I have called the scenario of the romantic cure, does not seem to differ radically from a variety of other mainstream narrative film treatments of desire.

MEMORY AND MODERNITY

However, it is our other thematic, of memory, that I believe holds the unique 'contribution' of the mind-doctor genre. Another film will carry us through some reflections on the significance of memory in the mind-doctor film, hopefully completing the bold claim at the outset to explore both the conversation and the structure of feeling expressed in this peculiar category of movie. To move towards that end, we may stroll back down the aisle to Ian Holm, Alan Bates, Julie Christie, Glenda Jackson and Ann-Margret, in Hugh Whitmore's production of *Return of the Soldier* (1985).

In *Return of the Soldier*, the film adaptation of Rebecca West's debut novel of 1918, Chris Baldry/Alan Bates returns home from the trenches of the Great War, yet another victim of amnesia. Major Baldry can recall nothing of the last fifteen years, nothing since an idyllic summer when he fell in love with a local girl. The Major returns from the war a shattered figure, the lord of the manor reduced to a nervous patient. Yet, he has also been freed from an oppressive present, transported to a time free of the coming burdens of wife, war and manor house.

This selective amnesia sets the stage for an intrigue of love. He pines for the girl of his youth, Margaret Allington/Glenda Jackson, spurning the 'comforts' of his proper yet apparently empty marriage to Kitty/Julie Christie. A devoted cousin, Jenny (played by a frumpy Ann-Margret), adds an undercurrent of incestuous intrigue to the story. The complex domestic scene is watched over by the kindly, if eccentric, Dr Anderson/Ian Holm. Dr Anderson offers worldly wise analytic help, ever mindful of the vagaries of desire and the hazards that a 'cure' might entail.

Anderson/Holm is brought in as consultant on what turns out to be a social as well as a personal disorder. Chris/Bates's yearning for Margaret/Jackson disrupts the Baldrys' ordered world of the landed aristocracy. We are presented with a striking opposition between Kitty/Julie Christie's cold and biting elegance, a pampered beauty who relishes her status, and Margaret's warm, earthy, if dowdy middle-class life, the rough-hewn contours of her small garden plot and kitchen hearth reflected in the lines of her face.

Kitty allows Chris his visits to Margaret – without which he says, 'I will die' – in hopes that the shock of the real Margaret will bring him around. However, Bates sees only the girl of his youth, a girl who called him from his stables and estate to proclaim the superiority of love over class division. Kitty takes to her bed, reduced to unleashing the fullness of her venom, as she proclaims of types such as Margaret, 'I hate them. They stink of poverty and neglect. They should be shot.'

Ian Holm's Dr Anderson embodies in character and profession the psychoanalytic atmosphere of Rebecca West's story. A review of the film by Steve Vineberg (1985) points to the central metaphors of surface and depth in the narrative. Holm is a man whose eccentric and innocuous surface covers a mind that plumbs the depths of experience. As psychoanalyst, he stands poised as the familiar of the depths, yet he also understands the problematic nature of a journey beneath the surface of the world. Anderson signals his awareness of the dilemma of 'diving into the wreck' (in the words of the poet, Adrienne Rich). Speaking to Julie Christie who asks that her husband be returned to her, he notes: 'You see, it's my profession to move someone from the various outlying districts of the mind to the normal . . . It seems to be the general feeling that that's where they ought to be . . . Sometimes, I don't see the urgency myself.'

Despite hesitations along the way, the 'cure' unfolds with the seemingly inevitable realization that Chris Baldry's fantasized escape cannot last. Margaret is enlisted in re-establishing the 'reality principle'. In a stroll in the manor grounds, Glenda Jackson sacrifices her own fantasies of escape by offering Bates a remembrance that she knows will spell the end of his amnesia. A trigger, a key in the shape of a past trauma unlocks the memory of time's passage. The death of the Baldrys' only child turns out to be the most painful of the experiences that Chris's amnesia cloaked and evaded. The key turned, Chris/Bates returns to time's movement, yet is left locked back into a world where love is ephemeral and pain inescapable.

On first approach, *Return of the Soldier* might seem to break the containing conventions of the romantic cure genre. We find a meditative film that approaches the subject of love with an eye for complexities and limitations. We have a highlighting of social themes rather than a retreat into the personal, and our 'cure' is ambiguous as opposed to miraculous.

Yet, in many ways our soldier's story opposes genre conventions only to return to them. While our protagonist's quest does not end with love's triumph, love for a woman remains the transformative force of the journey all the same. The ill-fated quest revolves around a romantic imbuement of suffering, an elevation of the lovers' sorrow which validates passion over reason, desire over conventional expectation. How far are we really from the themes of *Spellbound* or of *Random Harvest*?

As to the recognition afforded the social field, we again need to take a closer look at the actual conversation *Return of the Soldier* displays. We note the drawing of a rather rigid, easily appealing dichotomy between the brutish (as well as British) upper classes and the warm, genuine nature of the 'middling' strata. Julie Christie is positively venomous, with her narcissistic, empty and, as we have seen, occasionally genocidal concerns. We are allowed the existence of the good individual aristocrat, either those like Jenny who display a required asceticism or those like Bates whose fall from grace adds to his natural distaste for the likes of his own class who view war as an extended fox hunt.

The strength and good-heartedness of the lower middle classes are personified in Margaret's husband, a village schoolmaster played by the accomplished actor Frank Finley. William Grey/Finlay is well aware of the burdensome weight of his marriage's bland domesticity. In a gesture of sacrifice and patience, as much as passivity, he allows the young Margaret to emerge from their 'greying' life, so that she may join Bates in some final moments in the sun.

While such dichotomies tap our proclivities for splitting good and bad objects, one pauses at accepting the rather banal treatment of class conflict as morality play. Beyond these quibbles, *Return of the Soldier* appears torn between competing visions of memory. On the one hand, the character of Dr Anderson/Ian Holm expresses the ambiguities of remembrance, the complexities of establishing a relationship to the past. At the same time, the narrative ultimately resolves with a traumatic vision of history, and a representation of memory which locates the past as a moment of rupture, history as a repetition of trauma.

We might view the ending then as a failure to sustain a more radical, complex vision of historical consciousness. Yet, perhaps in the midst of this critique, we have discovered the strength of the film, namely, its capacity to offer differing visions of memory's tasks. Whichever direction we settle our judgement, I believe we can discern in our three film samples a mode of containment reductive towards the contradictions and problems memory poses for us. A wish is offered up to us by the romantic cure scenario: that the present may be healed by a gesture to the past, or by a revelation from that past that illuminates and cures.

What are we to make of such a striking wish? The history of psychoanalysis is filled with the problem of describing the nature of remembrance. As I have argued in a previous work (Sekoff, 1982), Freud throughout his career – from 'The studies in hysteria' (1895) and 'Screen memory' (1899), to late essays such as 'Constructions in analysis' (1937) – remained torn between competing visions of psychoanalytic history.

He wrestled with both an archaeological version of history that viewed the task of analysis as the restoration of an actual, registered past and an interpretive, 'hermeneutic' history that placed the narrative construction of a past at the centre of psychoanalytic work. Such tensions are still with us, whether in the current controversies over the seduction and trauma theories, the never-ending debates over the influence of environment vs. internal phantasy life, or in the confusions over the role of 'deficit vs. conflict' in psychopathology. All these controversies may be viewed as rooted in the difficulties psychoanalytic theory and practice have had in establishing an adequate 'historiography'.

Addressing the latter problem is clearly not the task of the present work. Here, I wish only to raise the idea that the tensions and ambiguities surrounding our ideas about remembrance are not simply the result of inadequate thought, but rather reflect difficulties in the path of appropriating a history that confront all of us in the modern era.

My assertion – and it must remain little more than that – is that the emergence of what might be termed 'modernism' shattered previous relations that had moulded the processes of creating both personal history and social memory. For better or worse, traditional modes of establishing historical consciousness were wrenched apart by forces of modernity. All of us – psychoanalysts or amnesiacs – have been struggling with this modern problem.

To define 'modernism' is an exacting task. It seems to me any adequate definition would need to account for a structure of feeling that dominates the landscape of industrialized societies of the twentieth century, a structure of feeling that reflects a shattering of the distances between subject and object, between interpreter and interpreted, between surface and depth, and (more difficult to theorize, if horrifically concrete) between the forces of power and those dominated by such power. The modern era brings to bear new forms of violence, that paradoxically remove force to its administrative and symbolic dimensions, yet all the while increasing the capacities and capabilities for physical violence, however close (torture) or distant (space weapons).

The loss of historical memory is a much lamented and not altogether newly noted phenomenon. For example, we find De Tocqueville's comment: 'Since the past has ceased to throw light on the future, the mind of man wanders in obscurity'. If many have noted the contemporary loss of memory, the origins, ramifications and possible remedies are not very well elaborated. To sketch out the disorder we might note some of its uglier manifestations: a) the call of the Right for a return to a past that never existed, to an oppressive and dangerous dystopia; b) the commodification of memory, the past as backdrop for everything from peanut butter to political advertisement; c) the loss of a popular memory of struggle. How many of us can call upon names like Ludlow, Lawrence or Selma? How many consider the idea that history can be amenable to human action?

The aetiology of this disorder is no doubt difficult to trace. Simple formulations – television, capitalism, industrialization, even our own 'modernist structure of feeling' do not really suffice. John Berger (1978, p. 213) argues that 'there is a historic role of capitalism, a role unforeseen by Adam Smith or Marx: its historic role to destroy history, to sever every link with the past'. Milan Kundera has pointedly underscored the capacity of socialist states (state capitalist or not) to efface memory – and with memory go both the individual and a public sphere of association, debate and political discourse. Henry Ford's comment that 'history is bunk' captures succinctly the fate of memory in the fractured consciousness of our time.

Our recognition of a disturbance in historical consciousness should not be taken as a romantic yearning for the good old days. To my mind, the most disturbing aspect of this fracturing of memory is the accompanying loss of a capacity to envision the future. As Christa Wolf (1977, p. 153) has written, 'The deeper our memory, the freer the space for the goal of all our hope: the future'. It is not simply a loss of memory that is troublesome, but the diminishing of our capacity to appropriate the past towards a transformative vision of the future.

It is my claim that the mind-doctor films may be 'read' as struggling precisely with our modern disturbance of memory. The figure of the mind-doctor is imbued with a symbolism of recollection and remembrance. We all know what we speak to the shrink about: we tell her our story, the bits and pieces of our past . . . we conjure up the child within and ghosts never laid to rest. The mind-doctor's fifty-minute hour, or hypnotic trance or whatever other manoeuvres are called upon, challenges the movement of time, peels back the given order to reveal the past disguised as the present. The unique contribution of the mind-doctor genre is its capacity to generate conversation about fractured states of our memory.

The central filmic symbols of this dislocated memory are the amnesiac and the traumatic backdrop of our world wars. The battlefields of our centuries re-present – concretely as well as figuratively – a rupture of our social and personal landscapes. Amnesiacs experience a fracture at the core of their identity. They have lost both who they are and the tools to find their way. Through the amnesiac's quest for remembrance we grapple with the problematic, stripped to its essential layers, of reproducing our identity, our subjectivity. The cultural rupture of remembrance is read back through the film amnesiacs' personal struggle with establishing – or avoiding – their history.

Though I have criticized the effacement of cultural struggle by personal journey in our film narratives, there may be a certain wisdom in this representation regarding memory. For history is not something that simply takes place out there, beyond us – but through us, within us. Fredric Jameson (1981, p. 102) has written that 'history is what hurts'. In John Ballantine, Major Smith and Chris Baldry, we are given access to the 'hurt' of history as it runs a course through their lives. Our view of this history may be truncated – 'war' as a force stripped of social, economic or political context; 'history' as great events or personal tragedies – yet we do get a 'feel' for a piece of our history, for the pieces of a disjointed structure of feeling whose shards we grapple to fit together.

Claude Lévi-Strauss wrote (see epigram to Gordimer, 1979): 'I am the place in which something has occurred'. This may serve as a reminder that in the midst of dislocation, 'something' is located within us. If we think of that 'something' as the 'hurt' of history, we are faced with the problem of locating this hurt, of describing the places where history occurs.

If our films explore particular personal 'locales' of historical process, they do so with a poor provision of charts and maps for those of us joining the expedition. Here, psychoanalytic inquiry may prove especially helpful. The analytic clinical method opens up more than an exploration of the psyche's depths, more than a charting of the unconscious. Fundamentally, analysis is concerned with the forging of subjectivity out of the crucible of personal history.

I want to call attention to only a small aspect of the complex processes that are involved in the construction and reproduction of 'I-ness', namely, the achievement of a subjectivity capable of historical consciousness. I use the word 'achievement' deliberately, for analytic experience shows again and again the hard and ever-present struggle to retain a sense of our histories. Indeed, the capacity to recognize one's subjectivity (or mis-recognize it for that matter) is also a profound achievement. To know one is thinking one's own thoughts, feeling one's own feelings, living in differentiatable outer and inner worlds – such knowing is often lost to many of us.[7]

For example, patients with 'borderline' or 'schizoid' diagnoses often see the therapist as a different person from session to session, indeed within a session. As one young woman often remarked to me, 'your face keeps changing', a 'fact' that made it difficult to trust that she could once again be safe with me.

Freud (1913; 1926) emphasized the fundamental human story as a movement from the biological immaturity and helplessness (*Hilflosigkeit*) of the infant towards the construction of an 'I' (*ich*/ego), of a human subject capable of reflecting (albeit within limits) upon its inner and outer worlds. Many other analytic languages have followed to describe the construction of human subjectivity. To begin with only one, Melanie Klein's history of the human subject charted a path from a 'paranoid-schizoid position' where experience is essentially fragmented and threatening towards a 'depressive position' where others could be experienced as whole entities (and thus be recognized, loved and needed, rendering the subject painfully vulnerable to loss).[8]

In the paranoid-schizoid position, as Thomas Ogden (1986, pp. 61–5) comments, 'danger and safety are managed by rendering experience discontinuous (by means of splitting) and by ejecting into another person unacceptable states of being' (the latter via the processes of 'projection' and 'projective identification').

Thus, in paranoid-schizoid states of being, grave barriers stand in the way of sustaining a historicity to one's experience. We may conceive of a realm of experience in which distinctions between the me and not-me, inside and outside, self and other, have poor footholds. This is a realm where the needs of the organism, rather than the wishes generated by a subject, dominate experience, a state of being wherein easily disrupted integrations of experience are accompanied by anxieties of fragmentation, disintegration and annihilation.

Might we now approach our amnesia films in a new light? Could they be providing a glimpse into a realm of psychological disruption and disintegration? We seem to have all the ingredients of the paranoid-schizoid realm. Our amnesiacs are thrown back toward *Hilflosigkeit*, a helpless tumble back through discontinuous experience. Distinctions that uphold identity are lost, mental integration gives way to somatic distress, anxieties of fragmentation and annihilation overwhelm our protagonists, and processes of projection turn the world dangerous, filled with threat and violence. Perhaps only the capacity to wish, the desire to love, remain somehow unscathed in the fall.

If our films give us a view of the loss of historical consciousness, perhaps they might also tell us something about the building of a subjectivity capable of sustaining a personal history?

Psychoanalytic theory poses a complex 'entrance' into the depressive position. Traced so richly in the work of D.W. Winnicott, the crossing of the depressive threshold is a movement dependent on an adequate 'facilitating environment' – and a process marked most pointedly by achievements of symbolic functioning that foster the capacity to be alone; by the ability to sustain both aggression and concern; and by the creativity to nourish a potential space between self and other where imaginative action (including the imagining of a personal history) might live (see especially Winnicott, 1975).

These 'depressive achievements' rest in turn on an array of other psychic and inter-personal processes, among them: the capacity to conceal and repress rather than disavow unbearable experience; the flexibility both to distinguish self from other and to dissolve such distinctions without overwhelming anxiety; the possibility of generating wishes/desires rather than being mired in insatiable need and demand; the ability to 'learn from experience' as opposed to the stasis of painting the world solely from our subjective palette; in sum, capacities of symbolization founded on a variety of intersubjective and intra-psychic integrations.

The scenario of the romantic cure touches upon basic elements of the movement into the depressive position. We find a facilitating environment offered by our lovers and therapists which 'holds' and 'contains' the needs and anxieties of our disrupted amnesiacs. We may discern portions of the steps that make up the piece by piece attainment of 'whole object' relatedness, starting from the elemental mergers between infant and mother (the inseparableness of our protagonists), through transitional phenomena (the facing of separations by each of our couples through love for the absent object – Coleman's second amnesia, Peck's jail term, Bates's manor house imprisonment), to depressive phenomena proper such as the 'surviving over time' of the loved object and the digestion of experiences of aggression, ruthlessness, guilt and concern. (Each protagonist carries the potential for violence. Peck and Bates lash out at their lovers. Each struggles with a guilt for past traumas and present pains.)

Conversely, we see the failure of transitional space in the use of the loved object as fetish and addictive object.

Other elements of 'depressive transition' are signified as well, such as the fundamental role of the oedipal matrix. Our couples face the tension of a movement between maternal embrace and erotic alliance. Castration looms in our amnesiacs' enforced passivity and from threatening rivals (the evil father-figure of Leo Carroll in *Spellbound*, the jealous psychiatrist of *Random Harvest*, and the threatening maternal phallus figured by the porcelain and rigid Kitty in *Return of the Soldier*). On the other hand, we find objects that nurture 'oedipalization', that is to say, who function as protectors/guides for desire and identification. These transitional guides are offered by the lovers of our films and by the 'mind-doctor' helpers, Dr Alex Bruloff and Dr Anderson.[9]

Now the entrance into history heralded by the depressive position is not an escape from hell into paradise, despite the promise of our amnesia films. History provides its own inferno, its own pains as well as pleasures. Though our 'historical subject' of the depressive position finds a realm of experience deeper, more textured, and with greater potential for satisfaction than the fragmented subject of paranoid-schizoid realm, suffering has not been banished from this best of all possible worlds.

If the quest in our amnesia films appears to trace the developmental path of entry into the depressive position, it also must be remembered that terms such as 'entrance', 'transition', even 'depressive position' itself must be understood as a kind of shorthand. Rather than a linear movement from one form of experience to another, we would better postulate a complex, textured and dialectical developmental process. Our celluloid journeys toward remembrance open a view of this dialectic – a process of contradiction and conflict that underlies our capacities to reproduce ourselves as desiring and remembering subjects.[10]

The reproduction of a desiring, remembering 'I' is an ongoing task, for our arduous climb over the threshold of the depressive position does not release us from the work of constructing ourselves. Indeed, from a psychoanalytic perspective each of us carries the burden of a ceaseless struggle with our fractured subjectivity. 'Divided subjects', we are susceptible to upheavals from inner and outer worlds, worlds only occasionally amenable to our wishes or control.

In this light, our mind-doctor films are expressions of our struggle to organize our basic self experience. From another angle, the mind-

174

doctor movies represent one site of the ongoing conversations out of which we construct and are constructed by our cultural and historical experience. Our exploration of particular portions of these conversations, primarily the scenario of the amnesia film, has highlighted the central roles of desire and memory in this dialectic of personal and cultural reproduction. It would seem that the modernist structure of feeling thrusts to the fore particular questions of memory.

If the disjunctures of the modern era have unhinged the self from previous attachments, it might follow that any new organization of the self may be dependent on cultural conversations which place the problems of desire and memory at their centre. Both the mind-doctor film and the practice of psychoanalysis itself represent two such conversations. These modernist practices remarkably fit the call of a structure of feeling which generates a search for others to touch and a history to remember.

In the case of the mind-doctor film, we have seen that the finding of an other through desire as well as the search for remembrance are recoveries that contain and constrict as well as liberate. Social and political issues are subsumed under personal imperatives. The organization of self is achieved at the price of remaining within limited boundaries of gender and desire. 'History' is reduced to the obvious, the graspable and the traumatic, with phantasies of 'cathartic cures' replacing a more ambiguous and uncertain struggle to appropriate the past.

The genre of the mind-doctor film offers us a romance. And romance, as Frye points out, is among the simplest of our tropes. Unfortunately, life is rarely so simple. Good does not always triumph over evil. Adventure cannot erase the problems of living day to day. And love depends less on a hazy lens and lush music than on the vagaries of the unconscious and the commitment of those willing to risk and compromise.

Freud chose tragedy over romance, offering psychoanalysis as a tragic lens on the quandaries and contradictions of the modern self. Yet all is not despair, for tragedy offers strengths that romance cannot yield. The tragic view opens us to the contradictions and complexities of experience, and thus offers us an enriched perspective for action and understanding.[11]

Both desire and memory 'hurt' – for each holds legacies of suffering and oppression. Yet, memory and desire also sustain – for they also carry us forward in struggle and in hope. Psychoanalysis – at its best – locates memory and desire within a dialectical tension between pessimism and hope, symptom and cure, stasis and potential. A liberatory transformative vision must sustain this tension if we are to appropriate memory and desire – their pain and promise – for the future.

POSTSCRIPT

While I have criticized the mind-doctor films for their narrowing of imaginative possibility, I hope I have recognized that these films are not of one piece, that they embody contradictions and complexities of their own. The film critic Jim Kitses (1969, p. 26) observed about genre that 'rather than an empty vessel breathed into by the film maker, the genre is a vital structure through which flow a myriad of themes and concepts'. If we traced the history of the mind-doctor genre more completely, we would find such a thematic flow – a myriad of conversations, questions, answers and questions again.

I want to point the reader to two films that strike me as breathing something vital into our rather tired genre. I offer only a preview, a short film clip to entice but not scare away the customers.

First, I recommend *Mine Own Executioner*, a little-known British film from 1948, starring Burgess Meredith as a lay psychoanalyst. We have all the ingredients of our amnesia scenario – an RAF pilot back from the war with shattered nerves and loss of memory, a pretty loving wife and a caring, committed analyst. Yet, the conventions of the genre are tested and challenged. Without giving away too much, we are allowed to see Meredith as troubled as well as talented. And we are given a sense of the limits of caring in a world where tragic events may overcome our best wishes and intentions.

The second film is a recent release, *Nineteen Nineteen*, written by Hugh Brody and Michael Ignatieff, and produced by the British Film Institute. As John Berger notes in his afterword to the script (Brody and Ignatieff, 1985, p. 93), *Nineteen Nineteen* attempts to speak to 'what we know about life, composed inextricably of the most intimate movements of the heart, accident, and the remorseless movement of history'. The movements of desire and memory are traced through the lives of two of Freud's patients (played by Paul Scofield and Maria Schell) who meet in Vienna in 1970 to recall past lives, a lost city and a famous analyst who remains as elusive as a century's history. The film stands as an intriguing attempt to bring together psychoanalysis and film, not only in content, but in method and structure.

NOTES

1. See also Anthony Giddens (1979), Raymond Williams (1977) for a discussion of 'structuration' – the ongoing interrelation of agency, structure and historical process.
2. See John Berger (1976) for a marvellous discussion of medicine, including the role of the physician as the familiar of death.
3. The list is easily extended with such movies as:

Somewhere in the Night	with	John Hodiak
As You Desire Me		Greta Garbo
The Third Day		George Peppard
Istanbul		Cornell Borchers
The Woman With No Name		Phyllis Calvert
Love Letter		Jennifer Jones
Hangover Square		Laird Cregar
I Love You Again		William Powell
Crossroads		William Powell
Mister Buddwing		James Gardner
Black Angel		Dan Duryea
Grip of the Strangler		Boris Karloff
The Morning After		Jane Fonda
Mirage		Gregory Peck
Captain Newman, M.D.		Peck on the other side of the couch.

My personal favourite: *Mine Own Executioner* with Burgess Meredith as the psychoanalyst, a film we will return to in a bit.
4. The detective story is perhaps the one true utopian American form. While detective fiction has world-wide appeal, it is in the hard-boiled, *noir*-style stories centred in the Los Angeles of Raymond Chandler and James Cain and the San Francisco of Dashiell Hammett that the American version comes into its own. The detective-hero embodied in a Philip Marlowe or a Sam Spade is wise to the ways of the world, toughened from personal hardship and a far too clear view of the tragic scope of life. Yet the hardened visage disguises a wistful eye and a utopian vision that longs for love, but above all for justice. Humphrey Bogart crystallizes this figure in films like *Casablanca*, *The Maltese Falcon* and *To Have and Have Not*.
5. For an excellent survey of cinema studies see Pam Cook, 1985.
6. For psychoanalytic studies of fetishism see the recent work of Janine Chasseguet-Smirgel (1985) and Joyce McDougal (1985).
7. I am indebted to Thomas Odgen's extensive discussion of the construction of subjectivity in his *The Matrix of the Mind*. See especially chapter 4, 'The depressive position and the birth of the historical subject'.
8. For discussions of *Hilflosigkeit* see Chasseguet-Smirgel (1985), especially the author's introduction and chapter two.

9. One must be careful about too strenuous a reliance on the type of reading just offered. Psychoanalytic criticism is littered with efforts that 'find' evidence of whatever processes are being looked for in a particular piece of art, literature or cinema. Classical Freudians will 'discover' instincts and compromise formations; ego psychologists will 'demonstrate' defences, resistances and attempts at mastery; and so on. There is no simple solution to this problem of interpreting from a pre-existing code. A turn to purely structural or formal aspects of art – recently so in vogue – does not elude the underlying necessity for a basic interpretive position. Perhaps all we can do is strive to keep in mind the tenuous nature of the interpretive process and make clear, as far as possible, the lenses that we bring to our readings. See Fredric Jameson (1981) and Elizabeth Wright (1984) for a discussion of this issue.

10. The work of Jacques Lacan has important implications for those concerned with retaining a psychoanalytic metapsychology that values a theory of contradiction and conflict as essential to an analytic enterprise. Contrary to many of the 'developmentalist' trends current in psychoanalysis, Lacan emphasizes that the consolidation of the subject is based on a fundamental misrecognition. We find ourselves, we build our 'I', only in the mirror of an other's desire for us, through their image of us. Thus, the ego is founded in alienation, misrecognizing itself in another – a founding that places a gap at the core of our subjectivity.

    Contemporary psychoanalytic theories that seek an over-eager merger with neurobiology, developmental psychology and psychiatry run the risk of 'normalizing' the complex dialectic that underlies the human condition. Lacanian analysis, however else one may criticize this school, cannot be accused of such normalization. The theory of the alienated 'I' offers valuable insight into the structure of repetition in life – in brief, repetition emanates from the doomed attempt to overcome the inherent gaps facing desire. Lacan also offers intriguing leads to a theory of aggression, rooted not in biology, but in the aggressive attacks on the 'lack' at the core of our alienated identity and desire.

    From a more classical psychoanalytic perspective, the work of Janine Chasseguet-Smirgel on the 'ego ideal' also offers a theory of repetition in psychic and social life based on the ego's attempts to overcome the gap between itself and its imaginary ideals. Given more space, Lacan and Chasseguet-Smirgel could help us explore questions regarding our susceptibility to, indeed striving for, the repetitive scenarios of desire and remembrance that the Hollywood film so successfully provides. See Jacques Lacan (1975); Ellie Ragland-Sullivan (1986); and Janine Chasseguet-Smirgel (1985).

11. For a discussion of tragedy from a psychoanalytic perspective see André Green (1979) and Roy Schafer (1983). Schafer: 'One might say that analysis raises the melodramatic or pathetic to the level of the tragic and

178

so changes the atmosphere or the quality or the dignity of an entire life'
(p. 192).

REFERENCES

Barthes, R. (1974) *S/Z*. New York: Hill & Wang.
—— (1975) *The Pleasure of the Text*. New York: Hill & Wang.
Beckett, S. (1957) *Proust*. New York: Grove Press.
Berger, J. (1976) *A Fortunate Man*. Writers & Readers.
—— (1978) *Pig Earth*. Writers & Readers.
Brody, H. and Ignatieff, M. (1985) *Nineteen Nineteen*. Faber.
Cavell, S. (1981) *Pursuits of Happiness*. Cambridge, MA: Harvard University
    Press.
—— (1988) 'The melodrama of the unknown woman', in J. Smith and W.
    Kerrigan, eds *Images in Our Souls: Cavell, Psychoanalysis and Cinema*.
    Baltimore: Johns Hopkins University Press, pp. 11–43.
Chasseguet-Smirgel, J. (1985). *The Ego Ideal*. Free Association Books.
Cook, P. ed. (1985) *The Cinema Book*. New York: Pantheon.
de Tocqueville, A. (1945) *Democracy in America*, vol. 2. New York: Random
    House.
Freud, S. (1905) *Jokes and their Relation to the Unconscious*. S.E. 8.
—— (1913) *Totem and Taboo*. S.E. 13, pp. 1–162.
—— (1926) 'Inhibitions, symptoms and anxiety'. S.E. 10, pp. 75–175.
Frye, N. (1957) *The Anatomy of Criticism*. Princeton: Princeton University
    Press.
Giddens, A. (1979) *Central Problems in Social Theory*. Berkeley: University of
    California Press.
Gordimer, N. (1979) *Burger's Daughter*. New York: Penguin.
Green, A. (1979) *The Tragic Effect*. Cambridge: Cambridge University Press.
Heath, S. (1977) 'Notes on suture', *Screen* 18(4).
Jameson, F. (1981) *The Political Unconscious*. Ithaca: Cornell University Press.
Johnston, S. (1976) 'Film narrative and the structuralist controversy', in P.
    Cook, ed. *The Cinema Book*. New York: Pantheon, pp. 222–50.
Kitses, J. (1969) *Horizons West*. Secker/British Film Institute.
Lacan, J. (1975) *Ecrits*. New York: Norton.
McCabe, C. (1974) 'Realism and the cinema: notes on some Brechtian theses',
    Screen 15(2): 8–15.
McDougall, J. (1985) *Theaters of the Mind*. New York: Basic.
Metz, C. (1982) *The Imaginary Signifier*. Bloomington: Indiana University
    Press.
Mulvey, L. (1975) 'Visual pleasure and narrative cinema', *Screen* 16(3).
Neale, S. (1980) *Genre*. British Film Institute.
Ogden, T. (1986) *The Matrix of the Mind*. Northvale: Aronson.
Pollock, G. (1977) 'Report on the weekend school', *Screen* 18(2).

Ragland-Sullivan, E. (1986) *Jacques Lacan and the Philosophy of Psychoanalysis*. Urbana: University of Illinois Press.

Schafer, R. (1983) *The Analytic Attitude*. New York: Basic.

Searles, H. (1975) 'The patient as therapist to his analyst', in P. Giovacchini, A. Flarsheim and L. Boyer, eds *Tactics and Techniques in Psychoanalytic Therapy II*. New York: Aronson, 1975, pp. 95–151.

Sekoff, J. (1982) *Remembering Against the Current*, Ann Arbor, MI: University Microfilms.

Trauffaut, F. (1967) *Hitchcock*. New York: Simon & Schuster.

Vineberg, S. (1985) 'Surface and depth', *Three Penny Review* 23.

Viviani, C. (1980) 'Who is without sin?: the maternal melodrama in American film 1930–9', *Wide Angle* 4(2).

Williams, R. (1967) *Modern Tragedy*. Stanford CA: Stanford University Press.

—— (1977) *Marxism and Literature*. Oxford: Oxford University Press.

Winnicott, D. (1975) 'The depressive position in normal emotional development', in *Through Paediatrics to Psycho-Analysis*. Hogarth.

Wolf, C. (1977) *The Reader and Writer*. New York: International Publishers.

Wright, E. (1984) *Psychoanalytic Criticism*. Methuen.

11 WITCHES AND SEDUCERS

Moral Panics for Our Time

Les Levidow

'REMEMBER, it's not just a moral panic.' Someone said this to me after attending my paper on the collective denial of child sexual abuse (which forms the second case study of this essay). True, nothing is ever just a moral panic.[1] At some level it always involves real distress, even authentic grievances, whose sources – internal and/or external – get personified in the form of folk devils. Yet, just as people in medieval times experienced the devil as if he were real, so too do people today experience illusory threats as if they were real, or (as some post-modernists might say) as even more real than their mundane everyday reality.

To some extent that paradox was acknowledged by 1970s studies of moral panics. While emphasizing the roles of the mass media in manufacturing news and thus the moral panics, those studies also analysed substantive issues that allowed the panic-mongering to resonate with deeply felt anxieties.

For Stanley Cohen (1973), public reaction to the Mods and Rockers illustrated how the mass media provide 'a main source of information about the normative contours of a society . . . the boundaries beyond which one should not venture and about the shapes the devil can assume'. At the same time, he also suggested how the moral panic ideologically displaced social tensions around new-found affluence and sexual licence. Refusing their allocated roles as passive consumers, youths were seeking excitement as a relief from dull, tedious jobs – a search for which they were feared as 'prematurely affluent, aggressive, [sexually] permissive and challenging the ethics of sobriety and hard work'. And such public delinquency seemed all the more threatening in the case of youths who held respectable jobs; for their role in blurring class boundaries, they were disowned as 'aliens'. Moreover, just as newly affluent families were flocking to package holidays abroad, rowdy youths were blamed for supposedly frightening them away from seaside resorts.

Suggesting a projection of suppressed desires, Cohen noted a typical behaviour of the lower middle class in condemning 'behaviour which is secretly craved': their expressed resentment concealed their jealousy. He concluded ominously, 'More moral panics will be generated and other, as yet nameless, folk devils will be created.' While the panic over Mods and Rockers (along with the subcultures themselves) seems to have disappeared without trace, more recent outbreaks have had profound effects, particularly in labelling entire categories of people as criminal suspects.

In the case of black youth, Stuart Hall (1978) described an 'amplification spiral' of public anxiety and criminalization. The mass media spread panic with the stereotype of the vicious mugger – to which the police responded by arresting more 'suspects', while judges responded by imposing lengthier sentences, which made the 'mugging' problem more newsworthy. Thus the mass media served to construct the events they were later to report as news. As he argued, such constructions lead people 'to experience and respond to contradictory developments in ways which make the operation of state power legitimate, credible and consensual'. Since his study we have seen that kind of panic made permanent and extended to other social groups – indeed, extending the definitions of criminality itself.

As the phenomenon proliferates, how useful is the term 'moral panic'? Simon Watney (1987) has rightly warned against invoking the term as a universal explanation for 'all conflicts in the public domain where scapegoating takes place', and against presuming that it is exceptional for mass media 'representation' to diverge from 'the real'. As he argues, a particular moral panic 'merely marks the site of the current front-line . . . in a permanent ideological struggle over the meaning of signs'.

For our purposes here, those signs will be analysed for their unconscious phantasy meanings – not mainly as a contrast to reality, but as an insight into how people experience reality, and how they reassert social identities under threat. This essay naturally draws upon insights from earlier studies about how public figures and the mass media have fabricated such panics. Yet it emphasizes what their success tells us about people's lived realities and phantasies – almost independently of whether the panic-carriers had legitimate grievances. (And, lest all this be taken as special condemnation of certain newspapers and politicians, let us remember that even the construction and selection of medical evidence have no natural immunity to the metaphorical meanings analysed here.)

As regards 'real' threats, my two examples of folk devils may seem as different as they could possibly be. In the case of Haringey's homophobic outbreak against rampant seducers, the panic-carriers lacked any rational basis for portraying gay people as a threat. In contrast, the Cleveland protesters had valid grievances against the 'witches' who personified the state's clumsy procedures for detecting child sexual abuse.

Nevertheless, the two phenomena had a common basis in unconscious phantasy. This involved projecting unwanted parts of ourselves on to supposed persecutors who actively undermine parental authority and threaten to annihilate our identity. While of course we all engage in psychic splitting and projection to some extent all the time, such a projective defence took a public, organized form in Haringey and Cleveland. In each case it attempted to alleviate anxiety by suppressing the devils, or at least their public authority. As this psychodynamic took over, it became almost futile to pose such otherwise constructive questions as 'How should the schools respond to children's prejudices about homosexuals?' and 'How should suspected instances of child sexual abuse be investigated?'

The political effects have run much further than banishing such questions and the folk devils who personified them. Although the opposing sides didn't correspond closely to party-political allegiances, certainly the panics strengthened 'the politics of fear' that helps provide the Conservative Party's basis of rule. That is, while lacking truly popular policies, the party rules through resigned acceptance – partly for lack of an effective opposition, partly for fear that only 'The Resolute Approach' can protect us from impending chaos. Within that psychic world, witches and seducers rank among a rogues' gallery of moral (even mortal) threats: feminists, black youth, Irish Republicans, trade-union militants, the 'loony Left', etc.

As in so many other cases, the two panics presented here have disoriented or even incorporated the Labour Party, to the point where it could not defend those who were truly being persecuted. By default, victory has been won by those who appeared to keep the threats under control, by those who could alleviate intolerable anxieties. Thus, as will be argued here, the Haringey and Cleveland episodes were more than 'just moral panics', in the following senses:
– that the panic extends to a level of unconscious phantasy which in turns expresses psychopathological aspects of this society;

183

– that these episodes exemplify a more general case of manipulating private fears, towards reducing us to helpless dependence upon state protection from psychic annihilation; and

– that any adequate political response must take that dynamic into account.

SEX AND DEATH: AIDS STORM SWEEPS HARINGEY

What underlies 'homophobia'? The term suggests simply a pathological fear of homosexuality, in others and in oneself. The labelling of AIDS as the 'gay plague' has deepened the fears of male homosexuality in particular – fears rich in death metaphors. Yet 'homophobia' is still largely treated as a matter of ignorance and prejudice, remediable through rationally informative education.

What more primitive emotions might be involved in 'homophobia'? Criticizing blanket use of the term as a reductive explanation, Simon Watney (1987) has pointed out the apparent paradox of this so-called phobia: 'far from avoiding a taboo and terrifying object, [its subjects] appear to rush to confront it directly'. He suggests that such behaviours 'result either from reaction-formations developed to defend the individual from some suppressed emotion or wish within him or herself, or else from other displaced or strictly speaking phobic anxieties projected on to gay men, about gender, sexual potency or even career prospects'.

As a way of investigating such dynamics, the second case study here will look at the frenzied reaction to an attempt at educating people out of their homophobic prejudices. By analysing the emotions and forces that erupted, we may be better placed to overcome them in the future, even to speak to the deeper social malaise that they express. Although this analysis is based mainly on key newspaper items from the second half of 1986 in one locality, it suggests a psychodynamic pattern which is far more widespread.

'Gay Lessons'
Britain's best organized, most intense manifestation of 'homophobia' has arisen in the north London borough of Haringey, ostensibly as a reaction against the council's policy of promoting 'Positive Images' of gays and lesbians in the schools. The policy identified the problem as 'heterosexism' and so proposed, for example,

– that classroom discussions reflect the range of children's real-life family situations; and

– that the schools challenge the insulting anti-gay phrases that children informally learn there (queer, pooftah, lezzie, etc.). In that sense, the policy was to extend existing anti-racist and anti-sexist initiatives to the realm of homophobia.

However, the extension nearly fell off the edge of the political map. The former initiatives sought to challenge stereotypes of race and gender differences, where the sexual overtones resonate mainly at a subliminal level. By contrast, the 'Positive Images' policy concerned the overt choices that different people make about their social identity based on sexual orientation. Here it is not sexuality as such but its metaphorical associations with death that operate subliminally, hovering between the unconscious and the conscious.

In this society, moreover, the whole area of sexuality is experienced as intrinsically threatening, bound up with projected fears and desires. We tend to demonize evil corrupters, while idealizing the morally pure. For a long time, male homosexuality in particular has been phantasized as a relation between predatory seducers and innocent victims: incurable aggressive homosexuals prey on the passive objects of their desire (Watney, 1981). Gay male sex is also seen to epitomize the unrestrained, amoral pursuit of physical pleasure-seeking – that is, the antithesis of responsible, faithful, romantic love.

Since the emergence of a 'gay pride' subculture, homophobic phantasies seem to have shifted from a paedophilia-type model to an epidemic model. That is, rather than the seduction victims remaining passive, they in turn become active agents in further spreading the perversion. According to this panic scenario, the insatiable threat extends to the entire society. With the rise of AIDS, panic-carriers could all the more easily associate homosexuality with epidemic, and in turn with annihilation threats personified by inherently immoral gay men. As noted by Simon Watney (1987), 'AIDS is made to speak on behalf of various social groups, whose moral opinions thus ostensibly emanate from the syndrome itself.'

Thus, in Haringey, perhaps predictably, what was intended as an anti-discrimination policy was readily construed as the most dangerous, even deadly kind of sex education, as 'homosexual education'. Apparently this was to mean 'Gay Lessons in HarinGAY', as announced by one tabloid newspaper. The intended challenge to 'heterosexism' was construed as an attack on heterosexuality, with that fine terminological distinction being lost on most people – wilfully or otherwise.

Indeed, it was considered possible to promote homosexuality by propaganda. As Education Secretary Baker proclaimed, 'When it comes to the aggressive promoting of homosexuality, it is wrong. That is the problem in Haringey and Brent. There is a difference between encouraging and accepting homosexuality' (*Sunday Telegraph*, 14 September 1986). This image of threatened contagion was eventually codified in Section 28 of the Local Government Act 1988, which prohibited local authorities from funding activities which 'intentionally promote' homosexuality.

As commentator Paul Johnson described the threat even more crudely, the problem of the commercial sex industry has been compounded by an 'official' sex industry, by the 'public promotion of promiscuity . . . designed to recruit the homosexual partners of the future . . . The immediate dangers of active, aggressive homosexual proselytising are obvious enough, given the alarming spread of AIDS' (*Daily Telegraph*, 6 October 1986). In the popular imagination, Baker's and Johnson's choice of words merges propaganda with seduction, contagion, disease, death.

In response to such widely felt fears, many otherwise sympathetic public officials have held back from supporting gay projects for fear of censure or legal sanctions. Labour leader Kinnock was clearly referring to such projects when he attacked 'zealots' for promoting 'extreme policies' (November 1986). In Haringey many groups have disavowed any contamination with homosexuality. Many otherwise sympathetic people have been thrown into a confused paralysis over exactly what the policy means, in the face of clear, determined opposition, albeit from a small minority. The policy's supporters (including Haringey Black Action) have made eloquent arguments in the local press and have organized demonstrations, but they have run up against the limits of a purely rational discourse.

Apparently the Positive Images policy has been relegated to a perpetual stage of 'public consultation', with full implementation on the far-off horizon. Education officers had no ready-made procedure for such public consultation, and the Positive Images policy was hardly a propitious issue for which to initiate such a procedure. Even this concession offered protesters little satisfaction. Parents' fears could hardly be allayed by reassurances that the policy remained at a consultation stage which itself lacked credibility.

Many parents seemed to react by taking the issue as an occasion for venting their resentment at the council's customarily autocratic behaviour. Some critics have attacked the council for wasting money on the 'Positive Images' policy when it can't even afford to buy enough standard school textbooks for children's basic education. Yet the 'backlash' itself has overshadowed other political issues, to the point of diverting attention from the need to fight ratecapping and massive, continuing public expenditure cuts. In this way, the panic-carriers have served to hasten the social disintegration that they were attempting to halt.

Speaking for Haringey's Tory councillors, Peter Murphy has repeatedly denounced the Positive Images policy as 'part of a Marxist plot to destabilize society as we know it'. Of course the Haringey backlash itself forms part of a nationally co-ordinated effort to discredit the 'loony Left' councils. However, to throw the 'conspiracy' charge back at the Tories won't suffice for understanding why they succeeded in spreading panic and disavowal of homosexuality – and why, at the same time, they failed to convert this feeling into increased public support for their party. For this understanding, it is essential to analyse how the 'backlash' involves pervasive feelings about a whole way of life . . . and death.

Sex and Death

As it happened, opponents of the Positive Images policy were unable to find any real signs of the 'gay lessons' that they so feared. They focused their alarm on such evils as a library book, denounced for subverting normal family values, as it portrayed a little girl living with two gay male adults. (This episode contributed to the clamour for Section 28, since enacted, which also prohibits local government from portraying homosexual life as a 'pretended family relationship'.)

In a period when the 'normal family' is being revealed as an endangered species, as well as a potential danger to many children who still live in it, how shall we interpret this response? In pursuit of its own interests, the local 'rabid Right' has played a catalytic role by evoking widely felt anxieties. Parents' fears that their children might become gay have symbolized various death fears: that of biological death from AIDS, death of innocence, death of heterosexual identity, death of parental/adult authority, death of the natural order – even a feeling that a child turned gay might just as well be dead. Within that psychic continuum, homosexuality doesn't simply cause disease: it *is* a disease, a deadly social disease.

Consider the imagery of the following: 'Tory Collapses in AIDS Storm' – one of the many suggestive headlines that have appeared in Haringey's local press since the Left Labour victory in the 1986 local council elections. This headline referred to a council meeting to debate a set of Tory motions as a demonstration and counter-demonstration gathered outside the town hall. The opposition was demanding, among other things, that the Labour council abandon its Positive Images policy and council funding for Reading Matters, a community bookshop selling gay and Left literature.

At the 'stormy' meeting, Councillor Murphy said of homosexuality,

> We do not wish these activities to be promoted as normal. We live in a period of violent plague and in this country 96 per cent of those affected are male homosexuals. When there are such dangers it is not the place for a local authority to start promoting a life-style that ensures you will end up dead a whole lot earlier. (*Haringey Journal*, 29 April 1988)

Earlier he had informed the public that in America 'AIDS sufferers are reputed to have on average 1,100 contacts' (*Enfield Advertiser*, 31 July 1986).

What shall we make of this simplistic equation, 'homosexuality = plague = death'? At a rational, empirical level, we might observe that the equation ignores the measures taken by gays to prevent the spread of AIDS, while exemplifying the homophobia that makes it more difficult for those infected to get the help that might save them, not to mention the still-widespread assumption that heterosexuality is entirely safe. At another level, however, it is important to see how the equation is about far more than gay sex and death. Indeed, that connection has been widely conveyed in ways which evoke a range of fears about sexual and violent impulses, contagious revolt and social disintegration – all of which conflate internal and external threats.

Violent Epidemic
Running throughout the entire controversy have been images of epidemic violence. For example, in the public meeting already mentioned, where Murphy warned of 'violent plague', another Tory councillor became ill with chest pains after accusing an openly gay Labour councillor of having 'vested interests' in spending money on homosexuals. The resulting headline, 'Tory Collapses in AIDS Storm', invites us to see him as an innocent victim of assault by an uncontrollable contagion, perhaps emanating from gay activist Peter Tatchell, shown demonstrating outside the council meeting. At an earlier meeting, a Tory implied that the pro-Positive Images demonstrators had turned up simply for violence: 'These people couldn't

TORY COLLAPSES IN AIDS STORM!

by Kevin Kavanagh

AMONG the demonstrators: Peter Tatchell, who lost a safe Labour seat in Bermondsey after an anti-gay smear campaign.
Picture: Tony Gay

PLANS for teaching Haringey schoolchildren about homosexuality are to go ahead — but only after a bitter row in which a Tory councillor collapsed with a suspected heart attack and Labour were accused of encouraging the spread of Aids.

At an emotionally charged Haringey council meeting on Monday night West Indian councillor Blair Greaves became ill after a speech infuriating that Labour's Cllr Philip Jones had a "vested interest" in spending money on homosexuals.

He was rushed to hospital in an ambulance, but later discharged.

The row hit fever pitch when Tottenham Tory leader Peter Murphy said the Labour group was not only trying to break up family life, but contributing to Aids statistics.

Cllr Murphy said: "We do not wish these activities to be promoted as normal. We live in a period of virulent plague

It's yes to gay lessons

and in this country 96 per cent of those affected are male homosexuals.

"When there are such dangers it is not the place for a local authority to start promoting a life-style that ensures you will end up dead a whole lot earlier."

Hypocrisy

By 33 votes to 13, the Labour group threw out a motion by Cllr Murphy to scrap the council's gay and lesbian unit, abolish the curriculum working party on

gays, cease "all promotion of homosexuality," stop the grant to Reading Matters bookshop and "any other homosexual group" and abolish all references to homosexuality in council policy.

To temper this hard-line approach, Tory opposition leader Cllr Bob Hall moved that the council should accept that Clause 28 was not intended to encourage prejudice or discrimination. Cllr Murphy accepted that amendment, but the Labour majority claimed it was sheer hypocrisy and Clause 28 was a deliberate attack on gay rights.

Cllr Toby Harris, the Labour leader said Cllr Murphy's reference to Aids was "repugnant, disgusting politics."

"Our work on the schools curriculum is not going to be declared gay and proud to

CLLR Greaves

replied: "He is not afraid to admit he is a homosexual."

Cllr Jones said in the council that he was an openly declared gay and proud to defend gay rights.

189

care less about the gay issue. It was simply Rent-a-Mob' (*Hornsey Journal*, 31 October 1986).

On another occasion the implicit accusation of violence became explicit. A married, pregnant woman was prevented from attending a gay meeting for a screening of the video, 'How to Become a Lesbian in 35 Minutes', whose title parodies the widespread notion that homosexuality as such can be taught or promoted. Afterwards she claimed that she had been punched in the stomach by the 'bouncer' (a term suggesting a sombre guard protecting an illicit, raucous event); and eventually she blamed this 'attack' for the miscarriage that she suffered two weeks later. Although she never identified the supposed assailant, at least one tabloid's headline gave her claim a factual status – 'Mother "Struck" by Bouncer Lost Baby' (*Daily Mail*, 22 April 1987) – a story which was then cited in a House of Commons debate. From sexual perversion, to violence, to death.

Similar connections have been suggested around the book singled out by the Parents' Rights Group, *Jenny Lives with Eric and Martin*. The book was stocked by school libraries and by the council-subsidized Reader Matters bookshop, which was also (unjustly) accused of stocking a book celebrating anti-police violence. The *Jenny* book contained photos such as the little girl sitting up in bed for breakfast with her father and his lover – described by critics as 'two naked men', thus suggesting a sex orgy rather than a cosy morning cuddle. Education Secretary Baker attacked the book as 'blatantly homosexual propaganda, not education' (*Sunday Telegraph*, 14 September 1986). Clearly this book contradicted his guidelines that sex education be taught in a context of 'moral considerations and the value of family life' – even though it wasn't even intended as sex education.

At a national level, and in popular imagery, all those elements came to symbolize links between 'gay lessons' and 'terrorism'. For example, for the cartoonist of the *People* (21 September 1986), some-how a veritable orgy of sex and violence develops to the point where children are running riot around a library full of such books as *Brian and the Brutal Policeman* and *Pop-up Samantha Fox* (reference to a tabloid newspaper 'pin-up girl'). Meanwhile the librarian offers a startled mother and child *Jenny Lives with Eric and Martin Again*, with a cheerful explanation: 'In this sequel Eric murders Martin with an axe, then slits his own throat. Jenny, now a gay herself, joins a squat, takes to hard drugs and dies – such an improvement on Enid Blyton, don't you think?'

Moreover, protests by the Parents' Rights Group eventually made a similar sex-violence link by citing two different council-funded videos, one giving voice to the ANC and the other to gay rights advocates. In July 1986 a local Tory MP, Hugh Rossi, sent his constituents a letter in which he opposed sanctions against South Africa (which of course would only 'injure the poverty-stricken black Africans') and opposed Haringey Council's plan to 'promote images' of homosexuals in the schools. Another Tory MP, Dame Jill Knight, told the House of Commons in March 1988 that Haringey Council was misusing Home Office funds to produce videos 'promoting terrorism in South Africa and homosexuality'. Again the sequence is sexual perversion, violence, death.

According to a cartoon in *The Times* (9 March 1988), the whole controversy focused on a bookshop stocking *Jill Lives with Joe and Horatio*, the latter two portrayed as balaclava-hooded men with machine gun and handgrenade, as well as such other violent publications as Blue Peter's *Let's Make a Bomb* and *The Big-Fat Anarchist Playbook*, perhaps based on the real-life *Playbook for Kids About Sex*. Although this cartoon seems intended to parody Jill Knight's phantasies rather than the Reading Matters bookshop, it starkly expresses the feared links: from sexual perversion, to violence, to death. The PRG may not have mentioned the 1985 uprising at the local Broadwater Farm housing estate, where a policeman was killed as youths fought riot police who had blocked their protest march, but we can be certain that many people held persistent memories of an event that symbolized a threat to the entire social order.

This threat was evoked from a different, quasi-religious angle by newspaper columnist George Gale (*Daily Mirror*, 9 July 1986). In 'Lessons That Threaten Life', he warned his readers about 'the left-wing conspiracy to brainwash children into the subversive belief that homosexuality is just as good, natural and desirable as heterosexual activity'. He railed against 'the falsehood that sterile homosexual behaviour is an alternative to the life-generating sexual exchange between men and women'. That is, his life-preserving appeal rested upon the quaint notion that heterosexuality is inherently (and purely?) procreative, or at least should be.

As with other manifestations of the moral panic, Gale's scenario of social sterility presupposes a homosexual promotion campaign of literally epidemic proportions, spreading to potentially everyone. The implicit missing link is gay sex as contagious disease. In this way, a conspiracy of political subversion becomes a perversion of the natural order, a veritable biological subversion, a threat to the very existence of the human species.

Thus, without needing to mention AIDS, his obsession with procreation resonates with the implicit message of much 'AIDS prevention' advertising: that casual, promiscuous, recreational sex leads to individual and species death. Or, according to George Gale's variation on the theme, only monogamous sex for procreation can save us from social and biological extinction. Just in case his readers hadn't got the message of the AIDS ads, the *Daily Mirror* took the trouble to lay out his column with an inset piece, 'Justice for the Death Dealers', about two Australians hanged in Malaysia for trafficking heroin, which warned readers that 'Trafficking in drugs is murderous'. Yes, just as is dealing in left-wing extremism, sexual perversion and AIDS: gay sex as war by other means?

The spectre of violence against innocent, decent family folk runs much further than newspaper commentary. The Parents' Rights Group has repeatedly evoked Nazi imagery by denouncing the Positive Images policy as propaganda, as indoctrination by a 'group of dictatorial bigots' who would impose their perversion on others and corrupt innocent children. Playing the victim, the PRG's leading black member made her protest at a council meeting by singing 'We shall overcome'. Yet around the same time another PRG leader gleefully announced the impending fate of the copy of *Jenny Lives with Eric and Martin* that she had taken from the local library: 'It is going to be part of a bonfire outside the education offices. I shall have great pleasure in doing it. It will be better than a Guy Fawkes night' (*Hornsey Journal*, 19 September 1986). Was this to be an anti-Nazi book-burning ceremony?

Beyond such symbolic attacks, gay men have become the targets of house-burning, murder, sackings at work throughout the country (see, e.g., HLGU, 1988). In Haringey in particular there have been open physical assaults on gay demonstrators. This onslaught has been legitimated by trial judges who describe the victims as 'promiscuous, effeminate, practising sodomites', etc., as well as by tabloid newspaper headlines about poofs and AIDS.

The *Sun* even published a cartoon of a man having hung his gay son from a lamp-post, with the mother commenting, 'I said your Dad wouldn't take the news so well, Rodney' (March 1988). Previously the same newspaper (14 October 1985) had run a photo of a man pointing a gun at a boy, with the accompanying story, 'I'd Shoot My Son If He Had AIDS, Says Vicar'. In this way the *Sun* makes it easier for us to

192

see that demonic images of violent homosexuals are projections of murderous impulses from inside those who promote such images.

Return to Normality?
Another pervasive theme has been the alleged reversal of naturally (or Godly) given distinctions between normality and abnormality. In one of many local religious outbursts over these issues, Pastor Godfrey Davis lent his church's hoarding to the cause of public education with the following warning: 'Homosexuality! AIDS? What does God say? Read the Book of Romans ch. 1 v. 27. They receive the due penalty of their sins.' Bible experts will know that this refers to the passage, 'Males behave indecently with males, and are paid in their own persons the fitting wage for such perversion.' Even non-experts will recall hearing something about the wages of sin.

Another local pastor announced he would fast, 'living on just water and prayers', until the council reversed its perverse policy . . . or until death. Thus the Reverend David Rushworth-Smith portrayed himself as yet another potential victim of left/gay violence. In the name of attacking the council's policy as unnatural, he seemed to be expressing some anxiety about what really is natural, unchangeable: 'If the council had said they would stop the sun rising in the east, it would be no less drastic.'

Natural law and religious truths have also guided the Parents' Rights Group but also probably limited their appeal as an organization. Having collected 1,500 signatures on their petition, the Parents' Rights Group was able to gather only fifty people for a demonstration in August 1986 where they displayed such placards as 'Bible Lessons, Not Gay Lessons'. At the same time, the group has attempted to give prominent roles to Afro-Caribbean, Cypriot, (Indian and Turkish) Muslim, Jewish and Irish Catholic members. Although this Rainbow Coalition seems to be composed of politically naïve moralists, their ethnic diversity may have served to generate wider opposition to the council's policy of Positive Images among groups afraid of being considered in some way abnormal.

One example strangely parodies the British characterization of male homosexuality as 'Greek sex'. Many of Haringey's Greek Cypriots reassure themselves that the local Cypriot Gay & Lesbian Group must have an entirely Turkish Cypriot membership, while of course Turkish Cypriots believe the opposite. For fear of community sanctions, many Cypriot gays continue to live in heterosexual couples, pretending they are heterosexuals. Here law parodies life, as

Section 28 prohibits local government from portraying homosexuality as a 'pretended family relationship'.

Representing older black people, the local West Indian Leadership Council condemned 'classroom lessons on homosexuality . . . or on any other sexual matter' (*Daily Mail*, 10 November 1986). And the chair of the Haringey Black Pressure Group on Education attacked the council for a 'racist policy aimed at breaking up the family . . . Homosexuality has its roots in a morally decadent white and European society', he stated, though without a clear mandate from the group's members. In addition, local groups of disabled people have seen their public image threatened by the council linking the Positive Images policy to anti-discrimination measures around race, sex and disability. By affirming such narrow definitions of normality, each group denies a part of themselves, in a desperate search for acceptance as normal.

The Tottenham Conservative Association itself attempted to organize a Campaign for Normal Family Life. This took the form of a petition which demanded 'a return to normal family values' and 'an end to ridiculous words such as sexist and racist and return to normality'. Their terminological objection paralleled the persistent attacks on items stocked by Reading Matters bookshop. Supporting the PRG's call for parents to boycott Haringey schools, one leaflet protested against the council's plan to turn 'normal abnormal and abnormal normal', 'the world turned upside down'. Thus, in the choice of words here, the fallen angel meets the Levellers of the English Revolution – an elision of moral and political subversion.

Moreover, in a July 1986 press release, the Association warned that Haringey Council's Gay and Lesbian Unit posed a 'bigger threat to normal family life than even the bombs and guns of Adolf Hitler'. Thus the Nazis' extermination of homosexuals, unacknowledged here, becomes psychically displaced by homosexuals' supposed attempts to exterminate the family. A similar historical reference was made by a letter writer claiming that Weimar Germany's permissiveness, symbolized by Berlin as the gay capital, led the German people to react by supporting the Nazis (*Hornsey Journal*, July 1986). Thus be warned: we must behave ourselves and not misuse our freedoms, lest we lose them.

Sensual Seduction

The Parents' Rights Group repeatedly proclaim that they are scared, and they certainly are – but scared only of 'homosexual propaganda'? At some level parents know that schools have always been a prime source of unofficial sex education, as well as anti-gay insults, with peer-group pressures and the mass media increasingly weakening the family's authority over their children. Similarly they will be aware of such 'normal' family values as wife battering and child abuse, problems now even taken up in mainstream women's magazines. Many mothers in particular face a sense of rage over their powerlessness, social claustrophobia and dependence upon husbands.

Apparently these negative feelings are displaced on to supposedly conspiratorial threats to their children's normality/morality. This displacement pretends that children would know nothing of sexual feelings, much less homosexual ones, were it not for dealers in propaganda and contagious perversion. As Tory councillor Dianne Harwood said, 'There is no reason I can think of for children to be aware of this. Let children be children first.' The 'predator/victim' imagery is expressed more starkly by the Parents' Rights Group, 'Our aim is to shield our children from any person or organization who would exploit their innocence.'

For understanding the frenzy over the pictures in *Jenny Lives with Eric and Martin*, we can consider the horrified comment by the PRG Treasurer, Yasmin Ahmed. Speaking particularly for Islamic women, she said, 'We would not even accept it with heterosexuals' (*Herald*, 25 September 1986). As one PRG member put it more personally, 'I wouldn't want my child to see me and my husband naked in bed!' We might wonder what psychic continuum is involved here: fear of corrupting one's own children, fear of corrupting oneself, fear of sensuality, fear of desires unfulfillable by the family?

Further clues to the underlying meanings can be found in the preoccupation with gay male sex, almost to the exclusion of lesbian sex. As one parent described the council's policy, it was 'like Sodom and Gomorrah all over again'. Although this focus could be explained in terms of the AIDS threat, far more metaphorical meanings are involved.

As suggested earlier, gay males are seen to epitomize the sexual pleasure-seeker, unrestrained by true family ties, and seducing on impulse, especially young initiates. Often the term 'seduction' has been used to imply that sex for pleasure (rather than duty, perhaps) is immoral, dangerous. Paul Johnson, a convert to Christianity, assures us that homosexuality 'is not a condition, it is something which is acquired by seduction in youth'; thus he reduces homosexuality to a temporary lapse of sexual restraint in youthful wild abandon, an otherwise passing phase which now refuses to pass because such practices are publicly promoted.

In a similar vein, the Parents' Rights Group has denounced another book, *The Milkman's on his Way*, for describing 'the successful homosexual seduction of a sixteen-year-old schoolboy by a male teacher', with 'explicit and obscene sexual scenes'. Given the group's traditional multi-religious outlooks, we have grounds for suspecting that it opposes all discussion or acknowledgement of sexual desire, particularly outside married coupledom, and that the term 'seduction' reveals the fear of such desire.

Whose Vulnerability?

The *New Statesman*'s writer Sarah Benton (1988) has suggested that the homophobic frenzy has arisen from misinformation and misunderstanding, especially public confusion over attacks on heterosexism, as distinct from heterosexuality: 'If the feared fantasy figures of homosexual seducers turning the natural world upside down were brought into the light, there to stand revealed as similarly ordinary, vulnerable people, a powerful, inarticulate force behind the backlash the government is promoting might be vitiated.' However, as she herself points out, the backlash has arisen partly in reaction to gay people's recent public campaigning – not just to win legal reform, but to win public acceptance of gay culture as equally legitimate. From a recent House of Lords debate, she quotes one member who in turn referred to another Lord speaking in the 1967 debate: 'He then asked the homosexual people in the future to comport themselves quietly and with dignity and to eschew any form of ostentatious behaviour or public flaunting.'

At that time it had been possible to build a consensus for 'tolerance', in favour of decriminalizing the behaviour of 'consenting adults in private'. The consensus involved an implicit reassurance that homosexuals posed no threat to anyone else because they formed an almost distinct subspecies, to be pitied and left in peace. Today, however, not only do we live in less tolerant times, but the psychic defence has broken down, to the point where 'public flaunting' generates intolerable anxiety.

That breakdown is about more than public display undermining conscious beliefs about the normality of heterosexuality. For deeper sources, let us consider the following: George Gale's presumption of procreative sex, the PRG members' avowed sense of shame about nudity, their anticipation of 'pleasure' at burning gay books, Councillor Murphy's attack on 'filthy, disgusting books' and the pervasive seduction phantasy – all linked to death metaphors. Taken together, these suggest a conflation of external and internal threats.

That is, public display of gay culture does far more than undermine a particular sexual taboo (e.g. anal sex) in an ideological sense. As a refusal to repress socially unacceptable impulses, it provokes anxiety within everyone, about all sexual taboos, all restraint on sexual expression. As the Positive Images policy implicitly approved the celebration of gay culture, even while attempting to fit it within the terms of an anti-discrimination approach, the policy itself was experienced as a conspiracy of seduction, even a mortal threat.

If the panic-carriers could not sympathize with the vulnerability of gay people, perhaps it is because the Positive Images campaign has evoked people's sense of vulnerability to their own feared, denied desires. These are symbolized by the male 'homosexual seducer' spreading a contagion of rampant desire *as* disease, which then becomes psychically inseparable from violence, AIDS, death. In this way, fear of catching AIDS merges with pre-existing fear of a rampant social-sexual disease. The threat extends far beyond homosexuality, whose public acceptance is experienced as an example for everyone to pursue immediate gratification of dangerous desires.

For this reason, or unreason, Tories and religious fundamentalists have succeeded in unleashing an epidemic, a moral panic whose effects go far beyond the small circles of fanatics who initiated it. For the same complex reasons, the Tories have been able to make little electoral success out of the reaction, which has mainly disoriented the Labour Party and diverted debate from the 'real' social disintegration underlying the panic.

What kind of understanding would be adequate for combating the backlash in a way that could lessen the anxiety it symptomizes? So far this analysis has described group psychodynamics at the level of transparent fears and desires, which often become explicit and acted out. To some extent this may be explained in terms of adult sexual desires being frustrated by repressive morality or by sheer embarrassment, then dangerously excited by seduction imagery, then projected on to an external threat, thus alleviating anxiety.

However, the sheer emotional intensity of the backlash, particularly the death imagery, can be explained only in terms of resonance with primitive, unconscious phantasy. That is, it would involve a repressed desire so dangerous as to risk annihilating the subject, or so dangerous as to generate murderous aggression which is then projected on to another who seems to threaten the subject with

197

death. The psychodynamics might involve the following primitive emotions:
– desired fusion with the maternal object, thus risking disintegration of the subject, then generating hatred of the object;
– murderous rage at the 'bad breast' for withholding gratification (i.e., as a counterpart of socially forbidden desires), thus experienced as persecuting the subject;
– forbidden oedipal desire for the maternal object, leading the subject to wish for the death of the father-rival; with the associated fear of being castrated, raped or even murdered by the father.

In any given individual, none or all of these processes may be involved. Whatever the source of the anxiety, it may be relieved by the homophobic group psychopathologies already described.

Any effective response to homophobia will have to find a way of acknowledging the unconscious feelings that the entire issue unavoidably excites. The task for us all, and not just for overt bigots, is somehow to accept and reintegrate those unwanted feelings back into our selves in a conscious manner. Does this mean consciously pursuing some 'forbidden' desires while consciously repressing others? This complex question can be answered only in the course of practically challenging our own infantilized dependence upon a state that psychically protects us from demonized threats.

What kind of society would not need such a state, and how would we construct it? These questions will need answering as part of any liberatory political project aiming to identify and overcome the fundamental causes of the real social disintegration that generates moral panics.

FREE THE CHILDREN FROM THE WITCHES:
The Cleveland 'scandal' according to the *Daily Mail*

> The idea that we are a nation of child abusers is very dangerous. The time will come, if this goes on, when half the parents in the country will be considered unfit to look after their own children. This is Salem.
> STUART BELL, Labour MP for Middlesbrough, June 1987

In the original Puritan settlement in Salem, Massachusetts, children were pressurized to invent accusations against certain envied women, who could then be branded as witches and burnt at the stake, thus purging the community of the imagined evil in its midst. In the 1950s Arthur Miller drew on those events as a basis for his play, *The Crucible*, as an indirect way of criticizing US Senator Joseph McCarthy's crusade against supposed 'Un-American activities' that were weakening the nation's moral fibre. By suggesting a psycho-dynamic interpretation of America's obsessive search for 'reds under the beds', Miller's play gave rise to the generic term 'witch-hunt'.

Such a dynamic recurred in mid-1987 Britain, after Cleveland Social Services (in north-east England) began 'obtaining Place of Safety' orders for removing several dozen children from their homes. At that point the professionals clarified that they weren't (yet) accusing the fathers of child sexual abuse. Further investigation was considered necessary for determining who had abused the children, now being kept in Ward 9 of Middlesbrough Hospital.

In the ensuring furore, however, the mass media gave far more attention to apparently innocent parents than to guilty ones. Much potential guilt both hid itself and found expression in a collective denial, amid accusations and counter-accusations of concealment and persecution. Soon the enforced disruption of families came to overshadow the reality of child sexual abuse that the drastic mea-sures were intended to reveal and prevent.

Although the Cleveland methods were clumsy (even brutal) and their medical diagnosis unreliable, the underlying reality of child sexual abuse has been obscured less by such inadequacies than by the emotions they generated. At an unconscious level, fear of one's own child being sexually abused merged with fear of being abused by the state's injustices, a feeling of being persecuted as if a helpless child; similarly, guilt over actual abuse, and over complicity with it, merged with potential guilt over unconscious sexual impulses to-wards children. Thus the intolerable guilt requiring denial ran much further than actual child abuse.

Through the psychodynamic of a moral panic, such threats from within the family were projected on to witch figures outside it, while sustaining an ambivalence towards the children's own moral-sexual purity. In this way, the collective denial took the form of a projective defence – defending parents from the threatened annihilation of their identities.

Witch Hunt

Backed up by the mass media, the local MP Stuart Bell quickly became the prime mover of that defence. When he mounted his crusade for the parents to get back their children, he protested at a 'Salem' rather than at the more familiar 'witch-hunt'. Why? Perhaps the latter term might have made it too obvious that he himself was promoting his own sort of witch-hunt against the professionals responsible for disrupting the families.

Moreover, he was defending the unity of the family, and thus the presumed innocence of the fathers, in the face of possible verbal evidence from children. Criticizing the Social Services Department's new guidelines for encouraging the children to make 'disclosures' of sexual abuse, he labelled these as 'confessions', as if to discredit such revelations. Yet his legalistic label unintentionally implied that any disclosures would be both truthful and signs of the children's own guilt; thus his term suggested a way to displace potential guilt away from parents.

At the same time, Bell's reference to Salem suggested alien societies where the state uses children to persecute parents. When an aggrieved parent first told Bell about the many children being removed from their families, some late at night, he reacted dismissively. As he later recounted the incident, he had replied, 'Don't be ridiculous – this is Middlesbrough, not Russia' (*Daily Mail*, 15 July). In a similar vein, local Tory MP Tim Devlin publicly compared the activities of the Cleveland Social Services workers to those 'of another body which carried the initials SS'.[2] Thus 'Salem' associated Cleveland with familiar images of totalitarian states interfering with the family.

When the controversy erupted, many observers criticized both Bell and the mass media for misrepresenting the issues. As some feminists have observed, certain newspapers attempted to discredit the central paediatrician involved, Dr Marietta Higgs, by emphasizing her 'unusual' domestic life (whereby her husband stayed at home to mind the children), her failure (refusal?) to use cosmetics and her foreign origins (from Australia). While newspapers' innuendo of 'collusive feminism' did help to cast Marietta Higgs and child sexual abuse consultant to Cleveland social services, Sue Richardson, as witches, a more comprehensive analysis would need to locate that aspect within the complex emotions stirred by the entire episode.

In order to do that, this case study will look more closely at how one tabloid newspaper, the *Daily Mail*, constructed a moral panic out of an otherwise much-needed controversy over the role of professionals, the state and the family itself. Over the course of several weeks, the paper featured frequent instalments of the Cleveland story, regularly including an inset box reminding the reader that this was 'The scandal the *Mail* revealed to the nation'. The scandal it revealed was not, of course, the possibility of widespread sexual abuse of children, much less its causes. Rather, the scandal was the false allegations, or at least misguided diagnoses, which unnecessarily disrupted the family unit.

The *Daily Mail* converted fears about child sexual abuse into fears about the family institution being abused by professionals, in particular by 'women doctors'. (Those whom the paper supported were called simply 'doctors'.) Although the paper did give some sympathetic coverage to the suspect professionals on the inside pages, the front-page coverage was consistently hostile.

The moral panic revolved around a series of key emotive terms – pain, innocence, collusion, accusation, secrets. Each of these can be seen as evoking people's inner fears about themselves and their families, in ways that displace those fears on to external authority figures, who are then seen as the sole sources of the threats that they face. For the millions of people who bought the paper every day, it offered both scandal and implicit reassurance that the Cleveland parents – and they, the readers – were innocent. As we shall see, the displacement of potential guilt conveyed the *Daily Mail*'s subliminal message, 'Free the children from the witches!'

Pain
The day after the *Daily Mail* first took up the story, the headline of its 'Femail' page defended 'Victims of the abuse "experts" ': 'There is a chilling and growing dossier of children who are victims not of abuse, but of the System' (24 June). The page presented the viewpoint of PAIN, Parents Against Injustice, founded by a couple whose child was wrongly diagnosed and removed from them. The founders were depicted, holding their children, as 'Loving parents falsely accused . . . Sue and Steve Amphlett, who've since documented hundreds of other cases'. She was quoted, 'Social workers are just not getting it right. They have awesome powers, yet seem unwilling to spend the time with families on their caseload which would enable them to do their jobs properly.' From the PAIN files the paper presented three case histories, which 'all involved educated, middleclass people who opened their doors freely to the professionals, believing that as they were innocent they had nothing to fear'. One reason for the *Daily Mail*'s selectivity might have been the parents' class confidence and financial resources that procured the expertise they needed to get their children back. As Sue Amphlett said of one case, 'the family only managed to get justice because they were able to find and afford an extremely good solicitor'.

However, the paper's selectivity had deeper meanings. Its message was that the parents' treatment was doubly unfair because they were well educated and had co-operated with the authorities: the night-mare could happen to anyone, even to middle-class families. This emphasis displaced a different fear evoked by the Cleveland events: that, equally, child sexual abuse could happen to anyone, not just to 'deprived' children. The *Daily Mail* shifted that fear to one of 'inno-cent' families being persecuted. Likewise, the pain of potentially discovering or acknowledging such abuse became the pain of suffer-ing false accusations.[3]

When pressure from PAIN led Bell to defend the Cleveland par-ents, he described his conversion in quite different class terms. As he later recounted his first visit to Ward 9, he saw that most of the parents were from local council housing estates, symbolized by the fact that 'The fathers had tattoos on their arms. They're my people' (15 July). Apparently their working-class status served as a sign of their innocent vulnerability to unjust treatment and thus their need for his special protection.

Lost Innocence
Throughout the several weeks of this episode, the *Daily Mail* pub-lished not a single account of child sexual abuse, nor even of parents' worry that their children might have suffered such abuse. Front-page headlines encouraged readers to identify with the parents' agony of feeling unfairly accused and of missing their children, or with the parents' elation at getting their children back by order of the High Court in Leeds. Consider how the wording leads readers to identify with abused parents:

HAND OVER YOUR CHILD (23 June)
THESE INNOCENT PARENTS (25 June)
THE FIRST CHILD IS SET FREE (26 June)
FREED CHILDREN TAKEN BACK FROM FAMILY (27 June)
9 MORE CHILDREN GO HOME (1 July)
THEY TOOK OUR TWINS AWAY (2 July)
Six More children 'not abused' (14 July)
NOW WE START TO LIVE AGAIN (31 July)

Those headlines contain implicit messages: that the family is the supreme 'place of safety', that children at home are 'free', and that children away from home are not.[4] Each time the court ordered the return of children to their homes, on grounds that corroborating evidence was (so far) lacking, the newspaper took the decision as vindicating those assumptions. And the more respectable status of

202

those parents who could employ lawyers lent greater credibility to them all.

Reading only the *Daily Mail*, one would not have known from other sources (e.g., Campbell, 1987)

– that the children's mothers were encouraged to sleep near them in the hospital grounds and to visit them;

– that child specialists were following up the doctor's physical diagnosis by giving the children relaxed, private sessions with anatomically correct dolls; and

– that many children did disclose sexual abuse (for which some adults were eventually arrested and charged).

The children had been separated not from their 'families' as such but from their fathers and any other suspect males, in an atmosphere where the children could speak more freely. Yet the *Daily Mail* focused readers' feelings entirely upon the parents' experiences of awaiting restoration of their family, in 'the continuing nightmare of parents who stand accused':[5]

> [A father] was sitting on the floor on the ward, rocking backwards and forwards saying he was going to kill himself (24 June).
>
> Social workers took back three children last night minutes before they were to be united with their parents (27 June).
>
> [A High Court judge] reunited four families torn apart . . . but for four other couples the agony goes on (1 July).
>
> There are no winners in this story. The children have lost most. They've lost their innocence and that is priceless. Some parents' trust in each other has been eroded . . . (13 July).
>
> My daughter was found to be a virgin and innocent (14 July).
>
> One couple hugged their three little angels . . . None of the children had a deprived unbringing (31 July).

In effect, the paper's emphasis reassured readers that they had ultimately nothing to fear about child sexual abuse itself. Their angelic children risked losing their 'innocence', and parents risked losing their mutual trust, solely through unfair accusations by misguided professionals. Without actually having to make such claims explicit, the *Daily Mail* could convey a collective denial of widespread child sexual abuse; mothers could avoid any sense of guilt over colluding in the dark secret.[6]

Colluders

Judging from published accounts of child sexual abuse, the mother understandably desires the evidence to disappear or be disproven, as the confrontational alternative to collusive denial seems unimaginably fraught (e.g., Cochrane, 1988). Were it not for the child's needs, it would be particularly tempting for the mother to remain a passive though collusive victim of the abuser's power. At some level, mothers can intuitively identify with this quandary.

The *Daily Mail*'s approach helped readers to displace the problem of collusion. If they unconsciously doubted their capacity to protect their vulnerable children from sexual abuse, they could put themselves in the role of vulnerable innocents seeking and deserving protection from abusing professionals. Their potential guilt could be projected on to those authority figures seen as colluding to persecute parents and children alike.

The suspect colluders were none other than a cabal of witches, led by Dr Marietta Higgs and social worker, Sue Richardson. On the front page of the *Daily Mail* (30 June), their photos appeared with the caption 'ACCUSED'. The occasion was Bell's charge that they 'conspired to keep police out of allegations of sexual abuse' – or 'plotted', as it was put in the first sentence of the lead article.

The *Daily Mail* never went as far as to deny explicitly that at least some of the removed children had suffered sexual abuse. But neither did the paper publish any evidence to encourage suspicions to that effect. Instead, the paper appealed to public suspicion about the fallibility of the professionals who had made such diagnoses.

In particular the *Daily Mail* emphasized that the local police surgeon disagreed with the diagnosis of sexual abuse made by Dr Higgs on the sole basis of the 'reflex anal dilation' (RAD) test; strangely, though, at the same time the police surgeon insisted that the police repeat the test on the children already removed from their homes. The paper mocked doctors' claims of widespread child sexual abuse by noting that the social services decided to remove children 'after apparently discovering an amazing upsurge in child abuse using the RAD method' (13 July).

It is entirely possible for us to doubt the adequacy of the RAD test and the social services' procedures, while at the same time reminding ourselves that right-wing tabloid newspapers usually treat experts with deference, at least when it suits their political purposes. It is rare for the *Daily Mail* to emphasize that the experts disagree, to malign certain 'experts' with inverted commas, much less to put them in the dock with banner headlines: 'THE CONSPIRACY' (30 June) and 'DEFEND YOUR METHODS', DR HIGGS' (30 July).

When an independent investigative panel was eventually formed to adjudicate the Cleveland procedures, the panel included Dr Jane

Wynne, who had pioneered the RAD method used by Higgs. After Bell protested at Wynne's inclusion, the *Daily Mail* described her as 'a woman doctor who holds controversial views' (27 June). Throughout the episode, the paper never applied the term 'controversial' to those who advocated different methods from hers, much less to those who doubted claims of widespread child sexual abuse.

Meanwhile the paper belittled the only relevant public survey, a MORI poll in which one in five of all women and one in ten of all men said they had suffered sexual abuse as children. Claiming that this was inadequate evidence, the newspaper complained, 'Nevertheless, one in ten is a figure that has now become part of the mythology of sexual abuse' (13 July). The paper implied that some professionals were colluding to find or even invent a sufficiently large number of cases to validate the MORI poll and thus present a threatening picture of family life.

Child Sex Secrets
Within the terms of the moral panic, what was supposed to motivate the witches to snatch away the children? Just as the *Daily Mail* didn't deny explicitly that some removed children had suffered sexual abuse, neither did it deny that Higgs and Richardson were acting out of sincere beliefs and concern for the children. It even ran an otherwise sympathetic biographical article, 'The Making of Dr Marietta Higgs, Crusader', on the same day as it quoted the Northern Regional Health Authority as denying that the Cleveland doctors were 'fighting some sort of crusade' (26 June). In this way, the paper suggested that someone had something to hide. What could it be?

The answer came several days later, when the *Daily Mail* promoted Bell's claims to have 'clear evidence of a put-up job as part of the empire-building strategy of Social Services'. The supposed evidence consisted of a memo, dated 29 May, setting out new procedures for dealing with suspected cases of child sexual abuse. At that time, the police surgeon had disagreed with the memo's provision that a second opinion from the police was considered unnecessary.

Although the guidelines were publicly available in the minutes of the Social Services Committee, the *Daily Mail*'s front-page headline announced the discovery of 'THE SECRET CHILD SEX MEMO' (7 July). The alleged secrecy neatly fitted the conspiracy theory, while displacing dark secrets from the family on to the witches-professionals. It also strengthened Bell's claims that the Social Services had exaggerated the abuse figures on the basis of the MORI poll, which would have predicted 14,000 girls and 7,000 boys sexually abused each year. 'These figures have no basis in fact and no substantiation in evidence', he said.

A week later Bell claimed that at least three-quarters of the removed children 'have been mistakenly taken into care' (15 July). He made this claim solely on the basis that the Director of Cleveland Social Services had privately told him that only about 20 percent of the parents were guilty. Neither Bell nor the paper said anything about how guilt could be determined, other than by a second opinion from experts who apparently did not hold 'controversial' views.

A similar theme appeared a couple of days later, when the Health Minister announced a public inquiry into the Cleveland affair. The *Daily Mail*'s headline declared, 'NOW THE TRUTH WILL COME OUT' (9 July) – that is, the truth about the professionals' guilt and the parents' innocence. Thus readers were implicitly reassured that the real abusers were 'controversial' professionals, backed up by 'empire-building' bureaucrats, all colluding to hide secrets.

How, then, could the family be protected from them? The paper trumpeted Bell's solution to the problem: 'MP warns parents: see lawyer before going to hospital'. It reported that Bell advised parents 'not to give consent to any intimate body checks and not to allow photos to be taken of their children' (21 July). Only in this way could other children be saved from the witches.

Such advice is more than ironic in the light of Bell's earlier accusation in Parliament that Dr Higgs was 'obstructing the course of justice'. The widespread emotional response of persecution and denial, encouraged by the *Daily Mail*, made it less likely that 'the truth' would come out through the public inquiry heralded by the newspaper.

Blaming the Messenger

Like all moral panics, of course, this one has a history and volatility. Not very long beforehand, newspaper editors considered child sexual abuse not a good theme for selling papers. According to journalist Jane Dibblin, as recently as 1980 the news editor of a regional paper told her not to bother to file a story on two incest cases then in the courts, as readers 'wouldn't want to read such a thing over breakfast'.

By 1986 attitudes had changed, at least superficially. Popular outrage focused on social workers for failing to protect abused children – in particular Kimberly Carlile in Greenwich and Jasmine Beckford in Brent – who were eventually killed by their fathers. Social workers came under increasing pressure to identify the affected children and remove them from danger. At that stage of popular awareness, it was widely presumed that the danger involved a tiny number of children, so the task seemed manageable. Many people, even some social workers, took comfort from the notion that the problem was culturally specific (or even endemic) to certain 'problem' categories, such as black people or 'the deprived', who merited special surveillance or fatalistic acceptance.

Many social workers, suspecting that the danger was far more widespread, faced a double-bind: while their suspicions about certain children might not be taken seriously, they would still get the blame for any insufficient vigilance resulting in obvious harm. When Cleveland social workers realized that the newly arrived Dr Higgs would treat the cases seriously, she received a large number of referrals. These in turn led to a drastic increase in 'Place of Safety' orders, which over-worked social workers must have found an easier option than a slow, careful investigation of each suspect family. In its own way, the unwarranted significance granted the RAD diagnoses evaded the complexity of child sexual abuse – its detection, its prevention – no less than did earlier approaches of social stereotyping or turning a blind eye.

With the confusing events around Middlesbrough Hospital, implicating apparently ordinary families, the target of concern reversed, from 'negligent' professionals to 'over-zealous' ones. Certainly both criticisms have some validity; as became clearer through the autumn 1987 Cleveland public inquiry, the social workers' over-reliance on medical expertise led the way to a veritable crusade based on ambiguous physical symptoms. Yet, in popular consciousness, the new criticism became a way of denying that child sexual abuse is widespread or extends far beyond special 'problem' categories – much less that the family itself may be structurally pathological.

Since then, the 'backlash' has frightened many doctors and social workers away from fully pursuing suspected cases of child sexual abuse. A Durham consultant, Dr Nigel Speight, described the quandary they face: 'The media and the public cannot have it both ways. On the one hand they lambast social workers for not taking children into care, yet when confronted by a conscientious paediatrician acting in good faith, they react with a hysterical backlash.' The problem is, they certainly will try to have it both ways, and any improved approach must take the double-bind into account.

For example, the ex-director of Brent Social Services, Valerie Howarth, took the ultimate blame for neglect in the Beckford case, and later left Brent to run the new Childline agency for abused children.

207

She describes the personal difficulty of facing a new kind of hostility: 'You are trying to do something for people's lives and you are depicted as a monster – that is what is really painful' (Laurance, 1987). As with the Salem metaphor, people see in her the monster that they fear in themselves or in someone they trust with their children.[7] Howarth, it seems, can only be wrong; people will have it both ways.

Early on in the 'scandal', Dr Higgs herself recognized that the messenger of bad news often gets blamed for it: 'I think what is happening to me, and all the anger that is directed against me, is a direct analogy of what happens to children when they disclose that they have been abused or when abuse is detected' (*Observer*, 28 June). Children's awareness of this threat was poignantly revealed on one occasion when a doctor used anatomical dolls to help a little girl to recount a suspected experience of sexual abuse, though without success; as the doctor was putting away the dolls, the girl said, 'If this doll had a secret and she told you, she'd get bashed up' (*Independent*, 28 August).

One commentary has suggested that parents' denial is intensified by removing the child:

> there is a danger with abusing parents that it may be interpreted as the expulsion of 'a core of moral evil' from the family. Once the child has left, the parents can cover up and deny their own emotional and sexual problems and scapegoat the child. The child is victimized in two ways: punished by being separated from its family and prevented from resolving its confusion about the abuse because this cannot be dealt with outside the family. (*New Society*, 3 July).

On the surface, this particular psychodynamic does not apper to have arisen in the Cleveland episode. Yet the idealization of 'innocent angels', with the scapegoating of witch-figures, may itself have been a defence against an inclination to scapegoat the child. This ambiguity broke through the surface in a slip of the tongue that also slipped past the *Daily Mail*'s sub-editor: one relieved mother said, 'My daughter was found to be a virgin and innocent' (14 July). If the girl had not been a virgin, who would have been guilty? The mother's verbal slip resonates with the guilt displacement evident in the term 'confession' used by Stuart Bell to describe children's potential revelations about being sexually abused.

Since the Cleveland episode, some social services departments have sought more tactful ways of protecting children from harm while identifying sex abusers. But the collective denial, encouraged by the mass media, will certainly persist. Improvements in medical evidence, in public surveys and in social work procedures will not suffice for overcoming a reaction of such emotional depth.

Moreover, we live in a period when harried social workers are being pushed into a neo-Victorian role of policing the poor, and when police have already used children's 'confessions' to prosecute adults for political violence.[8] Given such tensions, it will be increasingly difficult for people to demarcate between justified fears of state persecution, on the one hand, and a collective denial of child sexual abuse, on the other. In this situation, it becomes all the more important to identify those aspects of the public reaction explicable only as a psychic defence: appeals to the supposed safety of 'good family backgrounds', disavowal of children's sexuality, with projection of all guilt on to professionals or implicitly on to children – indeed, projection of dark secrets, conspiracies, persecution, etc.

Somehow ways must be found for bridging the emotional gap between two opposed views of child sexual abuse. As Bea Campbell (1987) said at the time, 'It is the difference between an exception to, and an expression of, our system of sexuality.'[9] And the gap lies somewhere between what people consciously know, what they unconsciously know and what they fear yet to learn.

Postscript: Beyond Panic?
In the year or more since this Cleveland study was first presented as a conference paper (October 1987), the collective denial and witch-hunt have persisted, if only by default. Meanwhile the major critical interventions have analysed the matter in a narrowly rationalist way, at the level of physical evidence and proper procedures.

When the Cleveland public inquiry culminated in the long-awaited Butler-Sloss report in July 1988, it dealt out some criticism to professionals and politicians on all sides of the episode, while reassuring us that all parties acted on their sincere beliefs. The only 'panic' mentioned was the hasty removal of children from their homes. The report barely hinted at the moral panic: 'We are also concerned about the extent of misplaced adverse criticism social workers have received from the media and elsewhere. There is a danger that social workers, including those in Cleveland, will be demoralized.'

The report partly vindicated Higgs and Richardson by noting that few of their diagnoses were based on the RAD test as the sole physical sign of sexual abuse, and that a majority of the separated children truly had been sexually abused. It also acknowledged that child sexual abuse occurs widely, 'frequently within the privacy of the family'. Yet it glossed over the contrary beliefs underlying the 'misplaced adverse criticism' of the witches. Indeed, it ominously stated, 'The role of the media in the Cleveland crisis is not yet complete . . . They have the last word.'

The report rightly located the problem at an institutional level: 'We make criticisms of individuals. Those criticisms must not be permitted to obscure the wider failings of agencies . . .' Yet it reduced those failings to faulty communication, co-operation and procedures. As a remedy, its recommendations featured an elaborate flow chart, 'intended to allow straightforward cases to be dealt with in a straightforward way' – as if the forces that exploded at Cleveland could be contained through better formal procedures.

Although the report recommended no disciplinary action, its narrow terms of reference have provided little basis for deflecting reprisals from those who sought to reveal child sexual abuse. Higgs's over-reliance on the RAD test and Richardson's blanket applications for Place of Safety orders left them still standing 'accused'. In the public imagination they appeared far more guilty of professional misconduct than their professional critics, not to mention those who for years had hesitated to act on evidence of child sexual abuse. The demand that they take responsibility for their procedural excesses has become conveniently conflated with the demand that they be removed from their posts, perhaps in the hope that the 'dark secret' would disappear along with its clumsy messengers. Such scapegoating has perpetuated the comforting notion that the children returned to their homes had not suffered abuse – a notion which the Butler-Sloss report did little to dispel.

Accordingly, the predictable stake-burning ritual has closed in on the witches, as they have been transferred to other posts, and Marietta Higgs has been banned from further work in child sexual abuse. All this holds a clear message to other paediatricians and social workers: either proceed with extreme caution ('watch your back') or be prepared to 'defend your methods' in the tabloid newspapers and public inquiries. The Butler-Sloss report's narrow focus on procedural defects and remedies can offer little confidence to professionals facing that choice.

From a more truly inquiring perspective, Bea Campbell has followed up her articles with a book, *Unofficial Secrets*, which uses personal interviews to convey some unpleasant behind-the-scenes realities. As one Cleveland mother described the quandary for children and adults, 'The only time our kids were believed was when they were lying' – that is, when they denied they had been abused. Contrary to the *Daily Mail's* account, not all the mothers joined in the active denial: 'The women were exiles in their own place . . . They fell silent, or rather, felt silenced.'

However, the book oversimplifies the problem of evidence by assuming that in retrospect 'the [RAD] diagnosis was largely vindicated', and thus rejecting all criticism of Dr Higgs as 'vilification'. Even in a sheer juridical sense the RAD test was not vindicated in all cases. And the problem goes far beyond the unreliability of a particular test. In a psychodynamic sense, the relentless denial – collective and individual, public and private, conscious and unconscious – obstructed the task of meaningfully following up the RAD diagnoses to gather stronger evidence.

As argued by one reviewer of the book (Scott, 1988), no straightforward, common-sense concept of 'truth' can guide us through the often inadequate or conflicting evidence involved in suspected cases of child sexual abuse. This is particularly true where adults conflate actual and unconscious guilt, and where terrified children remain silent or deny the abuse they have suffered. Moreover, when 'the spectre of feminism becomes folk devil', as Mica Nava (1988) described the Cleveland episode, empirical science won't suffice as a reply.

If suspicions about the psychopathology of the family are to be effectively pursued, we will have to resist the scientific temptation to adopt a single, simple guide to reality. Rather, that reality calls for a psychodynamic model, at least potentially capable of both relating and distinguishing different kinds of realities, of guilt – lived and phantasized, conscious and unconscious. Short of this understanding, investigations of abuse are likely to intensify the psychic threat that calls up the projective defence.

What would it take to untangle those aspects in a practical investigation? Within present administrative options, we could say that forced disruption of families should be abandoned in favour of more personal contact between a social worker and the entire family, so as to pursue suspicions with critical sympathy. However, if we take the MORI poll as a very rough guide to the extent of the problem, then the necessary resources themselves would symbolize a standing indictment of the family institution; the political obstacles would be not only budgetary but ideological.

211

Furthermore, we may glean some of the emotional difficulties for social workers by considering the 'pervasive and leaden sense of inner desolation' described by one psychoanalyst who had worked with incest victims (Brendan MaCarthy, quoted in Roith, 1988). In such countertransference dynamics, the professional comes to internalize the client's distress. Similar emotional difficulties experienced by the social worker, and the threat that they pose to present administrative structures, have already generated their own auxiliary form of collective denial and persecution by the social services bureaucracy. It strikes the bureaucracy as intolerable to imagine that the problem of child sexual abuse calls for an approach more complex than correct scientific-professional procedures; the inadequacy of such an approach has been denied and conveniently projected as the personal inadequacy of the harried social worker (Ernst, 1989).

Whatever the true extent and causes of child sexual abuse, the issue can take on a subversive character as soon as it exceeds its hitherto familiar role of stigmatizing a tiny minority of stereotypical 'problem families', who are to be monitored by coolly professional helpers. Hints of professionals' emotional involvement can induce a collective denial, as strong as parents' denial of widespread abuse. The prevalent reaction of projective defence exemplifies the impulse to maintain or restore the familiar social order, for fear of the apparent alternative: disorder, annihilation of professional or parental identity, of the family itself.

For understanding the moral panic, the causes of child sexual abuse may be less relevant than (though related to) the historical processes already undermining parental authority. Without necessarily joining Christopher Lasch (1979) in lamenting that decline, we can appreciate his account of how it proceeds through increasing commodification of social relationships, peer-group socialization and dependency upon experts for child-rearing practices. The current reduction of state-funded social services largely intensifies more impersonal forms of dependency, especially as people look to ever-new commodity gratifications and private experts to compensate for their lost social power as parents, workers, citizens. Both the Haringey and Cleveland moral panics have displaced that pervasive loss by projecting the threat on to those who supposedly seek to undermine the family; folk devils must be found to take the blame for snatching away one's child from parental protection and guidance.

Through such fear, the moral panics have served to strengthen the central government, sworn to protect us from all 'enemies within'.

Meanwhile its own truly persecutory policies – 'moneterrorist' austerity, criminalization, drastic rent increases, poll tax, labour 'flexibilization' – aggravate the decline of parental authority that leaves people vulnerable to such panics. How will the cycle be broken?

ACKNOWLEDGEMENTS

I would like to thank several people for their useful comments towards improving this essay, particularly Anne Gray, Robert Mitchell, Barry Richards, Ann Scott and Haringey's Lesbian and Gay Unit, who also gave me access to their clippings archive.

NOTES

1. As Stan Cohen (1973, p. 9) has put it,
   Societies appear every now and then to be subject to periods of moral panic. A condition, episode, person or group of persons emerges to become defined as a threat to societal values and interests; its nature is presented in a stylized and stereotypical fashion by the mass media; the moral barricades are manned by editors, bishops, politicians and other right-thinking people; socially accredited experts pronounce their diagnoses and solutions; ways of coping are evolved or (more often) resorted to; the condition then disappears, submerges, or deteriorates and becomes more visible. Sometimes the panic is passed over and forgotten . . . at other times it has more serious and long-term repercussions and might produce changes in legal and social policy or even in the way society conceives of itself.
2. Devlin's agenda became clearer several weeks later, when he implicitly blamed certain mothers by attributing child abuse to the absence of the original father and thus to deviant (= 'broken') families:
   Physical abuse is more often than not the result of a broken home. Unless we legislate to reinforce the concept of married life, and to discourage the prospect of unmarried couples being at a tax advantage, the number of one-parent families will grow (*Independent*, 1 October 1987).
3. A similar term was used by Dr Jane Wynne, consultant community paediatrician at Leeds General Infirmary: 'It is extremely painful to be an adult and have to acknowledge that adults do sexually abuse children' (*Guardian*, 1 August 1987).
4. Children are twice as likely to be sexually abused inside their home as outside it, according to first results of a government-funded survey (*Guardian*, 1 August 1987).

213

5. Some of these parents' reactions resonate with Elizabeth Ward's observations (1984). For example, after admitting abuse, fathers 'typically feel sadness and depression, rather than guilt'; they 'also feel the loss of the daughter, as well as the family group'. Her book quotes B.M. Cormier on such a father: 'There is great need to be forgiven, as if he were a child who must be reconciled to his mother' (p. 135).
6. Again, according to Ward (1984), her 'desire not to know is instantaneous, involuntary'; 'she is aware, however subliminally, that she will be blamed by the world of experts Out There' (p. 166).
7. The same term 'monster' has appeared in a High Court ruling, critical of Dr Higgs, that a father had been wrongly accused of child sexual abuse. The judge noted that the mother believed the father to be guilty 'and has possibly convinced her family and neighbours, who have now labelled him as a monster who would sexually abuse a mentally handicapped child' (*Independent*, 23 October 1987).
8. In the aftermath of the 1985 uprising at Broadwater Farm estate in Haringey, North London, police held children for days with no access to any other adult. Police decided to turn away social workers after they had encouraged the children to remain silent.
9. It has been suggested that child sexual abuse is an integral part of masculine sexuality as constructed in this society. See the articles by Campbell (1987) and Frosh (1987); also studies by the Child Abuse Studies Unit, Polytechnic of North London, Labroke House, Highbury Grove, London N5.

REFERENCES

Bell, S. (1988) *When Salem Came to the Boro*. Pan.
Benton, S. (1988) 'What are they afraid of?', *New Statesman*, 11 March: 14–15.
Butler-Sloss, Lord Justice (1988) *Report of the Inquiry into Child Abuse in Cleveland 1987*, HMSO, Cmnd 412.
Campbell, B. (1987) 'The skeleton in The Family's cupboard', *New Statesman*, 31 July: 10–12.
———— (1988) *Unofficial Secrets: Child Sexual Abuse – The Cleveland Case*. Virago.
Cochrane, S. (1988) 'Torn apart at home', *New Statesman & Society*, 1 July: 21–5.
Cohen, S. (1973) *Folk Devils and Moral Panics: The Creation of the Mods and Rockers*. Paladin.
Dibblin, J. (1987) 'The right of the father', *New Statesman*, 10 July: 15–16.
Ernst, S. (1989) 'Gender and the phantasy of omnipotence', this volume, pp 101–11.
Frosh, S. (1987) 'Issues for men working with sexually abused children', *British Journal of Psychotherapy* 3: 332–9.

Hall, S., ed. (1978) *Policing the Crisis: Mugging, the State and Law and Order.* Macmillan.

Haringey Lesbian & Gay Unit (1988) 'Putting the Record Straight' (available from HLGU, 48 Grand Parade, Green Lanes, London N4).

Lasch, C. (1979) *The Culture of Narcissism.* New York: Norton.

Laurance, J. (1987) 'The children's Samaritans', *New Society*, 10 July 10–11.

Nava, M. (1988) 'Cleveland and the press: outrage and anxiety in the reporting of child sexual abuse', *Feminist Review* 28: 103–21.

Roith, E. (1988) 'Freudian errors', *Observer* 20 November: 36.

Saraga, E. and McLeod, M. (1987) 'Abuse of trust', *Marxism Today,*' August: 10–13.

Scott, A. (1988) 'Hidden truths', review of Campbell, *City Limits*, 20 October: 84.

Ward, E. (1984) *Father-Daughter Rape.* Women's Press.

Watney, S. (1981) 'On gay liberation', *Politics & Power* 4. London: Routledge.

—— (1987) *Policing Desire: Pornography, AIDS and the Media.* Comedia/Methuen.

'In this sequel Eric murders Martin with an axe then slits his own throat. Jenny, now a gay herself, joins a squat, takes to hard drugs and dies – such an improvement on Enid Blyton, don't you think?'

215

12 THE PSYCHOLINGUISTICS OF DISCRIMINATION

Valerie Sinason

T HE WORD 'EUPHEMISM' is a euphemism in itself. It comes from the Greek and literally means 'fair-speaking', though its practical meaning is not to speak fairly but to be absolutely silent. It has a religious origin and comes from ceremonies where it was forbidden to speak in case the spirit would be offended by ill-omened words. The fear that saying something could make it happen, the fear that words or thought could concretely cause events to happen, especially bad events, is something we are all now especially aware of in young children's thinking. Freud used the term 'omnipotence' (1913) to describe this state. Klein (1952) underlined the way the young child enters such a powerful state as a defence against anxiety. Embedded in euphemisms, therefore, are psycholinguistic signs as to what evokes anxiety, guilty wishes and terror in any society.

We can also examine in what way euphemisms deal with *differences* that are intolerable. In fact, gender, sexuality, mortality, religion, mental illness, handicap and race are the areas where euphemisms have always clustered. These are areas of difference that wishes cannot change or put right; they are differences that thwart omnipotent wishes to be able to change and control. Therefore, to take a close look at our language can help our understanding.

There are universal differences we all experience that can help us in this examination. Firstly, there was the point when as tiny babies we had to see and acknowledge that we and our caretaking parent were not the same body; that we needed to be fed and were not able to succour ourselves. At the moment of weaning we all become displaced and lose our mother – country, cut off from the rich resources that we felt were ours alone. Then comes awareness of male

217

and female difference. This is hinted at earlier in our lives with the teat/nipple standing for a measuring hard principle and the breast/ bottle representing softness. The older baby also perceives that there is not only one other; there are several others who can engage together in dialogue and a new sense of difference is born. The existence of siblings in childhood, and fellow-students and collea- gues later on, brings in other areas of difference in intelligence, talent, physical, mental and emotional attributes. How we deal with these differences will affect how we cope with later issues of differ- ence that come our way.

Whereas early research in England suggested that external racia- lism could become internalized and destroy the sense of worth of Jews and blacks, later work (Stone, 1981) is more convinced that black children in general do not have poor self-esteem introjected from white society, and that with knowledge and awareness cultural iden- tity can be sharpened against the onslaught of racism (Kapo, 1981). In the second issue of *Gallery* (1975) I published a poem by the black poet Accabre Huntley who was then only seven. Called 'At School Today' it dealt with the racist abuse she received from the other children as well as physical abuse from the class teacher. But when the teacher hit her 'till I was dead in my heart' she could call on the 'Black mother' at home and in her own heart. Her inner strength and security could make her say 'I am Black, Proud and Beau- tiful'. In her language she chose the word 'black'; she discrimin- ated.[1]

From the 1660s onwards the word 'discriminate' meant to be able to differentiate, to perceive the difference between things. In the seventeenth and eighteen centuries, and still a little today, the ability to tell the difference between things was and is seen as a good quality and a person of discrimination was someone who could distinguish between things and therefore was distinguished. How- ever, in 1885 came the first use of discriminating *against*. Interest- ingly, this use of the term was coined to discriminate against certain imports from the United States (*Shorter OED*, 1972). Since then, the term 'discriminating' has largely lost its important original meaning of differentiation. The use of the term 'positive discrimination' has hastened the breakdown of the original meaning. To feel the need to add the adjective 'positive' means that differentiation is only seen in a negative, rejecting way. Freud has aptly commented (1909, p. 225) that 'the thing which is warded off invariably finds its way into the very means which is being used for warding it off'.

When a word deals with an area of difficulty, for example, the Anglo-Saxon word 'mad', it is allowed to have a historical life until the painful feelings connected with the word are no longer held by it, but leak. What happens then is that a new word is brought in, often from the Greek or Latin. In the fourteenth century the word 'insane' was imported to ease the pain of 'mad', but when that too became burdensome then 'mad' returned. There is a hope that the foreign word will be a blank which will be free of unpleasant associations: chemise for shift, intoxication for drunkenness, perspiration for sweat. Word changes are symptomatic, and as such they do not solve problems. The psychotherapy and mental handicap workshop which I co-convene with Sheila Bichard began life as a 'subnormality workshop'. A few years earlier it would have been called a 'mental deficiency workshop'. Some organizations now use the term 'learning difficulties', 'special needs' or 'print-impaired'. The school for maladjusted children where I used to work is now an EBD school (emotional and behavioural difficulty). ESN (educationally subnormal) is now MLD (moderate learning difficulty). There is often true hope that a new word could usher in a new climate. However, we must clinically take it as a diagnostic feature of difficulty when a word keeps changing.

With regard to handicap, mental illness and actual damage, we are often scared of facing differences because of guilt (Sinason, 1986). The guilt of the worker at not being handicapped turns into a collusive identification with the omnipotent self of the handicapped client. A true understanding that we are all equal souls and all handicapped in different ways gets transmuted into a manic desire to erase difference. My handicapped patients choose the word 'stupid' for themselves. The original meaning of 'stupid' is 'numbed with grief', and I feel the original meaning of the word does shine through because a lot of the pain and secondary effects of handicap are to do with the grief of internal and external trauma.

The original meaning of the word 'handicap' was a game of hand in the cap, where you put your hand in a cap and either got something or nothing. This is an accurate image of the genetic lottery that can at random produce handicap. In the late nineteenth century it was used for horse-racing with the meaning of penalizing a superior competitor so as to equalize his chances with those of inferior competitors. I feel there is a way, rather like with the word 'discrimination', that clearly perceiving that some people have handicap inflicted on them, genetically or environmentally, can be turned, through guilt at difference, into a inversion of values where differences, especially where negative, become the new dictators.

Similarly, the terrible way that the term 'suitable applicants only' implied white, middle-class English is now returning with a vengeance in some job adverts where every cast-off, disowned and damaged fragment of society is having to be specifically named. Cinderella returns, taking on the identification of her oppressors, and using similar means of exclusion. Just as the abused child identifies with the aggressor and can all too often become an aggressor, just as the abused country rises up and perpetuates the old abuse under a new name (from the Shah to the Mullahs, for example, the same torture continues), so the same process with words.

For example, this is from a poem by Sylvia Plath called 'The Applicant'.

> First, are you our sort of person?
> Do you wear
> A glass eye, false teeth, or a crutch,
> A brace or a hook,
> Rubber breasts or a rubber crotch,
>
> Stitches to show something's missing? No, no? Then
> How can we give you a thing?

Compare that with a job advert for an Afro-Caribbean child needing foster parents. The child has 'special needs'. Applicants are invited 'irrespective of gender, marital status, disability and sexual orientation'. Economic inactivity (the new euphemism for unemployed) or an unrelated criminal offence are also not ruled out. What is ruled out is anyone who is not Afro-Caribbean.

In Plath's poem she is savagely and ironically identifying with her damaged father whose leg was amputed. After her suicide attempt she saw herself as one of a deeply damaged group. In creating a dictatorship of the oppressed she is aware of the process. In the job advert there is deeply felt awareness of the injustice adults might have to bear, but no understanding of the emotional process. The damaged child is being offered not to a parent or parents who have the inner resources to care for her most, but other outcasts. Being marginalized does not carry with it inevitably the ability to care for others. There may well be unemployed, homosexual, disabled men and women who have committal criminal offences (though not against children) who have inner resources, although their circumstances are hardly optimum. However, the advert in its wording is hardly seeking out internal qualities. In its attempts to bring back from beyond the pale all outcasts, it transforms and corrupts the meaning of difference by seeking to idealize the experience of outcasts. The job adverts get longer and longer as more excluded fragments hammer for inclusion. The term 'open to applicants' is now meaningless. As retribution for the previous hidden rejection of some groups, those groups have now to be specifically named.

This dictatorship of the oppressed creates further casualties, by dealing with people according to outside skin and not by inner attributes. In other words, where racism is used to fight racism no progress is made. One piece of clinical work that made me ponder on this matter further was the referral of a fourteen-year-old Irish boy who was a keen National Front supporter when I worked in the East End of London. He was referred for truancy, failure to thrive and violence. Conceived by a sixteen-year-old Irish girl from a one-night stand with an English sailor, he was placed in an orphanage at birth and brought up by nuns for his first year. When his mother was ready to take him she already had another son from another brief liaison. A succession of violent cohabitees followed and Sean was placed on the NAI register (of children at risk of non-accidental injury). His school were very concerned by his National Front opinions and activities. These were intensified when he was moved with his mother and brother to appalling bed and breakfast accommodation, sharing a small, inadequate kitchen with a Bengali family. The Bengali family were an intact parental couple with ten children. They were in even more cramped accommodation, but Sean found it intolerable that they had breakfast first.

In one session he came in desperate and furious. 'My mother has taken the last bastard back. He beats her up, steals – we get away, and what does the woman do? She takes the bastard back. He sneers at me and said, "You said you'd take a knife to me if I came back" and he laughed and knocked me over and that's how I've got this mark.' I said how worrying that was and that I would ring his social worker. 'What's the point? Steve will stay and we'll all be stuck there.' I said he did not feel his social worker could do anything, she hadn't got him a council house and I hadn't got him a boarding school. He must feel, I suggested, that all women were weak and allowing bad, violent things to happen. He relaxed and said, 'I can't be cross with my mum. That's what happens when you have a working-class Irish woman. That's what she goes and does. That's how a whole family end up in homeless accommodation full of Pakis. If that man touches

221

me again I'll run to my grandparents in Ireland. They are not like that in Ireland.'

I said he was really upset at how his mother's actions had led to this decline. He had talked before about the poverty and violence in Ireland but right now he wanted to feel there was a country, a place inside him where he was biologically accepted and valued. He agreed.

Now, despite the appalling external circumstances, Sean's inner circumstances were amenable to change. By acknowledging the outside reality but also interpreting what the inner meaning was for him, the move towards racism and splitting could be halted. But then a new situation happened that was even harder to deal with and I would like to pay particular attention to the language. In the first session he was painfully aware of his own bastard, illegitimate position and his illegitimate home space. He projects his sense of disownment on to the temporary stepfather who becomes a bastard, and he longs for a country that will adopt him. However, although he uses the abusive term 'Pakis' his strongest feelings remain connected to his own family situation.

He arrived two sessions later in a fury, 'These special black ethnics. These fucking ethnics. Do you know what's happening? It's not enough that I share a stinking kitchen with them for breakfast. Now my fucking teachers have deserted me for them. It's all gone double-Dutch.'

I asked what had happened although I already knew because similar action was taking place in all the neighbouring schools. 'They have already gone on strike because they are capitalist money-grabbers anyway, pretending it is for us when they are glad to be shot of us. But now they have to come out in sympathy with another fucking school because some teachers were arrested for picketing against racism. So – special treatment again. If I were fucking Paki I'd get everything but I am only half-Irish.' I said maybe he feared I would just think 'Here comes poor white trash Sean', and not care anything about what was going on inside him. I'd only care about outside appearance. He simmered down. 'It's all double-Dutch.'

Now it may interest you to know that when William of Orange became King there was enormous anti-Dutch sentiment. Voices were raised that he and his guards were not True-Born Englishmen. In 1701 Daniel Defoe wrote a superb satire on the True-Born Englishman, protesting someone might claim to be true English, but not be true-born.

222

These are the Heroes that despise the Dutch,
And rail at new-come Foreigners so much,
Forgetting that themselves are all deriv'd
From the most Scoundrel Race that ever liv'd.
A horrid medley of Thieves and Drones
Who ransack'd kingdoms, and dispeopled towns.
The Pict and Painted Britain, treacherous Scot
By Hunger, Theft and Rapine hither brought
Norwegian Pirates, buccaneering Danes
Whose Red-haired Offspring everywhere remains
Who join'd with Norman-French, compound the Breed
From whence your True-Born Englishman proceed.

There was jealousy at the way William liked his own soldiers, and double-Dutch, meaning gibberish, was therefore an expression of discontent with this. Excluded from the love and patronage of the bilingual king, the deprived and envious subject could attack the royal language and try to render it meaningless. For Sean, deprived of his teachers who had put another race of siblings before him, the linking with William and double-Dutch was indeed apt.

Psychotherapists working in schools where anti-racist sympathy strikes occurred are well aware of the internal damage done to pupils which needs to be weighed strongly against the political damage that would have been caused by non-participation. The tenants became 'fucking ethnics' because they are engaged in adult union which excludes the omnipotent longing child. They are called 'ethnics' to savage the latest euphemism. 'Ethnic' started life meaning gentiles, i.e., it was a racist Jewish word. But then Christianity embraced the term to mean all heathens. It comes back apparently laundered by absence, but in the familiar way of euphemisms, the original meaning comes through. (It was in 1728 that 'ethnic' meant all heathens.)

The Pakistani family were rehoused before Sean and his family. When Sean was rehoused the violence of Steve sent his mother on the run again. Faced yet again with his mother's addiction to violent partners he could not bear to see her part in their predicament. By projecting blame on to the outside political world (which was also blameworthy) and black immigrants (who were not) he could hold an image of a good martyred mother. However, he was struggling, in his commitment to therapy, to give up these primitive ways of managing. The actions of his teachers, who were similarly, in my opinion, using the mechanisms of splitting to deal with their low morale, excited his areas of disturbance.

Having given the example of a racist boy struggling with deprivation of many kinds, I would now like to look at an eight-year-old Asian boy who suffered from racism. Here too I had to discriminate between the external and internal worlds in order to provide any help and meaning.

Ahmed, his widower father and his three sisters were all longing for a new mother. This was to be an arranged marriage. Mother was a young girl coming to England for the first time to take on a difficult, deprived, ready-made family living in poverty. Ahmed said, 'When they let my new mother come to England everything will be all right because I have not got a mother.' He was sure all teasing and bullying would stop because he felt children without a mother were seen as different and wrong.

Just before she was due anxieties appeared. 'We must not let the milksops see her because they might hurt us.' It was clear to me that his abusive use of 'milksops' for whites was a displacement of his infantile feelings about hunger and sharing. He said, 'Her coming will be another person in our flat and it is already crowded and they will be angry.' I had a difficult issue to deal with because I knew what he said was externally correct. But his choice of words and tone led me to say that perhaps people would be angry at her coming but perhaps he too felt worried about being crowded. 'Yes. I am in my father's room and my sisters but I will have to sleep in the hall maybe when she comes.' I said he might feel very excluded by her coming even though he wanted a new mother, and maybe he felt she took up all the room and all the milk, and I also took too much space. There was a pause. 'We might have to keep her in. My father said he will have to keep her locked in for safety.' 'Why?' I asked. 'People might throw stones at her or attack her because they do that to me and my sisters.' I said it was terrible that people did that to him and his sisters and he should tell the police, but he was not locked in – did he wish he was? 'If I was locked in I could be with my new mother all the time.' There was a silence. Then he cried. 'My new mother has already had a fight with my father in a letter. She can write and read. She said she wants to go visiting friends who live in Manchester and my father said she mustn't leave the house. She must stay at home and cook.'

There is terrible racism in the East End, but had I stayed with the external reality I would not have understood the extra, *internal* fear of displacement that Ahmed was suffering. If we keep our true sense of linguistic discrimination we will face more easily the terrors of hurt and subjugation.

My final example comes from an East End School for emotionally and behaviourally disturbed boys and girls from five to sixteen years old. At a certain point the teaching and psychiatric staff became very aware of an increase in swearing by pupils. It was the female staff who registered this first and one in particular mentioned Inner London Education Authority's commitment to anti-sexism. She felt the girls were most abused by the bad language. I asked staff to note the sexual words that were used so that we could consider the meaning of the choice. The decision to think about and note the disowned words lightened the atmosphere. It provided some means of dealing with the exhausted and battered feelings of staff who were being verbally abused throughout the day. The head was ill and there was uncertainty about when he would return. It quickly became clear that anal terms were the most frequent, followed by oaths about AIDS. 'I'll spit up your bum and give you AIDS.' 'Your willy is covered with shit.' 'Hello fucked-up bum.' The girls were using these terms equally with the boys.

It felt very much to me that the absent head was so strongly missed and worried about by these violently abused and abusive children that he became transformed into a persecuting presence who, instead of being away from the children, was anally penetrating them. Talk in assembly of how the head was, a message from him and an acknowledgement of how he was missed led to a reduction in swear-words, helped also by an assembly reminder that verbal abuse would lead to detention.

After the head returned, the school was in danger of being closed due to falling attendance and to political views about special education. Swear-words of a female kind then spread. 'Dirty spunky cunt', 'spunkbin', 'scabby tits' were the most frequent. The school, in danger of being closed, was seen as a weak and promiscuous woman, invaded and eroded. The swear-words, the litmus paper of communication going wrong, provided great help when their meaning was attended to. A girls' group was able to stem the self-abusive use of female terms by girls, but when the external situation deteriorated again the language also deteriorated and expressed it.

When England was a more religious country, a way of swearing in a euphemistic way was achieved by shortening words. Hence 'drat' came from 'God rot' and 'Zounds' from 'God's wounds'. However, unlike Anglo-Saxon or Middle English, we do not now have a rich source of taboo words. They seem to have diminished to four-letter words which are largely Anglo-Saxon. In some areas swear-words are used to make up for paucity in vocabulary and schools vary in how they deal with this. However, since they still are abusive as they are intended to be, any extra use of them highlights a lack of discrimination with language and a wish to break boundaries.

What the vulnerable, abused and abusive children had noted so painfully was difference and loss, firstly, the difference in the environment when the loved head was away, and secondly, the threat of loss of the school, their only safe environment. 'I don't care if they call this place a nutty place, a special school or what. I just want it to stay,' said Joyce, a West Indian girl. She could discriminate.

Each word we use registers a choice, an act of discrimination. We have to select the most suitable word. That does not mean we consider all the other words in our head inferior. It means only that we think to make an appropriate choice. If we have not chosen or selected *against* but *for*, our own disowned or outcast selves stay peaceful. However, we need internal resources to be able to make discriminating choices, because external pressures in the form of racism, poverty, death and unemployment stir up the dictatorship of the oppressed. The external attacks not only cause suffering in their own right but they also add to it, stirring up internal collaborators. Ahmed's jealousy of his new mother's relationship to his father found sadistic solace in seeing the racist stone-throwing re-enacted in his father's wish to see her locked up at home. Sean's feeling of dispossession was similarly displaced on to his stepfather and the Pakistani family. The schoolchildren, feeling discriminated against, turned their language against each other.

The wish that words could be a *tabula rasa* keeping only the meaning individuals ask of them is a mad wish. The borrowing of foreign words to serve as downtoners of indecent or frightening concepts is in itself racist. The primitive internal fears and the external political and social fears make their way into the nuts and bolts of daily language. As well as helping to change the outside reality, we need to attend to the internal realities, because real discrimination, the acceptance of difference, comes from internal resources.

NOTE

1. I am grateful to Dr Michael Sinason who first pointed out to me that 'discrimination', a term of distinction and differentiation, had become corrupted.

REFERENCES

Freud, S. (1909) 'Notes upon a case of obsessional neurosis. *S.E.* 10, pp. 153–320.

—— (1913) *Totem and Taboo*. *S.E.* 13, pp. 1–162.

Huntley, A. (1975) 'At school today', *Gallery* 2(10). Gallery Publications.

Kapo, R. (1981) *A Savage Culture*. Quartet.

Klein, M. (1952) 'Some theoretical conclusions regarding the emotional life of the infant', in *Envy and Gratitude*. Hogarth, 1975, pp. 61–93.

Plath, S. (1965) *Ariel*. Faber.

Sinason, V. (1986) 'Secondary mental handicap and its relationship to trauma', *Psychoanalytic Psychotherapy* 2(2):131–54.

Stone, M. (1981) *The Education of the Black Child in Britain*. Fontana.

13 PSYCHOANALYSIS AND RACISM

Stephen Frosh

T HIS PAPER is concerned with some psychoanalytic interpretations of racism. Its rationale is that understanding the psychodynamics of racism is an essential part of the anti-racist struggle. Racism is fundamentally a social phenomenon: it has roots in
economic oppression and imperialism, it is institutionalized in the
structures of Western society, it is widespread across gender and
class divisions, and it serves the specific political and economic
interests of dominant social groups. These characteristics make the
development of a socio-political theory of racism essential; indeed,
any history of racism can only be written from such a point of view.
However, while racism is a social phenomenon, it operates at more
than just the macro-social level. Just as sexism is something which is
institutionalized but is also manifested in the power-laden interactions between individuals, so racism is something which is acted out
both at the level of social organization and in encounters between
individuals. Furthermore, just as sexist beliefs, attitudes and emotions are present within individuals, so racism is something which is
deeply embedded in the psychology of each individual racist. A
psychological account of racism is not a substitute for a socio-
political account, but it is necessary for any complete description of
how racism is reproduced within society. The general point here is
that social forces do not operate solely on a structural plane, but they
become inextricably bound up with the subjective experience of
individuals, which in turn contributes to their perpetuation (see
Frosh, 1987; Banton *et al.*, 1985). The specific point is that racism,
which is the most vicious and dangerous form of social oppression,
achieves part of its power through being inscribed deeply in indivi-

229

dual psychology. A theory of what this means and how it happens is therefore necessary if racism is to be fully understood and combated.

THE RACIST HERITAGE

One doubt about the project of developing a psychoanalytic account of racism concerns the unpleasant history of psychoanalysis's own involvement with racist modes of thought and investigation. In some instances, overtly racist sentiments have been expressed in the name of variants of psychoanalysis; for example, Jung suggested that the Negro 'has probably a whole historical layer less' mind than the Caucasian, and warned white Americans that 'living with barbaric races exerts a suggestive effect on the laboriously tamed instinct of the white race and tends to pull it down' (Dalal, 1988, pp. 271, 276). Jung can also be found employing analytic concepts to bolster the racist philosophy underpinning Nazism. Take, for example, the following differentiation of Aryan from Jewish science, made in 1934:

> The Jew, as relatively a nomad, never has and presumably never will produce a culture of his own . . . Therefore the Jewish race as a whole has, according to my experience, an unconscious which can only conditionally be compared to the Aryan . . . the Aryan unconscious has a higher potential than the Jewish . . . In my opinion, it has been a great mistake of all previous medical psychology to apply Jewish categories, which are not even binding for all Jews, indiscriminately to Christian Germans or Slavs. (Jung, 1934, in Poliakov, 1974, p. 374)

Although Jung's is the best-known example of collaboration with Nazi racism, it is clear that it was by no means the only one among psychologists and psychoanalysts alike (Billig, 1978). The Nazi mythology of the will and of the power of the heroic personality to triumph over social constraints was one into which the individualistic focus of psychoanalysis could be made to blend.

In addition to explicitly racist formulations, there is also a more subtly racist trend in psychoanalysis which has been manifest in its anthropological branch. Here, the ideological determinant is an assumed equivalence between so-called 'primitive' people, children and the insane. As McCulloch (1983) points out, most researchers exploring the psychology of colonial people were motivated by a desire to understand the assumed origins of *Western* culture. In so doing, they reduced both the culture and the political condition of the people they were studying to the expression of 'primitive' psychological urges. Even progressive theorists can employ psychoanalytic notions to retrogressive ends. Mannoni (1950), for instance, suggests that the Malagasy people were tied to dependent personality structures by their worship of the dead and belief in magic and witchcraft. 'Wherever Europeans have founded colonies of the types we are considering,' he argued, 'it can safely be said that their coming was unconsciously expected – even desired – by the future subject peoples' (1950, p. 86).

Fortunately, among psychoanalysts and adherents of analytic theory there have always been anti-Fascists and anti-racists to oppose the tendencies described above: Reich and Adorno are the best-known examples, Fanon the most provocative. This is probably true, too, within the more private arena in which psychoanalysis has its practice. The common criticism that analysts impose supposedly value-free, but actually racist and ethnocentric, interpretive judgements on their patients is beginning to be balanced by respect for the attempts of some analysts and psychotherapists to ground their work in the culture and true subjectivity of their analysands. The fate of the concepts of attachment and the Oedipus complex will, perhaps, serve as touchstones for this development. There is a general message, however: it is when psychoanalysts, like everyone else, ignore the social and political context of their concepts that they become individualistic and are prone to the unquestioning acting out of racist ideology.

So far, I have provided reminders of how psychoanalysis can drift into racist theory and practice. In some ways, this is only to be expected: in a racist society, it is not surprising if intellectual disciplines dramatize racist ideas. Of more importance for anti-racists is the question of whether there are elements within psychoanalysis which can be employed to oppose racism – either in practice or in the sphere of 'ideological struggle', the provision of concepts and insights that can oppose the ideological givens that structure the racist world. In this area, I think psychoanalysis offers some remarkable insights which, when read alongside accounts of the economic and political interests served by racist practices, enhance understanding of the evil to be opposed. Particular questions worthy of attention here include the impact of racism on the psychological development of members of oppressed groups and the possible uses of psychoanalytic psychotherapy as an element in anti-racist actions. However, in the remainder of this paper I want to focus on areas

231

where psychoanalysis has contributed progressively to an understanding of the psychology of racism itself. My method is to take
some classic psychoanalytic statements on racist psychology and to
investigate their congruence with a view of racism as entwined
psychologically, as well as socially and economically, with the conditions of modernity. In particular, I am interested in the postulation
of a connection between racism on the one hand and fragmentation
terrors, sexual violence and masculine ideology on the other. The
psychoanalytic material, which has mostly focused on anti-Semitism
but which also includes an account specifically concerned with anti-
black racism, suggests that racism is, among other things, an expression of a deep and vicious fear of modernity.

MODERNITY AND FRAGMENTATION

One of the major contributions of contemporary psychoanalysis to
our understanding of the modern psyche lies in its vision of the
demolished ego. Lacanians, for instance, portray the ego as a fortress
against fragmentation, but one which is itself unstable, built upon an
imaginary identification with something outside. What the ego is a
defence against is the threatening condition of absorption in multiplicity and chaotic desire – the desire of the fragmented body, uninte-
grated and uncontrollable. Lacan (1949, pp. 4–5) notes that, 'This
fragmented body . . . usually manifests itself in dreams when the
movement of the analysis encounters a certain level of aggressive
disintegration in the individual.' Its form is of 'disjointed limbs',
organs which grow wings and take up arms for 'intestinal persecu-
tions', the figures of Hieronymous Bosch. This image of fragmentation, of a psyche which at best is tenuously integrated and at
permanent risk of collapse into warring pieces, is the strongest image
in the contemporary psychoanalytic heritage. For Lacan, it is present
both in the speciousness of the ego and in the fake symbolism of the
phallus: the ego is an imaginary representation of personal integrity
when underneath is contradiction; the phallus promises an order of
wholeness and oneness, with no differences and with infinite power
of definition and designation. A Fascist order, indeed. Many non-
Lacanians, too, have as their problematic the contemporary experience – the *modern* experience – of multiplicity, contradiction and
fragmentation. For example, Kleinians view infants as riven with
hatred and love, envy and guilt; the first experience is of split and
dangerous desires, with pressures towards fragmentation persisting
throughout life in the form of recurrent paranoid-schizoid processes.

At best we hold our ambivalent feelings together, recognizing their complexity and inconsistency, seeing in ourselves the conflicts that are dialectically reproduced in the social world. But we can never be sure of this integrity: in groups, in crowds, in dreams, psychotic disintegration reappears.

This is not the place to evaluate these alternative versions of the image of fragmentation. It should be noted, however, that they do not stand in isolation from images to be found elsewhere. Whether their theoretical framework is that of the new world of post-modernism (Jameson, 1984) or the long-standing one of modernity (Berman, 1982), the humanities are currently celebrating the multiplicity of things, their contradictions, realignments and flows. At the same time, this multiplicity presents each of us with stunning possibilities and terrifying prospects. In Marshall Berman's words, 'To be modern is to find ourselves in an environment that promises us adventure, power, joy, growth, transformation of ourselves and the world – and, at the same time, that threatens to destroy everything we have, everything we know, everything we are' (Berman, 1982, p. 15). What is so unsettling about the contemporary arena of the arts is also what is so disturbing about the modern psyche: to borrow Berman's title, itself borrowed from Marx, 'All that is solid melts into air'.

What has this to do with racism? Balancing the two faces of the experience of modernity are two types of response. Multiplicity, contradiction, flow, celebration of heterogeneity – this is only one side of what it is to live today. The other is rigidity, domination, totalitarianism. This side of things has a specific political manifestation as Fascism, and a general psycho-political expression in racism. It is one of the oldest tricks of psychoanalysis to interpret politics as a mode of defence, but here there is justification. What is present in the racist psyche is repudiation of modernity, of multiplicity and heterogeneity. Racist ideology is the building of a fort, and racist actions, an army to go with it – to defend, frequently through assault, the integrity of the disintegrated self. When all apparently solid things melt away or spiral kaleidoscopically, when the absolute truths on which we are built become uncertain and relative, the weak ego searches for something rigid to bolster it, to explain the disintegration surrounding it and to oppose that disintegration through absorption in a powerful totality. Psychoanalytic theorists of racism, whether explicitly or implicitly, have taken up this idea in a number of productive ways, to which I now turn.

233

PROJECTION AND CONSPIRACY

The most familiar psychoanalytic explanation of racism is as projection: the expulsion of disturbing or painful feelings from inside oneself on to the socially legitimized target of another. The classic account of this kind is that of Adorno *et al.* (1950), whose study of anti-Semitism, *The Authoritarian Personality*, remains one of the most substantial attempts at unravelling the racist psyche. Their notion of the significance of projective mechanisms is located firmly in an appreciation of the fragility of the psychological integrity of the racist, which they regard as a product of specific childhood experiences of (socially induced) authoritarian family relationships. The researchers argue that the authoritarianism of the father and the absence of affection interferes with a full resolution of the Oedipus complex and a gradual acceptance of ambivalence. Instead, a sado-masochistic structure develops in which the individual finds comfort in submission to authority while projecting much of her or his aggressiveness on to a culturally despised out-group. This projection is a *necessary* process: without it, the individual's aggressiveness will undermine the personality and destroy rationality to such an extent that psychosis will ensue. The prejudiced person *needs* her or his hated object in order to survive; indeed, the oppressed group is a product of the racist's need.

The postulation by Adorno *et al.* of a relatively straightforward link between certain family configurations and authoritarian personality structures follows in a tradition that has its most famous manifestation in Reich's *Mass Psychology of Fascism*. Where their model is more sophisticated than many, however, is in its recognition of the power of the threat which makes projection necessary. It is in order to protect the personality against psychotic dissolution that the extreme violence of racist psychology operates. Adorno provides an account of the processes occurring here which remains unsurpassed in its linkage of the social order with the desperation of the individual personality. First, the social link: the potential Fascist has no comprehension of social processes operating beyond her or his immediate experience; instead, the world appears as a buzzing and threatening confusion, offering no anchor points and no possibility of control. This is, of course, the modern experience generally called alienation. Adorno makes the link with anti-Semitism as follows: 'This alienation is experienced by the individual as disorientation, with concomitant fear and uncertainty . . . the [Jew's] alienness seems to provide the handiest formula for dealing with the alienation of society' (pp. 310–11). Anti-Semitic stereotypes are 'interpreted as means for pseudo-orientation in an estranged world, and at the same time as devices for "mastering" this world by being able completely to pigeonhole its negative aspects' (pp. 314–15). But this procedure requires that the pigeon-holing be absolute, that nothing creeps out which could destroy the precariously balanced ideology that makes the racist personality tenable. In this way, Adorno says,

> The extremely prejudiced person tends towards 'psychological totalitarianism', something which seems to be almost a micro-cosmic image of the totalitarian state at which he aims. Nothing can be left untouched, as it were; everything must be made 'equal' to the ego-ideal of a rigidly conceived and hypostatized ingroup. The outgroup, the chosen foe, represents an eternal challenge. As long as anything different survives, the Fascist character feels threatened, no matter how weak the other being may be. (pp. 324–5)

Eventually, the desperation of the racist's retreat from personality fragmentation leads to a process of internal rationalization in which the superego becomes filled with racist stereotypes to justify the attitudes and behaviours espoused by the rest of the psyche. This means that there are no longer any internal checks to destructive-ness: while the personality does hold together, it is at the price of becoming a spiralling, out-of-control mechanism of hate.

> Hatred is reproduced and enhanced in an almost automatized, compulsive manner which is both utterly detached from the rea-lity of the object and completely alien to the ego ... The extreme anti-Semite silences the remnants of his own conscience by the extremeness of his attitude. He seems to terrorize himself even while he terrorizes others. (p. 325)

This portrayal of the racist psyche meshes with the notion that racism is a manifestation of flight from the experience of modernity. Despite some of the more traditional social-psychological formula-tions adopted in places by Adorno et al., it is not so much the logical irrationality of the racist's ideas which is in the forefront of their account ('prejudice' as a series of erroneous judgements), but the emotional desperation that produces these destructive patterns of hate. Nevertheless, there is a form of irrationality too, and the direc-tion which this takes is equally revealing: it is the age-old ideological rationalization of racism found in the conspiracy theory.

235

When the world is crumbling all around, when all that defines reality seems to swirl away, the search for explanations is not just a cognitive strategy, but a deep emotional need. It is here that conspiracy theories appear: always they have been present in anti-Semitism, and at particular historical junctures (such as the defeat of Germany in the First World War or the challenge to the British imperialist ethos by colonial independence and the influx of black immigrants in the 1950s) they are generalized to other communities. One of the many striking results described in *The Authoritarian Personality* is of the centrality of the idea possessed by anti-Semites that Jews are *threatening*. This threat is of two kinds. First, Jews present a *moral* threat to the anti-Semite, appearing as immoral, sensuous and prying, and liable to contaminate the purity of the gentile. Adorno *et al.* perceive this sense of moral threat as so powerful that they propose that it must be generated by a projective mechanism: 'It is possible . . . that anti-Semites are struggling to inhibit in themselves the same tendencies that they find so unbearable in Jews. Jews may be a convenient object on which they can project their unconscious desires and fears' (p. 96).

As well as perceiving them as a moral threat, anti-Semites see Jews as a *social* threat, having immense power which links with their clannishness to present an organized challenge to the autonomy of the non-Jewish world. It is this element, the 'Jewish conspiracy', which has the most visible place in the history of anti-Semitism. Billig's (1978) study of the National Front in Britain demonstrates how powerful a hold such conspiracy theories continue to have over Fascists and racists. In the case of the National Front, the foundation for racist ideology is still belief in a world-wide Zionist conspiracy, with black people often seen as pawns of the Zionists, used to encourage the 'mongrelization' of the white race (p. 194). But the general features of conspiracy theorizing can be seen in many ordinary racists' attitudes, particularly towards Asians. What is very striking about this material, however, is not so much that racists go to the trouble of creating a rationalization of their attitudes in terms of belief in the conspiracy, but that in the process they mix derogation of the objects of hatred with a barely disguised *admiration*. It is the *power* of the hated group which is emphasized: the cleverness of the Jew, the physicality of the black. The conspirators are brilliant schemers, worthy enemies: to the Fascist they are opponents who must be crushed because they are dangerous. Indeed, they are often fascinating: the obsession of anti-Semites with Jews is extraordinarily out of line with the extent of actual exposure to Jews of most of these anti-Semites; Jews represent for them the deepest principle of destruction and degeneration, and of a subversive, unnerving power. Kleinians will recognize what is happening here. The racist ego is one which has to deal with the violence of unfulfilled internal desires in the context of a world which is experienced as threatening rather than containing, as confusing rather than secure. Faced with this, the experience of inner destructiveness is defended against by projection on to external objects, selected for this purpose by their visibility as socially legitimized objects of denigration. The affective content of this projection is envy, regarded by Kleinians as the pure culture of the death drive – a spoiling hatred which is directed at one and the same time against the admired (for its fantasized cohesion and power) and the despised (because it contains the projected rejects of the self). It is, therefore, not just that negative aspects of the racist's identity are projected outwards and then attacked, but also that the rejected group is fantasized as possessing idealized features, for which it is hated and which the racist strives to crush.

Billig proposes that the force behind the projection cannot be that of denied impulses, but is rather an admiration for the superego qualities of the enemy. Discussing the racist's belief in the existence of the conspiracy, he argues that, 'Sexual fantasy cannot be claimed to be the dominant motivating force behind this particular belief. The image of the conspirators themselves often depicts an enemy who is dangerous because he is without the frailties of human passion' (p. 337). But what if this image is itself a defensive one? The context of all this, it has to be remembered, is one in which the forces of modernity stir up passions which are both thrilling and terrifying; these passions are constantly threatening to run amok, to destroy the precariously sustained ego and thence the fragile integrity of the personality. Under these circumstances, groups which are fantasized as in control, as hard and unmoved by the fragmenting forces of the world, can become idealized and envied. The admiration of the racist for the conspirators is precisely that they are secret, organized, impermeable, unfeeling and without passion. All are attributes desired by the threatened ego; all, of course, imaginary attributes, and all part of the world that rejects the intense uncertainties of modernity. If the racist's deep fear is of disorder – disorder within as well as without – then the admired enemy is the one who has overcome disorder and created an efficient and ruthless world. Racist violence under these circumstances can then be seen as an outpouring of the racist's own disorder, directed against the boundary of the other to prevent it being directed against the self. Projection and projective identification: these are indeed the mechanisms at work here. But what of the desire that underpins them, the disturbing impulse that makes the defence necessary? Although Billig may be right to reject a simple formula that explains racism as projection of unwanted sexual feelings, he has perhaps underestimated the power of sex to figure the elements of boundary loss and ego-destruction that the racist so fears. To approach this idea, it is necessary to look at a psychology of racism in which biological and sexual images of the black person are regarded as the core components of racism's emotionality.

SEX AND THE OTHER

One of the many problems inherent in reading the works of Frantz Fanon is the uneasy imbalance between psychological and political explanations of colonialism and its effects (see McCulloch, 1983). Certainly, there is a difference in level between the accounts presented in *Black Skin, Black Masks* (1952) and in *The Wretched of the Earth* (1961), which calls into question many of the earlier work's perceptions. Nevertheless, it is in *Black Skin, White Masks* that Fanon deals most fully with the psychology of the racist, so it is this work which is relevant for my argument here.

Fanon is in no doubt that what he calls 'Negrophobia' has sexual origins. 'For the majority of white men the Negro represents the sexual instinct (in its raw state). The Negro is the incarnation of a genital potency beyond all moralities and prohibitions' (p. 177). In part, this is a matter of projection. Fanon uses the Freudian idea that civilization is built at the expense of sexual urges:

> Every intellectual gain requires a loss in sexual potential. The civilized white man retains an irrational longing for unusual eras of sexual licence . . . Projecting his own desires on to the Negro, the white man behaves 'as if' the Negro really had them . . . The Negro symbolizes the biological danger, the Jew the intellectual danger. (p. 165)

Negro and Jew are both phobic objects for white society and, like all phobic objects, are sources of attraction as well as repulsion. They represent the underside of society, the hidden aspect of human nature, containing all the projected impulses that, if released, hinder the progress of civilization. The Negro is the scapegoat for social

238

failings, but more than that he (for in Fanon it is always *he*) is a reminder of the instinctual basis of all energy, once again the 'dark side of the soul' (p. 190). This is where Jew and Negro differ: it is the abstract idea of the Jewish race that disturbs the anti-Semite (the idea of conspiring Jews who will rob white Christians of the world), but it is the *physicality* of the Negro that threatens. In Fanon's words:

> every time that a Jew is persecuted, it is the whole race that is persecuted in his person. But it is in his corporeality that the Negro is attacked. It is as a concrete personality that he is lynched. It is as an actual being that he is a threat. The Jewish menace is replaced by the fear of the sexual potency of the Negro. (pp. 162–3)

The white man projects his repressed sexuality into the Negro, constructing him in fantasy as a sexual paragon and an object for his homosexual desire. The white's relationship to the black is then mediated by this sexuality; the existence of the black man is a constant threat to the potency of the white man, a stimulus to the desire of the white woman. Racist persecution of the black is, therefore, sexual revenge.

For Fanon, then, anti-black racism takes as its form a vicious sexual hatred which arises as the white man projects his sexual fantasies on to the body of the black. The black then comes to represent biology – to be the incarnation of sexual power. To explain the systematic way in which it is black people who become the repositories of these fantasies, Fanon makes use of the Jungian notion of the collective unconscious, albeit with a social rather than a biological underpinning. At the heart of European civilization, he proposes, there is a shared fantasy of the black man which is founded around a deep, unconsciously structured image of baseness and vileness, associated with the sexual imagery described above. Fanon makes explicit reference to Jung here: 'European civilization is characterized by the presence, at the heart of what Jung calls the collective unconscious, of an archetype: an expression of the bad instincts, of the darkness inherent in every ego, of the uncivilized savage, the Negro who slumbers in every white man' (p. 187). Where Fanon differs from Jung is in his explanation of how this collective unconscious, this shared channel for projection, is formed and perpetuated. In Jung's theory, the mode of transmission is biological, a process inherent in the accumulated matter of the human cerebrum. Fanon, however, converts the notion of the collective unconscious into a theory of ideology by arguing that the archetypes he is dealing with are produced through historically specified cultural processes, notably those of colonialism and the linked sexual repressions of Europe. The perpetuation of racist archetypes then derives from processes of social reinforcement. Thus, what makes Fanon's theory possible as a socio-political explanation of racism is its awareness of the way social practices can be translated into ideological givens which can reproduce particular sets of feelings – complexes – that are vitally racist.

To this point, the focus has been upon Fanon's description of the sexual fetishizing of the black man by the white, as it expresses the intensity of racist fear and the construction of the black as a biological 'other'. It is this way of reading Fanon that has made his work amenable to Lacanians, who have their own method of describing the disintegration of the contemporary personality. Fanon provides an explicit starting point here in his own references to the way the black is constructed as the other for the white. At one level, Fanon describes simply the inability of the white racist to tolerate difference:

> The white man is convinced that the Negro is a beast; if it is not the length of the penis, then it is the sexual potency that impresses him. Face to face with this man who is 'different from himself', he needs to defend himself. In other words, to personify The Other. The Other will become the mainstay of his preoccupation and his desires. (p. 170)

This concept of The Other is linked both to psychoanalysis and to existentialism. It represents here the way that history and oppression produce a divide between people, creating The Other as an alienated image of the self. As Bhaba (1986) discusses, Fanon's treatment of otherness is an ambivalent one, mixing a form of existential humanism with a more modern awareness that it is in the context of otherness that subjectivity is formed – that The Other contains the divisions which desire produces within each psyche. Fanon expresses this side of the argument in a footnote on Lacan's mirror phase:

> When one has grasped the mechanism described by Lacan, one can have no further doubt that the real Other for the white man is and will continue to be the black man. And conversely. Only for the white man The Other is perceived on the level of the body image, absolutely as the not-self – that is, the unidentifiable, the

unassimilable. For the black man . . . historical and economic realities come into the picture. (pp. 161–4)

In other places, Fanon discusses the absorption of the racist image of otherness to the image of the Master, particularly in the consciousness of the oppressed black. But in this quotation, he is concerned to differentiate between black and white psychology, arguing that the black man represents to the white all his own otherness – the threat that arises from the mystery of his own body and its desires. As in Lacan's mirror phase, it is the visual image of The Other that makes it possible for it to become a container for the racist's internal otherness, for the fragmentation that is central to the experience of infancy and, indeed, to the experience of modernity itself. The immense terror around which the psychology of the racist centres derives, in this account, from the threat to the precarious sense of ego-integrity that proceeds from an encounter with the black other: the *visibility* of difference undermines the abstract sense of homogeneity which so shakily supports the ego. Into this is poured the sexual distress of the white; supported by the economic and political pay-offs of oppression, racism becomes a fortress for the fragments of the self.

SEXUAL TERROR AND THE MASCULINE ORDER

One of the troubling doubts that a reading of Fanon produces is his neglect of femininity or – more strongly – his adoption of misogynistic positions. Fanon, too, has an aversion to fluidity and multiplicity; his assault on racism is through an ironic and bitter attack on the way specific sexual impulses are projected on to the black *man* from the white. Of the woman of colour he says, with more than a slight echo of Freud, 'I know nothing about her' (1952, p. 180). His language is fragmentary, poetic and strong – fluid, in its way – but it is a language that takes masculinity as its concern. Yet it is worth considering again the nature of the threat to the ego that produces the benighted racist defences considered here. The threat is of disintegration in the face of a fragmentary world, one which offers no firm ground for the construction of a strong self, one in which the potential joy of multiplicity is obscured by the terror of disappearance in the heterogeneous. What is this threatening world if not that of the fantasized feminine principle, that image of the feminine which sees in it anti-phallicism, fluidity and heterogeneity? To a considerable extent, this is a male romanticization of femininity, but it is also an image adopted by feminists seeking to destroy masculine 'mastery'.

241

Cixous' (1976) image of womanhood, for example: 'Heterogeneous, yes. For her joyous benefits she is erogenous; she is the erotogeneity of the heterogeneous: airborne swimmer, in flight, she does not cling to herself; she is dispersible, prodigious, stunning, desirous and capable of others, of the other woman that she will be, of the other woman she isn't, of him, of you' (p. 260). What this image plays upon is the terror of dissolution which is defended against in the discourses both of masculinity and of racism. The fantasy of heterogenous womanhood, essentialist idealization though it is, gains its strategic and disturbing power by its representation as a pole of opposition to the rigid phallocentrism of masculine ideology, but also to the controlling boot of Fascism. The two, it seems, go together. Masculinity as an ideology, as a fantasy of how the world can and should be, like Fascism and racism, idolizes mastery, ordering reality into firmly held blocks, kept down, kept predictable, kept subordinate. This is the phallic mastery that Lacan so clearly describes, the ideal of oneness, of clarity and of single, intended meanings. This is the opposite of metaphor and of the unconscious.

The link between racist and masculine ideology – between the repudiation of two forms of fantasized otherness – is what is revealed most clearly in Theweleit's (1977) analysis of the writings of the men of the Fascist Freikorps of Weimar Germany. First, there is the deadness of the language of these men and their fetishizing of the Fatherland and of the all-male soldier world – and of violence. Then there is their idealization and rejection of womanhood in all its sexual forms: not only the conventional splitting of women into good and bad, mothers and whores, but a desperate and vicious fantasy of total annihilation of the 'red woman'. This woman is partly phallic, armed and violent. But she is also part of the 'red flood' (compare the image of 'floods' of immigrants), the tumult that breaks down the dams protecting both the nation and the self. As with all things modern, the flood produces ambivalent feelings: excitement at the sweeping away of things which are frozen and dead, but terror at the dissolution of identity that this brings in its wake. In the end, it is all of unbridled life that poses the threat to Fascism. Theweleit says, 'The monumentalism of Fascism would seem to be a safety mechanism against the bewildering multiplicity of the living. The more lifeless, regimented and monumental reality appears to be, the more secure the men feel. The danger is being-alive itself' (p. 218). Later, dealing with the energy displayed in the mass rallies of Fascism and Nazism, Theweleit comments,

Men themselves were now split into a (female) interior and a (male) exterior – the body-armour . . . What we see being portrayed in the rituals are the armour's separation from, and superiority over, the interior: the interior was allowed to flow, but only within the masculine boundaries of the mass formations. (p. 434)

As with the external forms of mass Fascism, so with the internal forms of racism. The hater of flow and multiplicity also hates women, hates the whole image of the feminine other, hates the dangers and unpredictability of contemporary life. Because of the fantasies of femininity and of ethnic otherness (particularly blackness) that are ideologically sanctioned in a society partly structured around oppositions of gender and race, these become the carriers of the threat to the safety of the psyche. Thus the racist defence, along with the fantasy of 'masculine' order, is part of the hatred of all that modernity brings – of its terrors and disconnections, of its promise and its fertile creativity. Racism, consequently, is not just anti-Semitic or anti-black; it is anti-world, anti-desire, anti-modernity itself.

NOTE

1. An extended version of this chapter can be found in Frosh, S. (1989) *Psychoanalysis and Psychology* (Macmillan Education).

REFERENCES

Adorno, T., Frenkel-Brunswik, E., Levinson, D. and Sanford, R. (1950) *The Authoritarian Personality*. New York: Norton, 1982.
Banton, R., Clifford, P., Frosh, S., Lousada, J. and Rosenthall, J. (1985) *The Politics of Mental Health*. Macmillan.
Berman, M. (1982) *All That Is Solid Melts into Air*. Verso.
Bhaba, H. (1986) 'Remembering Fanon'. Foreward to F. Fanon, *Black Skin, White Masks*. Pluto.
Billig, M. (1978) *Fascists: A Social Psychological View of the National Front*. Harcourt Brace Jovanovich.
Cixous, H. (1976) 'The laugh of the Medusa', in E. Marks and I. de Courtivron, eds *New French Feminisms*. Brighton: Harvester, pp. 245–64.
Dalal, F. (1988) 'Jung: a racist', *British Journal of Psychotherapy* 4: 263–79.
Fanon, F. (1952) *Black Skin, White Masks*. Pluto, 1986.
——— (1961) *The Wretched of the Earth*. Harmondsworth: Penguin, 1967.
Frosh, S. (1987) *The Politics of Psychoanalysis*. Macmillan.
Jameson, F. (1984) 'Postmodernism, or the cultural logic of late capitalism', *New Left Review* 146: 53–92.

Lacan, J. (1949) 'The Mirror Stage as formative of the function of the I as revealed in psychoanalytic experience', in *Écrits*. Tavistock, 1977.

McCulloch, J. (1983) *Black Soul White Artefact: Fanon's Clinical Psychology and Social Theory*. Cambridge: Cambridge University Press.

Mannoni, O. (1950) *Prospero and Caliban: The Psychology of Colonisation*. New York: Praeger, 1964.

Poliakov, L. (1974) *The Aryan Myth*. Heinemann.

Reich, W. (1946) *The Mass Psychology of Fascism*. Harmondsworth: Penguin, 1975.

Theweleit, K. (1977) *Male Fantasies*. Cambridge: Polity, 1987.

14 REASON, RACISM AND THE POPULAR MONSTER[1]

Philip Cohen

BEYOND RATIONALIST PEDAGOGIES

THERE IS a famous etching by Goya entitled *The Sleep of Reason Produces Monsters*, which shows a writer slumped over his desk surrounded by a crowd of eery bat-like creatures, representing phantoms of the imagination which have escaped the grasp of the conscious mind. This picture has come to symbolize the project of the Enlightenment – to make the more recalcitrant and hidden aspects of the human personality yield up their secrets so that they can be better understood and controlled, and so that society can be organized along more orderly and rational lines. Today that project survives nowhere more strongly than in the role assigned to education and social science in the struggle to overcome the monstrous images of popular prejudice. If the etching were to be redone today it would show reason and racism locked in mortal combat to win the hearts and minds of the young.

If we are setting out here to challenge this Enlightenment model it is not because we do not believe in the importance of educational interventions against racism, but precisely because 'the heart has its reasons which Reason does not know'. All the evidence to date shows that the racist imagination as it works through popular culture is not accessible to rationalist pedagogies, and almost effortlessly resists their impact. This kind of reasoning simply does not work against the ideological forms of common-sense racism as these are manifested in the everyday cultural practice of young people. Secondly, and even more seriously, the very notion of 'enlightenment' is deeply implicated in a practice of reason which is historically rooted in certain dominant forms of European race thinking.[2] In fact, it is not the sleep of reason which has produced 'monstrous races'; rather it is the creatures of the racist imagination which have periodically aroused the European intelligentsia from its slumbers, if only in order to rationalize them as the basis of new technologies of surveillance and control over subject populations. The dominant forms of scientific rationality in western society are not only consistent or complicit with racist ideas; they have played an active role in producing and relaying them.This is not down to an aberrant historical moment – the moment of 'scientific racism'; it is part of a continuing process. Reason has been made part of a civilizing mission, the prerogative of the 'educated classes' (white professional), in such a way that 'unreason' becomes an 'inherent trait' of 'non-European' and 'uneducated' (i.e., working-class or black) people, who are then regarded as 'lacking control over bodily impulse', or possessing 'primitive mentalities' and 'low intelligence'.

It is not as easy as it looks for anti-racist education to divorce itself from this set of hidden assumptions. For example, if teachers operate with deficit models of working-class culture, and equate racist attitudes with infantile and irrational impulses, then inevitably the two become associated and an expectation is set up that it is white working-class children (rather than middle-class adults) who are the problem. This in turn may lead to forms of intervention which reinforce working-class children's resistance to the 'civilizing mission' and make their racism a major medium of resistance to schooling. It is in and through such self-fulfilling prophecies that the dominant-class racism is both realized and, at the same time, disavowed.

If such tangles are to be avoided then we need a new approach to understanding the relations between reason, racism and the monster, and a set of alternative strategies for tackling some of the deeper and more unconscious roots of popular prejudice in the classroom.

One starting point must be the recognition that, although almost every culture makes use of monsters for the purpose of representing basic human fears and anxieties about 'The Other', in Western cultures this function has taken on an added and quite specific dimension: the monster is not an archetype of the collective unconscious, but a site in which key contradictions of gender, race and class are played out.[3] In the Middle Ages the 'monstrous races' who were held to inhabit the edges of the known world were the object of popular fascination and wonder, and ranked alongside the mythical creatures of classical antiquity. But by the eighteenth century the prevailing attitude had changed to one of fear and hostility focused on the 'monstrous consequences' of any kind of affiliation between apes, Europeans and black people. This change was not due to the realities of the colonial encounter (which in one form or another had been taking place since the First Crusade). What was new was the way the civilizing mission connected practices of reason and refinement, uniting bourgeois and aristocratic versions of human individuality in a single code of breeding.[4]

This code drew a new line between those with breeding and those who merely bred. It enabled the English upper classes to define themselves as the sole standard-bearers of culture and relegate everyone else to the realm of Nature, whether as Noble Savage or wild beast. The opposition between Culture and Nature not only took on a specific class/race connotation, but affected images of sexuality too. If breeding was 'in the blood' it nevertheless became an almost mystical property of inheritance transmitted from generation to generation in a way which repressed any reference to sexual reproduction. That very absence was the mark of the body's refinement, of the fact that it left nothing to be desired. In contrast, the body of subject races was associated with unrestrained powers of sexuality, as a symptom of their generic degeneracy. Thus, a sexual double standard was inscribed in the heart of the racist enterprise.

It is in this context that the history of the monster in popular culture must be read. The monster represents the return of the repressed, uniting elements of nature and culture, animal and human, female and male, which are split off and opposed within the code of breeding, subverting its practices of reason and refinement by means of a 'polymorphous perversity'. In this sense the monster is part of a wider strategy of popular resistance to the dominant culture of Anglo-Saxon societies. But this is only one side of the picture. Because of its hybrid form, the monster also articulates fears and fantasies about miscegenation; it can become an 'heraldic device' for popular racism, and the direct embodiment of negative stereotypes.

For example, in racist propaganda Jewish people have routinely been portrayed as vampires, and are often drawn with Dracula-like features. One of the most infamous caricatures of the Irish is a drawing by Tenniel which shows The Fenian in the form of Frankenstein's Monster. More recently, the National Front produced a poster showing a Rastaman with Medusa-like dreadlocks, and blood dripping from his mouth, in an obscene plagiary of Caravaggio's painting. Today in primary schools, black children with or without locks are often nicknamed 'Medusa'.

This contradictory or 'two-faced' aspect of the monster is reproduced within the structures of feeling and belief which characterize children's basic attitudes to the world. At one level the monsters which appear in fairy tales or dreams have a therapeutic function, in enabling the child to objectify and hence gain control over sadistic fantasies centred on intimate bodily relations between self and other; but where the monster ceases to function in this mode it becomes a device for projecting these 'bad feelings' on to real others, and thence becomes available for capture and further elaboration by the racist imagination.[5]

The educational strategy indicated by this analysis is clear. We must mobilize the monster against racism, by allying it to those cultural practices and those positions of identification which make it possible for children to gain greater control over both their inner and outer environment. As a result, the monster gains a new, and specifically educational, *raison d'être*; rather than being used in an aimless and non-specific way (every primary school teacher has at one time or another told a class to 'draw a monster' to keep them amused), we are setting out to deploy the monster strategically within a programme of learning activities which systematically *works through* the social and psychic conflicts which it represents. In this way we seek to deprive the racist imagination of one of its most powerful and popular supports.

THE MONSTER IN CHILDREN'S STORY BOOKS

Our task has been made somewhat easier by the appearance of a new type of monster book in recent years, so I propose to look at a few of them in the light of the foregoing remarks.[6]

Aimed at five- to eight-year-olds, these picture story books attempt to give children some insight into the role which monsters play in organizing their inner experiences of self and other. Young readers are invited to explore the emotional conflicts which monsters represent, and sometimes resolve. In doing so, they come to recognize the monster as a creation of their own phantasies, rather than as simply a figure of external threat. The monster is thus relativized, and made integral to the child's everyday world, no longer part of an exotic bestiary, but a friendlier figure, working closer to home.

The pioneer of this new genre is Maurice Sendak's famous *Where the Wild Things Are*. A small boy puts on his wolf suit and goes on the rampage until his mother sends him to bed without any supper. In revenge Max turns his bedroom into a forest and sails off to become

King of the Wild Things. He quickly learns how to tame the monsters (by staring into their eyes), and once he is sure he can stop them when he wants to, orders the rumpus to begin. He then promptly 'gets his own back' by sending the wild things to bed without any supper. The story ends with Max realizing how much he misses his mum; he gives up his privileged position and returns home, where of course he finds that all is forgiven and his supper is waiting for him on the table.

At one level this is a simple morality tale about how children should deal with the anxieties aroused in them by their destructive phantasies and actual naughtiness. Max learns how to tame the wild child within, first by setting limits to the monsters' behaviour, and then by relinquishing his omnipotent position in favour of recognizing his dependency needs. More problematic is the way this inner scenario is unfolded in terms of the cultural landscape in which the story takes place. For many children who read this book, where the Wild Things are is quite simply 'the jungle'. Max's relation to his monsters is an almost exact replica of the white colonists vis-à-vis their 'noble savages'; both go off on a voyage of discovery and end up by lording it over natives whom they have 'befriended' and whose savage customs they have learnt to 'master'. Max, of course, abandons the Wild Things to their primitive cannibalistic state, in order to return to civilization and supper, an attitude not uncommonly found among ex-colonial missionaries even today.

At a deeper level Sendak's story line, like that of William Golding in *Lord of the Flies*, underwrites the recapitulation theory which informed the developmental psychology of Victorian imperialism. According to this theory, in moving from 'stone age baby' to 'civilized man' the psychological development of the individual child is supposed to recapitulate the stages of historical development from tribal to modern society. At the heart of this bizarre idea is the association between non-European cultures and primitive or infantile behaviour, a link which has been made into common sense precisely through the figures of the monster and wild man. Max is initiated into the rituals of the Wild Things for much the same reason as Kipling and Baden Powell encouraged white middle-class boys to undergo a dose of tribal ritual and roughing it in the 'wilderness': only by regressing to these more 'primitive states' – and by learning to master them – could they properly advance to more civilized standards of behaviour. The fatal equation between an internal process of psychic integration and an external process of 'civilization' is here cemented into place.

249

David McKee is careful to avoid such traps in his picture books. For him the monster remains a metaphor or metonym of real power relations rooted in actual social or political situations. *Not Now Bernard* takes a look at the family. Bernard is frustrated that his parents are too busy to bother with him. To everything he asks they give the stock reply which gives the book its title. So he goes out into the garden and is promptly eaten by a monster. Thus incorporated, he goes indoors, roars at his mum, bites his dad, breaks his toys, but is still ignored. In fact the parents persist in treating the monster as if it was Bernard; it has his dinner in front of the TV, and is eventually tucked up in his bed with a glass of hot milk. 'But I'm a monster', it says. 'Not now, Bernard', his mum replies, as she turns out the light.

This story deals with the same issues as those in Sendak's book, but treats them in quite a different way. Max goes wild for no apparent reason and is then shut away on his own. With Bernard it is the other way round. He feels excluded because his parents are so preoccupied with their own affairs, and then gets angry. The preferred emotional strategies also differ. Max's parents are conspicuous by their absence, and it is this, which, in a sense, permits him to escape into a secret, split-off phantasy world where 'wildness rules OK'. Bernard, in contrast, has to work through his 'monstrosity' in terms of his real relations to his parents. The fact that they do not take flight, but carry on as if nothing much had happened, conveys a double message, at once reassuring and frustrating. For they are saying 'Yes, this monster is a normal and integral part of our child, we will not be destroyed by "Its" rage'; but they are also refusing to be budged by the monster's demands for attention, precisely because they continue to recognize and meet the child's needs. In Sendak's story the power of the Wild Things is celebrated in order to highlight Max's sacrifice in giving it up. But in McKee's story there is a wry recognition of necessary limitations on the power of both monster and child; to hold the child within a loving framework within which s/he is not always the centre of attention is also to help cut the monster down to size. In that way, the story tells its readers, a true sense of human proportion can be maintained.

In his second monster book, McKee elaborates this message on a wider geo-political stage. *Two Monsters* live on opposite sides of the same mountain; they sometimes communicate through a hole, but never get to see each other face to face. They both see the same sunsets which the blue monster living on the western side refers to as 'day departing' while the red monster on the eastern side talks of

250

'night arriving'. What starts as a quibble over words quickly escalates into a slanging match, with each insult being capped by an even
more elaborate one. The whole situation soon reaches ludicrous
proportions, with the monsters chucking stones at each other, then
boulders, until at the end they have completely demolished the
mountain and see each other for the first time. They both realize how
stupid they have been and meet in the middle of the mess they have
made to watch the arrival of night and departure of day together.

It is a simple but telling parable which manages to make some
connections between the language of ritual insult and prejudice in
the playground and the institutionalized rivalries of the Cold War.
Both operate in terms of what Freud referred to, somewhat ironically,
as the 'narcissism of minor difference'. Indeed much of the humour –
and children do find this book very funny – comes from the ever-
widening discrepancy between a trivial or non-existent 'mole hill'
and the 'mountain' which is made out of it. The absence of any figure
with whom the reader could identify – unusual in a story for this age
group – is used to demonstrate that both points of view, in the
symmetry of their obsessions, are mutually – and monstrously –
absurd. A defining feature of the monstrous – its lack of human
proportionality – is here mobilized against the dehumanizing consequences of ideologies founded on such split perceptions of the
world. Yet we are also watching a war of attrition as each side tries to
wear the other down, but only succeeds, against their own worst
intentions, in destroying the very conditions of their enmity. Consequently the conclusion, however conventionally 'happy ever after' it
looks, remains somewhat ambiguous. Two wrongs do not make a
right. The destruction of the mountain, the mess that has been made,
stands as some kind of monument to the childishness of the whole
enterprise. But the actual ending fails to do justice to the importance
of the theme. 'That was rather fun', giggles one monster to the other.
'Yes, pity about the mountain.'

In the stories discussed so far the monster remains a more or less
allegorical figure, and this is often emphasized in the style of the
drawings which carry so much of the story's message for young
readers. However, in *Jack and the Monster*, there is a return to a much
more naturalistic style of illustration in keeping with the story's
intimate domestic theme – the arrival of a new baby in the family.
Partly this is possible because this 'monster' is never seen, until right
at the end, when he is recognized by Jack as his baby brother.
Instead the story details the disruptive effects of the baby's presence

on Jack's everyday life, as first his room and then his whole world is turned upside down.

Casting the monster in this sibling role is quite an effective device, not only to explore the intense feelings of hatred, jealousy and rivalry which are generated in this context, but to help older children to locate these feelings in the more infantile aspects of their self. Where the book falls down is in not looking further at the dialectics of envy. For if envy can make a sibling or friend seem like a monster, it also disfigures the envious, and makes them behave in a quite monstrous fashion. In this case Jack is shown doing a lot of mild moaning, but he never has so much as a temper tantrum, even when he is told off for something he did not do. Somehow the display of murderous feelings would seem incongruous in the rather cosy middle-class setting of the story. This is not an Agatha Christie story for eight-year-olds, though it might be rather more use if it was. Moreover, the picture which is drawn of the family life and its sexual division of labour is decidedly conventional. Daddy is shown reading a bedtime story sitting in his armchair with his slippers on while Mummy hovers round with his supper on a tray.

It is perhaps not surprising that the majority of books in this genre still focus on boys and continue to underwrite the notion that the monster is essentially a male phantasy. Nevertheless the monster has been successfully recruited by feminists and used as an ally in the battle against sexism. For example, in *Maggie and the Monster*, the latter still has the regulation hairy feet and tail, but in all other respects looks and behaves like an eight-year-old girl. Maggie gets quite cross with her visitor at first as it blunders around in the dark and keeps her awake. But anger turns to sympathy and identification when she discovers that the monster is merely looking for her mum. With Maggie's help, daughter and Ma Monster are reunited, and everyone goes off to have a good night's sleep.

Here then, separation and loss set in motion a reparative strategy which pre-empts the kind of oral sadism which is so central to boys' stories. The monster is not befriended in order to be overpowered, but made to feel at home, a welcome, if uninvited guest. The monster is recognized as a double, not as the other in the self. This perspective is developed in another feminist text, *My Grandmother the Monster*. Told in the first-person singular, this depicts the changing attitudes of a girl to an elderly relative who comes to stay. Prejudice and resentment give way to sympathy and shared excitement when she discovers that her grandma's favourite game, when she was little,

252

was Monsters. So here the monster is not only feminized but mobilized to slay the dragon of ageism as well by providing a living cultural link between the experience of different generations.

In this book as in some others, the monster is made to belong to a special field of secret knowledge shared only with other children, and those few adults who are on their wavelength. Only within this privileged frame is the monster allowed to have a past. This idea is explored in *A World Full of Monsters*, which purports to be a potted history of the species, from the days 'when there weren't any cars or electricity' up to 'modern times', as told to and by a ten-year-old boy. In the good old days, monsters, it seems, were everywhere; they did every conceivable sort of job from policeman to farm labourer. They even played tennis. But with the advance of science and technology (not to mention MacDonalds hamburgers) monsters have become a dying breed, until they only appear at night times and to children who are 'in the know'. They just say 'Hi monster', and go back to sleep.

This story involves a rather sentimental portrayal of children's culture as a repository of traditional values otherwise destroyed by adult and/or modern society. To suggest that modern technology has driven the monster underground is not only to make it the symbol or instrument of the worst kind of nostalgia but to ignore the actual role which it plays in the contemporary popular culture to which children are exposed. For example, there is a new wave of mega-monster movies, in which the traditional features of the monster are indeed 'technologized'. This is carried over into the toys which are designed to enable children to re-enact scenes from these films in the 'privacy' of their own bedrooms. With the advent of 'Zoids' and 'Transformers' the most archaic forms of the monster are married to the most advanced weapons technology, in a way which is no doubt wholly appropriate for the 'post-modernist' age, but which may not be so beneficial for children themselves.

One of the problems with most of the books I have discussed is the rather old-fashioned and stereotypical images which they use. Invariably the monster is drawn with fangs, a long tail, a knobbly face, hairy body and pointed feet, a bogyman composed from a bricolage of all the more conventional and classical parts. In *Well I Never*, we are introduced to a slightly wider, if still traditional cast – a vampire, a ghost, a witch, and a werewolf. The story revolves around the make-believe character of monsters. Polly, who doesn't want to get dressed and go to school, invents some monsters who are haunting ` her bedroom. Her mother dismisses the idea as sheer superstition,

253

CRISES OF THE SELF

but when she goes upstairs to investigate, she is wholly convinced of their existence by Polly's performance. Polly, of course, promptly does a double-take, and chides her mother for being so gullible. 'Who on earth believes in monsters, these days?' Polly says as she goes off to school, followed by Dracula and co.

Such strategies of disenchantment are unlikely to rob monsters of their power in and over children's phantasies. If young readers find the monsters pictured in these books to be unbelievable, it is not because we are living in a scientific age, but simply because the stories are not frightening enough. The trouble with these monsters is that they are *too* friendly; they clearly would not hurt a fly. Only the monster in *Not Now Bernard* looks as if it has real teeth, and would be likely to bite. Compared with the frightening images which surface in their dreams, not to mention the horror movies they watch on TV, these story-book creatures are very tame indeed. Consequently the processes through which the more destructive or punitive aspects of the psyche are transformed into a more benign form are foreclosed. The narrative domestication of the monster has paradoxically tended to limit its usefulness in helping children withstand its wilder forms of seduction.

This is a pity because these books do explore with some sensitivity the sources and sites of children's negative feelings, and indicate ways of dealing with them which do not depend on splitting, projection, denial or repression. Although some of them focus explicitly on the monstrous roots of various kinds of prejudice, their main use is in working through the underlying images and structures of feeling on which ageist, sexist or racist constructions depend for their common sense. By showing ways of dealing with basic anxieties about identity and difference without resource to strategies of domination, this kind of children's literature can help deny these ideologies their ontological supports.

INTO THE CLASSROOM

In discussing this work[7] with teachers and others a number of concerns have been voiced regarding both the methodology and the theory of ideology and racism on which it is based. The first is simply that it does not privilege the black experience as a perspective for understanding racism. It is certainly the case that our approach, in so far as it seeks to develop and communicate a historical perspective on Anglo-Saxon racism, does not privilege any one of its modalities. Anti-Semitism and anti-Irish racism have unfortunately played an equally important role, and are given equal emphasis. Nevertheless, in the choice of input materials we have accorded Asian, Afro-Caribbean and Chinese cultures pride of place in representing non-European forms of the monster, in particular to illustrate the positive role which monsters can play in constructing difference without recourse to strategies of domination.

A more serious objection is that we are engaged in a covert form of indoctrination, secretly manipulating children's minds 'without their knowing it'. This is first of all to credit teachers with Svengali-like powers – itself an interesting fantasy but one which has no bearing on reality. Secondly, it is to ignore the fact that the aims and objectives of each curriculum unit are clearly and explicitly spelt out to the children at the outset; there is no 'hidden agenda'; indeed there does not need to be. For, far from attempting to 'brainwash' children, the aim is to bring the hidden role of the monster, i.e., as an unconscious link between certain forms of reason and racism, to the surface so that it can become the object of conscious reflection and debate. The whole approach is designed to make children more aware of the way their behaviour and attitudes are unconsciously shaped by such images and by cultural practices in general, not to conceal from them the processes of change.

A final worry is that by focusing on monsters we are in danger of opening up the floodgates of the racist imagination. Better let sleeping monsters lie. This is to fail to understand that the racist imagination can only exploit the monster as long as the truth of its other functions remains dormant or concealed. This is not to say that racist chains of association may not be released in the course of the working-through process. But we have taken great care to devise *framing procedures* to hold any such material within a context of interpretation which points to alternative non-racist readings while at the same time rendering racist articulations highly visible.

Most of the classroom exercises are based on games, story-telling, mask-making, etc., symbolic forms which both impose constraints on the acting out of feelings or beliefs, and provide a shared space of representation which the teacher can enter, in order to negotiate about meanings. It is indeed one of the main aims and claims of this approach that it encourages in children a practice of reason which is more attuned to the task of taming – and relativizing – the monsters which people their imagination, while giving them greater confidence in handling a variety of expressive media, which is important not only for their personal development, but for understanding the dimensions of power which operate in their everyday lives.

In that respect this approach is part of a wider attempt to reclaim the civilizing process from its capture by élitist forms of knowledge and ethnocentric standards of 'reasonable behaviour', by placing the cultivation of critical sensibilities at the heart not only of anti-racist work with children but of popular education as a whole.

But perhaps the last word should be left to Bruno Bettelheim whose study of the possibilities of children's stories and fairy tales has done so much to open up this field (despite his masculinist pronouns):

> Those who outlawed traditional fairy tales decided that if there were monsters in a story told to children, these must all be friendly. But they missed the monster a child knows best and is most concerned with: the monster he feels or fears himself to be, and which also sometimes persecutes him. By keeping this monster within the child unspoken of, hidden in the unconscious, adults prevent the child from spinning fantasies around it. Without such fantasies the child fails to get to know the monster better, nor is he given suggestions as to how to gain mastery over it. As a result the child remains helpless with his worst anxieties – much more so than if he had been told stories in which these anxieties are given form and body, and which also show how to overcome these fears. (Bettelheim, 1988)

NOTES

1. An earlier draft of this text was published in *Racism and Popular Culture: Working Paper 9*, published by the Centre for Multi-Cultural Education, University of London, 1988.
2. On the role of western reason as a form of power, see Foucault (1965; 1975). See also Lewontin *et al.* (1982).
3. On the scientific construction of the monster as a strategic site of articulation between the practice of reason and the ideologies of racism, see Tort (1979). For its more general history as a popular cultural form, see Lascaux (1983). For a study of the role which the iconography of the monstrous races played in the relations between European and non-European cultures from the early Middle Ages, see Wittkower (1977).
4. This argument is developed at greater length in 'The perversions of inheritance' in Cohen and Bains (1988).
5. The original psychoanalytic theory of the monster was sketched in Freud's paper on the Medusa's Head. From a Lacanian perspective, the

work of Daniel Sibony offers fresh insight into the contradictory structures of the racist imagination. See in particular his (1976) 'Quelques remarques sur l'affet ratial'.

6. The following books are discussed in this section: Sendak, M. *Where the Wild Things Are*, McKee, D. *Not Now Bernard* and *Two Monsters*, Graham, R. and Varley, S. *Jack and the Monster*, Winthrop, E. and dePaoloa, T. *Maggie and the Monster*, Davis, A. and Powell, A. *My Grandma the Monster*, McQueen, J.T. and Brown M. *A World Full of Monsters*, and Eyles, H. and Ross, T. *Well I Never*, I am greatly indebted to conversations with Margaret and Michael Rustin, and to their book *Narratives of Love and Loss*, for much of what follows.

7. The Cultural Studies Project is funded by the Sir John Cass, YAPP, Gulbenkian, Baring, Hilden and Cadbury Trusts, and is developing anti-prejudice teaching materials for use with primary school children. This work is reported in detail in the project's annual reports, available from the University of London Institute of Education.

REFERENCES

Bettelheim, B. (1988) *The Uses of Enchantment*. Harmondsworth: Penguin.

Cohen, P. and Bains, H. eds (1988) *Multi-Racist Britain*. Macmillan Youth Questions.

Davis, A. and Powell, A. (1964) *My Grandma the Monster*. Toronto: Women's Press.

Eyles, H. and Ross, T. (1988) *Well I Never*. Andersen.

Foucault, M. (1965) *Madness and Civilization*. Tavistock.

—— (1975) *Discipline and Punish*. Harmondsworth: Allen Lane, 1977.

Freud, S. (1922) 'Medusa's Head'. *S.E.* 18, pp. 273–4.

Graham, R. and Varley, S. (1988) *Jack and the Monster*. Andersen.

Lascaux, G. (1983) *Le Monstre dans l'art occidental*. Paris: Flamarion.

Lewontin, R. *et al.* (1982) 'Bourgeois ideology and the origins of biological determinism', *Race and Class* 24:1–15.

McKee, D. (1987) *Not Now Bernard*. Arrow Books.

—— (1987) *Two Monsters*. Arrow Books.

McQueen, J. and Brown, M. (1988) *A World Full of Monsters*. Collins.

Rustin, M. and Rustin, M. (1987) *Narratives of Love and Loss*. Verso.

Sendak, M. (1970) *Where the Wild Things Are*. Puffin.

Sibony, D. (1976) 'Quelques remarques sur l'affet ratial', in Macciochi, M. -A. ed. *Eléments pour une analyse du fascisme, vol. 1*. Paris: UGE.

Tort, P. (1979) *L'Ordre et les monstres*. Paris: PUF.

Winthrop, E. and dePaoloa, T. (1987) *Maggie and the Monster*. Andersen.

Wittkower, R. (1977) *Allegory and the Migration of Symbols*. Thames & Hudson.

15 PSYCHOANALYSIS AND THE THREAT OF NUCLEAR WAR[1]

Jane Temperley

PSYCHOANALYSTS in this country have on the whole avoided the public sphere – certainly as a collective body we have not engaged in politics or taken part in political controversy. We have concentrated on the practice of psychoanalysis and on the development of psychoanalytic understanding of our patients and of ourselves. We do have a section of the BPAS (British Psychoanalytical Society) which interests and informs itself about the application of psychoanalysis and which does give expert evidence on issues in the mental health sphere. It is, however, unprecedented that a large number, over 130 in a society of 400, should decide to form a group, Psychoanalysts for the Prevention of Nuclear War (PPNW), to express publicly our views as psychoanalysts about a matter of political controversy. The issue which caused us to go public is the danger of nuclear war.

Our concern is that at a technical level we now have the means to destroy human life on this planet – an irreparable act, the possibility of which distinguishes nuclear war from all previous war. However catastrophic the damage produced by previous wars – the genocide of the Aztecs or the massacres of the First World War – human beings and human society did survive and in the course of generations recover. Those who died could envisage that their children or the physical world they knew and loved would survive them. It was possible to think in terms of just wars, but, as Archbishop Runcie has pointed out, there can be no such thing as just mutual obliteration.

It is, of course, pointed out that awareness of the horrors of nuclear war is exactly what has protected Europe from war since 1945. This argument presupposes, however, that human beings are rational and that, since nuclear war is tantamount to suicide, it will not be resorted to. It is because of our clinical understanding of the relative weakness of human reason and reasonableness in the face of the largely unconscious forces which determine our states of mind and our behaviour, both as individuals and as groups, that as psycho-analysts we have observations which it is our responsibility to make to the public debate about the dangers of nuclear war. We make them in the same spirit as the Medical Campaign against Nuclear Weapons, to which we are affiliated, and the corresponding group of scientists who have made public their concern about the possibility of nuclear war. We feel our perspective is particularly important because, as Einstein remarked, nuclear weapons have changed everything except men's minds.

The revolution produced by Freud was the unseating of our belief in rational thought as the primary determinant of our attitudes and behaviour. He compared our conscious knowledge of our minds to that of early medieval man's knowledge of the earth and its relation to the planets and stars: if we concentrate on what is conscious and rational, we have as little knowledge of the largely unconscious forces which determine our mental life as medieval man had of the nature of the solar system and of the relative insignificance and peripheralness of the earth he, medieval man, saw as its centre. Freud stressed how our mental attitudes are heavily determined by unconscious emotional forces and how our capacity to think ratio-nally can be disturbed and disrupted by powerful feeling.

Further than this he pointed out that as individuals we have a much greater capacity to think and behave in a considered, rational way than we are usually able to maintain in groups or in nations. Reality testing – the capacity to perceive others in the world about us as they really are and not primarily in terms of our fantasied antici-pations – tends to deteriorate in groups and the power of emotion to swamp reason also increases. The capacity to think, to exercise moral judgement and to tolerate frustration deteriorates. Freud, in his paper on group psychology, remarked on 'the tendency to the imme-diate carrying out of intentions as they emerge'. Regression to more primitive states of mind is another feature of large groups. Alix Strachey pointed out an example of this in Shakespeare's *Julius Caesar* where the crowd lynches a man called Cinna, despite his establishing that he was Cinna the poet and not Cinna the conspira-tor. When we regress, as we do in our dreams and as we are able to do as members of large groups, our unconscious minds take over and we cease to be concerned with these precise and tiresome distinctions which characterize secondary process rational thought.

At the international level an example of the frailty of human reasonableness is the fate of a book much read in the years preceding the First World War. Called *The Great Illusion*, written by Norman Angell and published in 1910, its contention was that war had become impossible. In view of the financial and economic interdependence of nations the victor would suffer equally with the vanquished and therefore no nation would be foolish enough to start a war. A twentieth-century war, Angell contended, would be on such a scale that its inevitable consequences of commercial disaster, financial ruin and individual suffering would be so pregnant with restraining influences as to make war unthinkable. The book had a great cult. It was translated into eleven languages and its most influential proponent was Viscount Esher, a friend and adviser of the King and chairman of the War Committee assigned to remaking the British Army after the Boer War. The book anticipated what suicidal madness a European war at that time would be, and its argument is an interesting forerunner of the theory that nuclear terror has prevented and will prevent a European War in the second half of this century. Many very influential people saw and argued that war would be ruinous for Europe, but the forces of reason had very little to do with the riot of excited mutual destructiveness which launched the First World War.

To judge from history war seems endemic to human nature. It provides a socially sanctioned outlet for violence and aggression which would in other circumstances be inhibited or punished. It also allows people and nations to relapse into the very dubious satisfactions of the state of mind Melanie Klein called the paranoid-schizoid position. Instead of having to wrestle with the complex feelings we all have within ourselves and towards other people, in situations of war (and I include the 'cold' war we have had since 1945) we are encouraged to project the ugly aggressive aspects of ourselves on to the enemy and we then see ourselves and those on our side in an exhilarating aura of goodwill and idealization. Such a mental posture has great appeal – it evokes the glorious moral certainties and simplicities of the comic strip and the nursery story, of all the goodies versus the baddies stories that delight and relieve and reassure children of all ages. It is a tremendous strain emotionally and intellectually to aspire to the depressive position, to recognize that we all have to struggle with loving and hating responses and need to take responsibility for them; that we are not innately and morally superior, however comforting that might be to our national narcissism, that the issues between nations as between individuals are complex and may involve painful self re-evaluation. It is so much more exhilarating to live in a world that contains 'evil empires' than in the one which John Kennedy evoked when he urged that 'every thoughtful citizen who despairs of war and wishes to bring peace should begin by looking inward'. In that speech he spoke of the Russians as fellow human beings whose apprehensions about further invasion were comprehensible in terms of their recent experience.

The lure of the paranoid-schizoid position is great. The British people seem to believe that a nation which cannot, after all these years, subdue Afghanistan on its own border is really intent on trying to annex western Europe and is deterred only by nuclear weapons from doing so. On the other hand, it is all too easy to idealize ourselves as sane Europeans between the insane 'superpowers' or to idealize Gorbachev and see the USA as the Great Satan.

Melanie Klein traced how the individual at first structures his perception of the world in terms of the paranoid-schizoid position and gradually, if all goes reasonably well, is helped by good experience to withdraw projections of his own frightening emotions and see himself and those around him in more realistic terms. This latter state she called the 'depressive position'. One can see how societies, too, struggle between these two psychological positions on such matters as attitudes to criminals, to the mentally ill and to foreigners. There is at one level a comfort and simplicity in being able to differentiate the right-minded members of one's society, including oneself, from these disturbing deviants who should be mistrusted, avoided and restrained if not actually attacked. Clearly they become the carriers of what is aggressive, mad and alien in oneself and it is a powerful test of a society's maturity to begin to withdraw the primitive projections which lead to this scapegoating. It is conversely a great test of a group's maturity to be able to withstand the experience of receiving these projections without lapsing in turn into excessively paranoid states of mind. It seems that American military planners have consistently made calculations of Russian capacities and intentions in terms of the 'worst case', attributing to the Russians the weapons and the hostile intentions that their most pessimistic imaginings and calculations could construe. It has subsequently become clear that for decades they vastly over-estimated Soviet nuclear capacity, which was always inferior to their own, and they are likely to have similarly overestimated Russia's aggressive intentions. When asked to justify their insistence that Russia is only stopped from attacking western Europe by our nuclear superiority, western spokesmen all too often cite the extent of the Russian military arsenal. If they are *that* heavily armed they must be intending to attack us, the argument runs. The converse argument, that they also construe our huge arsenals as indications of our intention to attack them, is overlooked. Out of such escalating paranoias, impulsive and violent action can all too easily arise whether within the family or between neighbours, communities or nations.

Fornari, in his book *The Psychoanalysis of War*, stresses that if we are not able as nations to achieve and maintain the depressive position we will destroy ourselves. Our possession of nuclear weapons may all too easily mean that a severe lapse into the paranoid-schizoid position may be irrecoverable – there could be no reparation, no recovery. He feels that the mental re-orientation required of us is to recognize that the ultimate threat we face is the danger of nuclear war which is far more hideous than any particular nation's hostile intent toward us. It has been well stated that 'such things deny and pollute the very things they purport to defend'.

Freud shocked the world by his exposition of the extent to which our conscious motives and thoughts are determined by more primitive and emotional unconscious forces. He particularly shocked and disturbed people with his emphasis on the power of infantile sexual desires and conflicts to determine adult attitudes. To a large extent public knowledge of Freud's thinking remains fixated at his delineation of the Oedipus conflict and at a very early stage of his theorizing about the conflict between the demands of our sexuality and of our desire for self-preservation. Conflict and the possibility of a neurotic resolution of it arose, according to this early theory of his, when infantile libidinal desires, often suffused with primary process thinking, came into conflict with the ego, the part of the mind which is concerned with the nature of reality and which is the seat of the self-preservative instincts. For example, the boy child, intent on possessing his mother and eliminating his rival father, has, under the influence of the self-preservative instincts and of his ego's recognition of his need for his father and of his father's superior strength, to subdue or repress those sexual impulses. From 1910 Freud revised this theory several times. He introduced the notion of narcissism and he became increasingly troubled by something in human nature which he felt did not tend, as he had always supposed, towards the pursuit of pleasure or contentment. He was troubled by the problem of sadism and more particularly of masochism, by suicide and by

evidence of people's attachment to bad experience and of a reluctance to change that went beyond the resistance set up by repression.
To cope with these issues he re-cast his instinct theory radically. He
introduced the notion of the death instinct and thereby caused as
much controversy among analysts as his original theories on infantile sexuality had caused controversy outside analysis.

Whereas his original theory had taken the conflict between sexuality and self-preservation as the crucial issue in human psychology,
in his new theory he saw the tension within us as being between the
life instinct and the death instinct. The life instinct underlies our
wishes to make new combinations and includes sexuality, creativity
and the desire to explore and have new ideas. The death instinct
represents an urge to return to the inanimate, to the inorganic, to
dissolve connections. It is profoundly conservative and constantly
strives to return us to the state from which we emerged. It attacks and
is opposed to the life instinct and is the source of both self-
destructive and outwardly aggressive behaviour. At first he seems to
me to stress its lethargic, conservative nature but increasingly he
attributes to it a virulence from which the individual seeks to defend
himself by projecting it outwards and expressing it in aggression to
others. Melanie Klein was to add that one of the defences against the
death instinct is to project it outwards and attribute it to others and
become paranoid of their intentions. By the time Freud wrote *Civilization and its Discontents* he saw the problem of human aggression as
the main threat to which society has to address itself and the main
source of human unhappiness. The sexual instincts seek to bind
people to one another and are re-directable for socially cohesive
purposes. It is the problem of man as *homo lupus homini* which he
identifies as the major issue both for the individual and for society.

Freud's theory of the death instinct remains extremely controversial, but many practising analysts in this country have found it
very illuminating clinically. Beyond the effects of adverse childhood
environment, there seems to be a variable factor in all of us which
can react with hatred and resentment to what the healthier parts of us
recognize as opportunities for change and development. Rather than
give a clinical example, I am taking a powerful literary one, Sartre's
Huis Clos. In this play the three characters discover that they have
died and that they are in Hell. Hell is in fact the misery of their
relationships with each other. To me the most profound part of the
play is when they discover that the doors out of Hell are in fact open:
they are free to leave but they do not do so, because they are so
invested in the destructive relations they have with each other. This

conservative investment in the bad relationships that are familiar to us, which Freud to my mind rightly described as deathly, is what one fears may prevent the Western nations and the Soviets from using what appear to be hopeful initiatives from Mr Gorbachev.

That murder and destruction are exciting is obvious from the popular press and from the popular mood at times like the Falklands War. A more subtle and possibly more dangerous manifestation of what Freud called the death instinct is apathy. It seems to me that our state of mind since we discovered nuclear weapons is like that of a man who has been given a possibly fatal diagnosis. There are intermittent spells of lucid recognition of the appalling danger – 75 percent of American college students think they will die in a nuclear holocaust – but such intervals of recognition are extremely difficult to maintain. There is a great wish to regress into dependence on some all-wise authority and to abdicate to him or her our responsibility for informing ourselves and for taking action. One of the few things Psychoanalysts for the Prevention of Nuclear War has achieved is that those of us who have undertaken to give papers have actually bothered to inform ourselves of some of the facts. I am ashamed that until I did so I did not realize that the Russians had consistently offered no-first-strike undertakings and that the West had consistently refused to reciprocate. I felt less ashamed and more worried when I found that most of my friends were equally ignorant. A few years ago it did leak through into public consciousness that the Americans were talking of limited nuclear war in Europe. It also became public knowledge that in their calculation of the consequences of a nuclear attack on Russia, the USA regarded the deaths of 50 million of their own population as 'acceptable'. There was a sizeable mass response but I think we have now relapsed into a state of 'it won't happen; the politicians know best.' In Britain the inability to face and engage with the deadly truth takes the form it often does with ageing individuals. We live in projective identification with an idealized version of our former younger self, re-fighting the Second World War and posturing with our independent nuclear weapons as if we were still the super-power we once were. Alternatively we comfort ourselves by projective identification with the first of our imperial offspring, the United States, like a parent forfeiting the independent wisdom that he has despite his declining strength, for the false comfort of living excessively through his strong but naive child.

That there should be such a factor in human nature as an instinct or urge for death can seem preposterous. I was interested, therefore, to look at the correspondence between Freud and Einstein in the 1930s. Einstein wrote of 'political power hunger' supported by groups who 'regard warfare, the manufacture and sale of arms, simply as an occasion to advance their personal interests and enlarge their personal authority'. It is he and not Freud who adds that these groups could not arouse such wild enthusiasm and sacrifice of life if it were not that 'man has within him a lust for hatred and destruction', which is normally latent but which 'it is a comparatively easy task to call into play and raise to the power of a collective psychosis'. Wilfred Owen recognized its force when he rewrote the story of Abraham and God's instruction that he should sacrifice his son Isaac. The angel appears

> Saying Lay not thy hand upon the lad
> Neither do anything to him. Behold
> A ram, caught in a thicket by its horns
> Offer the Ram of Pride instead of him.
> But the old man would not so but slew his son
> And half the seed of Europe, one by one.

It is only by recognizing the extent of these sinister forces within ourselves as well as in others, that we may give a chance to the other great force, the Life Instinct. To quote Freud's concluding words in *Civilization and its Discontents*, 'and now it is to be expected that the other of the two Heavenly Powers, eternal Eros, will make an effort to assert himself in the struggle with his equally immortal adversary. But who can foresee with what success and with what result?'

NOTES

1. In addition to being presented at the 1987 'Psychoanalysis and the Public Sphere' conference, this paper was delivered as a lecture to the Scottish Institute of Human Relations on 20.2.88, and published by them as a pamphlet in 1988.

REFERENCES

Fornari, F. (1966) *The Psychoanalysis of War*. Bloomington: Indiana University Press.

Freud, S. (1921) 'Group psychology and the analysis of the ego'. *S.E.* 18, pp. 67–143.

—— (1930) *Civilization and its Discontents*. *S.E.* 21.

———— and Einstein, A. (1933) 'Why war?' *S.E.* 22. 197–215.
Owen, W. (1977 'The parable of the young man and the old', in *Collected Poems of Wilfred Owen*. Chatto.
Sartre, J.-P. (1944) *In Camera*. Hamish Hamilton, 1946.

Notes on Contributors

PHILIP COHEN is a Research Fellow at the Institute of Education in London, where he currently directs the Cultural Studies Project, developing anti-racist work with primary school children. He was an editor of and contributor to *Multi-Racist Britain* (1988), and has written widely on historical and contemporary aspects of popular culture in Britain.

SHEILA ERNST is a psychotherapist at the Women's Therapy Centre, London, and has worked as groupwork consultant to a social services department. She is co-editor of *Living with the Sphinx* (Women's Press, 1987) and co-author of *In Our Own Hands* (Women's Press, 1981). She is a group analyst.

KARL FIGLIO formerly lectured on the history of science and medicine at the University of Cambridge, and on the sociology of medicine at the University of London. He is an Associate Member of the Association for Group and Individual Psychotherapy, and is in private practice as a psychotherapist. He is Managing Editor of *Free Associations*, and a Fellow of the University of Essex, where he teaches on sociology and community mental health.

STEPHEN FROSH is Lecturer in Psychology at Birkbeck College, University of London, and Academic Organizer and Principal Clinical Psychologist at the North West Thames Health Authority In-Service Training Course in Clinical Psychology. He is author of *Psychoanalysis and Psychology* (1989) and *The Politics of Psychoanalysis* (1987), and co-author of *Child Sexual Abuse* (1988) and of *The Politics of Mental Health* (1985), all published by Macmillan Education.

269

R.D. HINSHELWOOD is a psychoanalyst and Consultant Psychotherapist at St Bernard's Hospital, London. He is founder of the *International Journal of Therapeutic Communities*, founder and currently editor of the *British Journal of Psychotherapy*, author of *What Happens in Groups* and *A Dictionary of Kleinian Thought* (both published by Free Association Books), and co-editor with Nick Manning of *Therapeutic Communities: Reflections and Progress.*

PAUL HOGGETT has been actively involved in nearly all strands of left politics for almost twenty years. He is on the editorial boards of *Free Associations* and *Chartist*, and works at the School for Advanced Urban Studies, University of Bristol.

LES LEVIDOW is an editor at Free Association Books. He is managing editor of *Science as Culture* and a member of the editorial board of *Free Associations*.

MARIE MAGUIRE works at the Women's Therapy Centre in London and in private practice as a psychotherapist. She is a member of the Guild of Psychotherapists.

BARRY RICHARDS lectures in the Department of Sociology at the Polytechnic of East London, and is an editor at Free Association Books. He edited a previous collection of papers on psychoanalysis and politics (*Capitalism and Infancy*, Free Association Books, 1984) and is the author of *Images of Freud: Cultural Responses to Psychoanalysis* (Weidenfeld Dent, 1989). He is a member of the editorial board of *Free Associations*.

JED SEKOFF, when not watching movies, is a psychoanalytic psychologist. He trained at the Wright Institute, Berkeley, California. Currently he is Director of Psychological Medicine at the Department of Family Medicine of the University of Miami.

VALERIE SINASON is a poet and child psychotherapist. Her poetry collection *Inkstains and Stilettos* was published by Headland Press (1987). She is Senior Child Psychotherapist at the Tavistock Clinic Child and Family Department and Day Unit. She co-convenes the Tavistock Mental Handicap Workshop, and is currently writing a book on mental handicap for Free Association Books.

JANE TEMPERLEY is a member of the British Psycho-Analytical Society. She has a degree in modern history and trained as a psychiatric social worker in the United States. She worked for thirteen years in the Adult Department of the Tavistock Clinic, where she was a principal social worker. During that time she trained as a psycho-analyst at the Institute of Psycho-Analysis and is now in full-time private practice as a psychoanalyst, also teaching Freud at the Institute of Psycho-Analysis.

AMAL TREACHER worked as a clinician in the field of mental health, then read for a cultural studies degree. Now she is undertaking PhD research which centres on developing an understanding of the contemporary focus on the interior self.

ROBERT M. YOUNG is the author of *Mind, Brain and Adaptation* (Oxford University Press, 1970), *Darwin's Metaphor* (Cambridge University Press, 1985), and other studies in the history of ideas of human nature. He is a psychotherapist, editor of *Free Associations* and *Science as Culture*, and managing director of Free Association Books.

INDEX

273

This first edition of
Crises of the Self
Further Essays on Psychoanalysis and Politics
was finished in August 1989

It was set in 10 on 12 pt Palatino
on a Linotron 202
printed on a Miller TP41
on to 80 g/m^2 vol. 18 Book Wove

The book was commissioned by Robert M. Young,
copy-edited by Gillian Wilce,
designed by Martin Klopstock,
indexed by Fiona Barr
and produced by Miranda Chaytor and Martin Klopstock
for Free Association Books.